WHAT PUPPY?

Sara John

INTERPET PUBLISHING

Published by Interpet Publishing,
Vincent Lane, Dorking,
Surrey RH4 3YX,
England

ISBN-10 1-84286-241-4
ISBN-13 978-1-84286-241-4

Editor: Philip de Ste. Croix
Designer: Philip Clucas MSIAD
Production management: Consortium, Suffolk
Print production: 1010 Printing International Ltd,
   Hong Kong
Printed and bound in China

The information and recommendations in this book
are given without any guarantees on behalf of the
author and publisher, who disclaim any liability with
the use of this material.

The Author

Sara John has been associated with dogs all her life.
Her main love is the Soft-Coated Wheaten Terrier,
which she has owned, shown and bred for 30 years.
She is a Kennel Club-accredited breeder and judges
the breed in the United Kingdom. A tutor for the
Animal Care College in Ascot, she holds several
canine subject certificates and diplomas. She is
the author of *The Puppy Pack* (2008).

Height at
withers

Throughout the book silhouettes of the 100
selected breeds are shown in relation to the
profile of a Wire-haired Fox Terrier (above)
which stands around 38cm (15in) tall at its
withers. This is to allow the reader to get an
impression of the relative sizes of the dogs
being described. It should be understood
that the sizes given in the data tables are
averages and that inevitably some individuals
will grow to be smaller or larger than this at
maturity. The sizes are for general guidance
only. Where breed standards stipulate a
height, allowance has been made beyond this
to include the sizes of typical pets.

CONTENTS

Introduction To A New Puppy

Owning a puppy is a wonderful experience if you are prepared to love and care for your pet, but please never take this decision lightly. Be realistic, ask honest personal questions. If it goes wrong, there will be heartbreak ahead for you and your puppy. *What Puppy?* offers useful information to help prospective owners think about what having a puppy involves, and advises on how to choose the right puppy for them, their family and their circumstances.

Why do you want a puppy?

Humans choose dogs as friends and companions who will offer unconditional love. Dogs ask only for companionship, exercise and food. Dogs come in all shapes, sizes and coat types: small, medium, large and giant-sized, smooth- or long-coated. And they have so many individual attributes that it is difficult to decide which puppy will suit you. So it is important to be clear before buying one: why do you want a dog?

- As companion or playmate?
- As a guard dog?
- For exercise and improving your health?
- For enjoying shows, competitions, or walking companionship?
- Fulfilment of a childhood wish?
- Need for a working dog?
- To get out and about socially?

What kind of puppy do you want?

The choice of a puppy should focus on which breed or variety suits your lifestyle. With so many pedigree breeds, designer dog crosses and mongrels available, careful choice to match your circumstances is essential. Some breeds need more walking, for others training is paramount, and some need time-consuming grooming and involvement in activities. Puppies demand lots of time and attention during the first two years of their life for house-training, obedience training, socialising and grooming so that they become well-behaved members of the community and not a walking liability.

Think about:

- How much time do you have?
- Would a puppy be home alone?
- Is there enough space?
- Time and frequency needed for daily exercise?
- Is there a garden or open space nearby?
- Cost of food and equipping a home for an adult dog?
- How much time is there for grooming and training?
- Will your puppy have a home for life?

If you cannot contemplate positive answers to these questions, please ask yourself:

Should I really have a puppy?

What kind of puppy will suit your circumstances?

If you decide that you can commit to a puppy for life, think what your main considerations are in choosing a puppy to join your family. The table alongside may help you to decide what dog would best suit your lifestyle.

Can puppy come on holiday?

Puppies cannot go into kennels under six months old, so you will have to take the puppy with you, providing you are not travelling abroad, or get someone to look after him. Older puppies can be left in boarding kennel but need current inoculations. You can use house sitter but that will probably be more expensive than kennels.

POINTS TO BE CONSIDERED WHEN SELECTING YOUR PUPPY

Pedigree Dog
- Size and nature will be apparent
- Health may need more attention
- Breed features are known
- Characteristics are predictable
- Knowledgeable breeders are involved
- Increased costs

Designer or Mixed-Breed Dog
- Unknown origin or two combined breeds
- Usually healthy (but not always)
- Individual features appear on dog
- Character may be difficult to determine
- Limited background information
- May or may not be within budget

Large Dog
- Will need plenty of space
- Will need plenty of exercise
- Higher fencing may be essential
- Unsuitable for changing circumstances
- May have dominant natural behaviours
- Less likely to cause trips or falls
- Food costly and storage more problematic
- More 'poo' to pick up and dispose of

Small Dog
- Less space needed
- Exercise level comparable to size
- Limited or average containment needed
- Will be easier if circumstances change
- More manageable natural behaviours
- May not suit active family life
- Economical to feed
- Less 'poo' to pick up and dispose of

Male Dog
- May be stronger or more dominant
- May seek female company
- Marks own territory
- More inclined to guard the home

Female Dog
- Often more submissive with children
- Season occurs at regular intervals
- Urine burns the grass
- Possibly less territorial

Long Coat
- Long grooming sessions often needed
- Skill may be needed for trimming
- More effort to bath the dog
- More dirt brought into home
- May need cleaning after toileting

Short Coat
- Only occasional brushing needed
- Occasional bathing only
- Cleaner with respect to dirt in the home
- May shed more copiously than long coat

● Dogs come in all shapes and sizes, and suit lots of different purposes. With so many on offer, it can be difficult to choose.

Selecting Your Puppy

Most breed standards tell you what you can expect to get with dogs of a specific breed. Generally, every puppy has potential to be a good or bad puppy, but the outcome depends very much on how the puppy was bred, socialised and trained, how the owner raises him and any other environmental influences.

Buying from a reputable pedigree dog breeder

Never buy from puppy farmer breeders: their puppies are not always pure bred, many are raised in poor surroundings or suffer poor health. Good breeders explain their breed to new owners and provide advice on care, feeding, health matters, socialising, training and grooming. Owners should not be left alone to learn about caring for their puppy. These are points you want to tick off when choosing a breeder or a puppy from a good kennel.

- The breeder gives advice on the breed, health matters and preparing to take your puppy home.
- The litter looks happy, healthy, well fed, clean and wormed.
- Appropriate paperwork is available for the puppy.
- Puppies are well socialised and human-orientated.
- Dams, and possibly sires, are available to inspect.
- Puppies' living area is light, airy and clean.
- Puppies are leaving their birth home for their owners.
- Puppies bought for a specific reason, e.g. showing, are suitable for that purpose.

Choosing a designer breed

Remember designer breeds are 'cross breeds' not pedigrees, and have no registration papers. Some designer breeds are available from trustworthy breeders, some are not. Many designer breeds are advertised as being healthier than their parent breeds, but this is not always so. Research shows that the incidence of eye problems in Labradoodles is higher than in the parent breeds. Ask breeders for evidence that they have checked this, and ask to see health certificates for both parents. Non-shedding coats are determined by genetic inheritance and which generation level you have reached after first crosses, so check how many puppies bred previously have actually been non-shedding.

Choosing an older or rescue dog

There are many sources for buying rescue dogs, reputable charities often deal with re-homing and may expect to vet owners' homes, so puppies only go to long-term homes. Retired breeding dogs, Greyhounds and abandoned dogs and puppies are often available, but they may have no history, so get to know their character before making a decision. It is important to know the dog's estimated age, and about any problems that may appear later, or potential health problems that may cause unexpected costs.

BREED TYPES AND THEIR CHARACTERS

Breed group	Family suitability	Natural behaviour
GUNDOGS e.g. Retrievers, Setters, Spaniels	Good temperaments, calmer demeanour, often easier to train, child friendly, some need plenty of exercise, enjoy family life. Most popular breed group.	Hunting, training, good companions, take part in many canine activities.
HOUNDS e.g. Dachshund, Elkhound	Various sizes, friendly, some gentle breeds suitable for most families.	Natural scenting or sight abilities, fast runners and need plenty of exercise.
PASTORAL e.g. Border Collie, Sheltie	Sheep-herding breeds, many types of coat and temperaments, highly trainable, ideal for competitions.	More in touch with natural behaviours.
TERRIER e.g. Airedale, Soft-coated Wheaten	Intelligent, devoted and loyal, mostly good with children, small and medium sizes to choose from.	Enjoy digging, need training in short sharp bursts, can challenge dynamics if two family terriers disagree.
TOY e.g. Chihuahua, Pekingese, Pug	Small breeds need less walking, more suited to small homes and apartments. Not all ideal as family pets.	Home-loving. Some long coats need time spent on grooming.
UTILITY e.g. Poodle	Variety of sizes available, good family dogs, loyal.	Larger breeds need more space, some may be more difficult to train.
WORKING e.g. Bernese Mountain Dog	Larger sizes available, intelligent, highly trainable so ideal if you want a dog to train for canine activities.	Often have a natural instinct for herding and guarding, vary in reactivity, not all suitable for families.
DESIGNER BREED e.g. Labradoodle, Cockerpoo	Often have best of both breeds, mixed breed groups can unite advantages of character from one with coat of the other.	May not be as healthy as the parent breeds, some unpredictability in size, temperament and character.
MIXED BREED DOG	Mixed parentage, but a dog's looks give clues to its nature, often pretty colours, healthier, puppies and adults available.	Rescue homes may know the background; if not, you pick by what you can see: looks, size, behaviour.

Bringing Your Puppy Home

When you collect your puppy, the breeder should provide:

Pedigree registration documents (not designer breeds)
All pedigree puppies have them, unless breeders have specific reasons why they do not, which they should tell you. You need the documents to change registered ownership with the appropriate Kennel Club.

Contract of sale, receipt for payment Conditions of purchase should be clearly stated, and show how much you paid to make the puppy legally yours.

Puppy diet sheet and often a small supply of food Diet sheets should be provided before collecting the puppy to enable new owners to stock up with the right foods. Some breeders provide several days of food to ensure the puppy has enough of the same provisions, in case some foods are difficult to obtain or need ordering.

Puppy pack/guidance notes on how to care for your puppy Notes should be provided that advise about socialising, training, food, grooming and exercising your puppy for at least the first few months. Some breeders may provide books to help too.

Preparing your home for your puppy

- Select a suitable quiet site that is easily cleaned as a place for puppy's bed.
- Put away anything a puppy could chew.
- Make sure puppy cannot chew electrical leads.
- Use stair gates to prevent access to 'off-limit' areas.
- Store chemicals from the garden or home safely and securely out of the way.
- Make sure gardens are well fenced.
- Register with a local veterinary practice.

Essential items of equipment

Dog beds Cardboard boxes initially. There are various sizes, types and styles of bed from which to choose: wicker, plastic and fabric baskets, beanie bags or cage crates.

Blankets Probably available from around the home or charity shops, but they must be washable, and several are needed to manage during puppy's early days at home.

Towels Old towels for wiping a wet puppy are ideal, as they run and splash around in anything interesting they find.

Pet carrier (above) A pet carrier to bring your puppy home is a useful accessory. Big enough for small or large puppies, it should be lined with newspaper and a blanket for the journey.

Pen Useful for containing puppies at night, particularly until house-training is accomplished.

Water and food bowls At least one of each is needed. Water must always be available; the food bowl needs washing between meals.

Newspaper For lining pens or putting in front of baskets in case of any little accidents.

Food Check out local sources of puppy food before bringing the puppy home, as some are cheaper to order for direct delivery, or may

● Puppies learn to walk best when attached to a light lead. This should be long enough for owners to hold comfortably. Collars should be checked frequently for fit.

be regularly available at a local source in smaller quantities if storage space at home is difficult.

Collar Small puppy collars are useful for puppy to wear as soon as he arrives home. Puppy will be so busy getting to know his new home, he will not have time to wonder what is around his neck.

Lead and harness Puppy leads can be bought along with the collar. Harnesses may be purchased later as these need trying on the puppy to find a suitable fit.

Coat Some breeds feel cold more than others, but coats may need fitting on the puppy.

Grooming kit Some breeds benefit from particular brushes and combs suitable for their type of coat, but small puppies may need softer brushes than adults. Take advice from the breeder on what is best. Soft children's toothbrushes, nail clippers and dog shampoos can be found at pet shops or supermarkets.

Poo bags, shovel and kitchen roll For cleaning up after your puppy when you take him outside – available from local shops or supermarkets.

Choosing toys

A variety of toys in different shapes and sizes are ideal, but try to choose something suitable for the natural behaviours of your puppy's breed. Terriers, for instance, enjoy shaking rag toys; working breeds like to run after balls; Retrievers appreciate dumb-bell shapes to retrieve.

● This 9-week-old puppy enjoys shaking rag toys as it appeals to his natural behaviours.

Ragger toy

Remember when you buy or make toys:
- No sharp edges to damage soft mouths.
- Try to choose 'indestructible' toys and avoid things like decorative bells and tassels which may be detached and swallowed.
- Balls should be large enough not to present any risk of swallowing.
- Old boxes should have any metal staples removed.
- Never give plastic bottles as playthings – puppies can break them into shards.
- Children's toys are unsuitable for puppies to play with and should be avoided.

Food To Keep Your Puppy Healthy

A puppy's food must provide a balanced diet to support growth and development. Dogs are omnivores. Early canine ancestors ate mainly rumen (ruminants' stomach contents) and meat from prey, with the addition of seasonal berries, grains and grass for vitamin and fibre content. Diet is important because food consumption can cause health problems (allergies, obesity, skin problems) and behavioural difficulties (hyperactivity, aggression) if nutritional balances are not correct. Sometimes manipulating the diet can help to balance dietary chemicals, and make puppy training easier. Fresh water is essential, and should always be available. Change the water every day.

● *Dinner time is an ideal time to teach a puppy good manners, but never tease a puppy with his food.*

A balanced diet contains:

Protein For maintenance, growth and regulating the body metabolism.

Carbohydrate Converts to glucose for energy metabolism.

Fat Essential fatty acids maintain skin and coat, and provide energy.

Minerals and vitamins For bone formation, development and good blood chemistry.

Fibre To support digestive function.

Puppies need combinations of these constituents for adequate growth and development, but they do not all eat the same. Different breeds have different needs and a lot depends on size, activity level, adult body needs and growth requirements. Health and condition must also be maintained.

Choosing from the options available

Ideally puppies should remain on the same diet for at least two weeks, while they settle into their new home. Once settled, owners can change the diet to one of their choice, but this must be done carefully and gradually over a period of days:

- 3/4 of old diet, 1/4 of new diet for 3–4 days
- 1/2 of old diet, 1/2 of new diet for 3–4 days
- 1/4 of old diet, 3/4 of new diet for 3–4 days
- All new diet

If at any point the puppy refuses food, go back one step increasing the old diet and decreasing the new for three to four days, then gradually increase the new diet in the same graduated steps.

With so many varieties of food available, owners should think about their preferences, taking into account convenience for feeding, ease of purchase, food storage and any breed nutritional requirements. The table outlines what is available for you to help you decide what might be best for your puppy – but do also discuss this with the breeder. Take care with bones – small raw bones like chicken wings crunch up safely, cooked ones may splinter.

WHAT CHOICES ARE AVAILABLE?

Wet food   Canned

- Contains meat and offal plus 80 per cent water
- Often need an additional mixer or meal
- Supposedly a lower incidence of allergies
- Brands specific to country of manufacture
- Digestion takes around nine hours
- Bulky to store tins
- Will attract flies if left down for long

Sealed semi moist packs

- Similar to canned but usually more meat
- Food is not sterilised in packaging
- Stabilised with preservatives or chilling

Frozen

- 100 per cent meat or animal parts included
- Requires a mixer
- Used with vegetables for a natural diet
- Must be stored in a freezer
- Defrosted before use

Dried food   Kibble

- Contains animal by-products
- Contains around 20 per cent meat base
- Convenient to weigh out and clean to serve
- Free access to bowl as dog requires
- Brand leaders available worldwide
- Can be used for training treats
- Digestion takes around 16 hours
- Less needed, means less faecal output
- More acceptable for vegetarian owners

Natural/Mixed diets   Raw meat, vegetables and small raw bones

- Home-made from fresh/frozen meat
- Variety of vegetables to prepare
- Adding vitamins and minerals is necessary
- More time-consuming to prepare
- Digestion takes around five to six hours
- Reduced allergies and digestive problems
- More benefits to health as it is a natural diet
- Less faecal output, more goodness absorbed

Looking After Your Puppy's Health

Puppies need regular health checks, particularly as they grow. Different checks are needed either daily, weekly, monthly or yearly.

DAILY CHECKS

Eye cleaning Some puppies have 'goo' in their eyes after sleeping; remove this daily with damp cotton wool to prevent infections. Continual runny eyes can indicate infection, allergy or a dietary problem and need veterinary treatment.

Summer/winter checks Check between the toes for grass seeds or stones in summer and ice particles in winter. Also check for seasonal parasites, broken nails or hardened lumps of mud stuck in the hair between the toes.

Handling experience Regular handling of a puppy encourages socialisation. Different breeds may need more handling, but this develops a puppy's understanding and acceptance of being handled from a young age. It also helps if puppies are used to being handled when they visit the vet for health checks or treatment, and they are more likely to accept grooming, training or other necessary attention calmly as they mature.

Teeth cleaning Chews and bones help to keep teeth clean, but brushing teeth *(above)* twice a week with a toothbrush and dog toothpaste is beneficial. Teeth should look clean with no tartar build-up and gums should be pink and healthy-looking. Check for biscuit pieces or bone segments stuck in the gums. Good diet, teeth cleaning and some homeopathic remedies used regularly, along with the provision of bones and chews, will prevent costly veterinary treatment and keep puppies healthy.

Paw pad condition Pads can easily be injured, cuts may become infected and need cleaning. Dipping the paw in a little warm salty water or an antiseptic cleansing wash will prevent infections and may avoid a trip to the vet.

Encourage your puppy to sit for handling.

● *All puppies should be well handled before they go to their new home, and should enjoy this contact. If they are nervous, encourage them by gentle stroking and giving a small titbit.*

WEEKLY CHECKS

Lumps and bumps Check skin, tummy, testicles, nipples and between the toes weekly to detect lumps from injuries, or any other problems. Early detection keeps treatment costs down.

Safe Nail Clipping

Take several small clips, so you do not risk cutting the quick.

2nd

1st

QUICK

If cut, the quick will bleed profusely. Blood flow can be stopped with styptic powder.

● *Bath small puppies in the sink or a bowl, larger puppies can go in the bath.*

Nail cutting Dog's nails grow and need trimming just like ours. Use proper dog nail clippers (weekly for puppies, monthly for adults) and remember to do both paw nails and dew claw nails on the inside of the leg. Walking on hard surfaces like pavements helps to wear nails down, but young puppies will not have this opportunity until they are fully vaccinated.

To cut nails: pull the hair away from the nail base, find the quick (the pink tube in the centre of the nail that contains nerves and blood supply) and trim small bits off the end of the nail leaving a gap of at least 5mm to the start of the quick. **Do not cut into the quick** as this is painful and causes bleeding.

Ear cleaning Clean ears regularly, particularly on dogs with long floppy ears or long coats where hair grows in the ear canal. This can be plucked out by hand.

MONTHLY CHECKS

Bathing Puppies enjoy rolling around in the dirt while playing, and love snuffling in the garden or undergrowth and paddling in muddy water. Some breeds can go without a bath for some time, a good brushing being sufficient to keep coats clean. Long coats, however, are likely to need bathing with reasonable frequency to keep them looking good. Use dog shampoo from pet stores, choosing one suitable for the type of coat, age of the dog, colour of the coat, length of the coat and so on.

Gender checks Perform these monthly, particularly in breeds more prone to lumps and bumps. Checking around the testicles and nipples is important. Entire (not spayed) bitches can be prone to mammary tumours, which if surgically removed early will prevent the size of the lump increasing and perhaps becoming malignant.

Faeces and urine checks These checks can pick up quickly on early health problems, so it is worth taking time to do them every so often. Faeces needs checking as loose motions could indicate an upset tummy, the wrong kind of diet or worm infestation. Irritated bowels may present as a loose, mucus-covered, sometimes blood-stained motion; a very dry stool could indicate a diet too high in fat. Somewhere in between is about right! Also check urine colour, quantity and frequency of passing urine, particularly if a puppy starts drinking a lot of water unexpectedly.

Puppy's Health *continued*

YEARLY CHECKS

Inoculations While they are costly, inoculations early in life are recommended, although opinion is divided on the need to continue them after the first year; some people prefer homeopathic remedies for safety reasons. However, puppies holidaying in kennels will need their yearly inoculations kept up to date. Trips to the vet for inoculations will usually include a yearly veterinary check. First visits could include micro-chipping with a small chip that holds identification details and information about you as the owner of the dog (*below*). Owners wanting to take their puppy abroad for holidays should ask their vet about procedures for rabies injections (which lasts three years) as these cannot be done at the same time as yearly vaccinations. Non-compliance could cause problems when you go abroad.

Puppies travelling abroad need:
- Pet passports
- Micro-chipping
- Rabies vaccination and blood testing
- Tapeworm treatment, 24–48 hours before return
- Travel with approved transport companies on authorised routes

Veterinary health checks Most vets listen to the heart and lungs, check the mouth and teeth, feel the tummy for lumps, look at coat condition, ask questions about general conditions, worming and flea regimes or inquire about any problems occurring since the last check. They will weigh the puppy, ask about eating habits and possibly suggest a blood test.

LIFETIME CHECKS

For many breeds health checks are needed to identify problems that occur in specific dog breeds. This is particularly the case with dogs used for breeding as this prevents puppies being born that perpetuate health problems. Some breeds have genetic illnesses and specific tests can help to identify them. They include blood tests to check kidney and liver function; hip X-rays (at one year old) to advise on the joint condition; eye testing (done in the litter or later); DNA testing from blood specimens to identify a predisposition to any inherited conditions. Copies of the parent dogs' health checks should always be shown to prospective owners when they purchase their puppy. Breeding stock checks are costly, and not needed for pets unless problems are suspected. It's best to teach puppies to stand still on a table beforehand for this.

Neutering

Neutering dogs or bitches is personal choice. The advantages are that males are less inclined to seek bitches, and bitches stop having messy seasons, and accidental litters are prevented. Some changes may occur after neutering, such as weight gain, or coat texture changes, but generally many dogs enjoy better health, and both genders have a lower incidence of cancer. Bitches avoid phantom pregnancies or womb infections, which are serious.

Worming

Puppies need worming every three months until they are two, and then every six months, unless they are in a household with young children when the three-month regime should be maintained. Broad-spectrum wormers from vets are the best option, and worming records help you to remember the frequency of treatment. Worming protection covers roundworms, tapeworms, hookworms/whipworms and heartworms.

● *Puppies biting around the base of the tail need checking for fleas.*

● *Gentle petting encourages puppies to wait while you do daily checks.*

themselves to the skin and are often grouped together on areas of the body. They suck blood from the host and can cause serious conditions, such as Lyme's disease.

Grooming

All dogs need grooming at least weekly, and often more frequently. Grooming puppies encourages them to accept handling for physical examination and visits to the vet, and also helps them to bond with owners. Puppies learn that their owner is 'boss', because they learn to behave while standing on a table. Some breeds need grooming daily; others with increased frequency when they are shedding copiously and dead hair needs removing. Some have low- or non-shedding coats which mat and tangle if dead hair is not brushed out. Dogs with ears that flop down over their ear canals should have them

Fleas, ticks and lice

Treat your puppy for fleas, ticks and lice in warmer weather, when they can migrate to humans. Various treatment choices are available from vets or good pet shops, including flea collars, drops, spot-on treatments and insecticidal baths.

Flea infestation can cover puppies, and the fleas may take up residence in carpets and furnishings. Puppies suffer intense itching as the fleas suck blood causing allergic reactions. Fleas breed quickly, and are seen on skin as moving specks of dirt.

Different lice and mites affect different parts of the body but, depending on their type, they can cause irritation with erupting or flaky skin problems.

Ticks are round bean-shaped parasites that attach

cleaned and wiped weekly to prevent ear infections, and any smell from the ear should be investigated. Long-coated dogs benefit from having long ear hairs plucked out weekly to prevent infection occurring. Some breeds may need to be seen by a professional groomer which can be costly, but many breeders are willing to show you how to do this yourself.

Puppy Growth and Development

Dogs exhibit more variations in height and weight than any other animal does. Puppies can be as small as Chihuahuas at 16–20cm (6–8.5in) in height and 0.5–3kg (1–6.5lb) in weight or as big as a Great Dane at 76–86cm (30–34in) and 45–54kg (100–120lb). Larger breeds take much longer than small toy breeds to grow to adulthood, but the principles behind their growth and development differ very little. In larger breeds, however, nutrition is even more important because diet can greatly influence bone growth and structure over the longer period of development. Bone disease can result if their diet does not have the correct nutritional balance.

● *Best of friends and stemming from the same ancestral source, but this Great Dane needs more time to grow than small dogs like Chihuahuas, and has different nutritional needs to achieve his lofty height.*

The right diet

For this reason, owners bear a weighty responsibility to choose the correct balanced diet to suit the size of their dog. Specific nutritional components of diets are crucial, and owners should seek advice from the breeder on what to feed their puppy for at least the first six months of life. There are plenty of nutritional dog foods available, which owners can try, but do observe your puppy carefully to make sure he is putting on the right amount of weight and bone growth and is developing normally. Calcium, for example, is critically important for healthy bone growth and development, because bone stores calcium. Some foods are provided specifically to address this requirement in certain breeds of dog, but they may not suit all breeds. A dog given too much calcium in its diet may even develop deformed bone and joints, because growth rate becomes uneven, while too little calcium and phosphorus may cause weak, deformed bones. Energy levels are affected too, depending on the breed's size and level of activity. Medium and large breeds fed too much energy-rich food may suffer obesity and skeletal problems as a consequence.

The graph illustrated will help you to estimate the projected pattern of growth of your type of dog, but it should not be taken as an exact measure.

| 1 day | 10 days | 4 weeks | 6 weeks | 9 weeks | 14 weeks | 5 months | 24 months |

Body Weights of Growing Dogs of Different Breeds

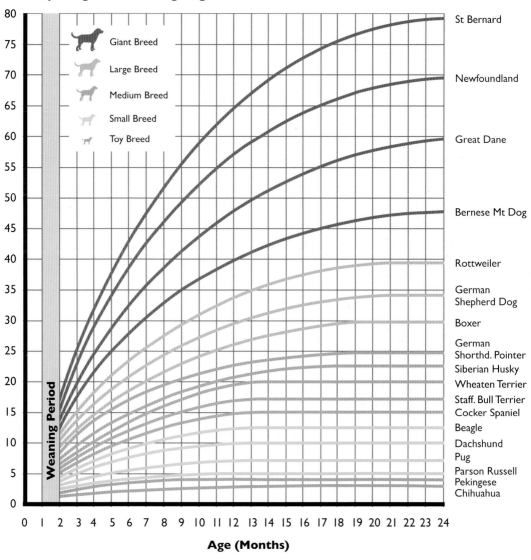

Keeping Puppy Fit and Trim

Obesity can be a real problem for your puppy if you overfeed him, or give the wrong kind of diet, because most fat cells are laid down during puppies' critical growth phase. It is best to control this problem by not allowing it to start in the first place. Around 25 per cent of dogs are known to be overweight, and they suffer the consequences of poor health, which may well include costly treatments at the vet. Obese puppies are more likely to suffer from joint problems, a reduced quality of life and shorter lifespan, all of which can be avoided by selecting a sensible diet. Some breeds are particularly prone to problems if they are long-backed because of the double whammy of the strain on their spinal joints from carrying the extra weight and the consequent lack of exercise. All dogs are at risk of obesity, but breeds that are particularly susceptible are Cairn Terriers, Dachshunds, Cavalier King Charles Spaniels, Beagles, Basset Hounds, Labradors and Rottweilers.

Just like humans, puppies avoid all sorts of problems if they are maintained in the right environment to enjoy a healthy lifestyle.

Maintaining your puppy's weight

It is important to check your puppy's weight regularly to avoid him becoming too thin or too fat. A healthy dog has bright eyes, a healthy 'bloom' on his coat, and a skeleton covered in the right amount of flesh. If this is not the case, owners should:

- Make sure quantities of the diet are correct.
- Increase or reduce the essential fat components of the diet.
- Take more exercise, or play more with the dog.
- Provide more toys for stimulation.
- Avoid too many treats.
- Avoid overfeeding the puppy during its crucial growing phase.

Growing up healthy

Most owners expect their puppy to grow up healthy, and if they are feeding correctly, exercising carefully, training appropriately and spending the right amount of time on play, grooming, love and attention, then all should be well. However, there may be occasions when for some reason a puppy fails to thrive, and owners may be left wondering what they have done wrong. The table on the opposite page gives ideas of how your puppy should look and behave if it is in good health.

● *The healthy Pug (left) is a good example of how to care for a puppy's health by not overindulging him with too much food.*

HEALTHY PUPPY CHARACTERISTICS

What to look at	What you should find
Eyes	Clean bright inquisitive eyes with no evidence of dullness, no 'goo', crusts or infection in the corners.
Nose	Cold nose, with a moist feel.
Mouth	Clean pink healthy-looking gums with clean white teeth, sweet-smelling breath.
Ears	Clean ears with no evidence of dirt or wax and no smell.
Skin and coat	Slightly pink in light-coloured dogs with healthy hair growth. Coat and skin look clean with no crusty skin and with a healthy 'bloom'.
Paws	Trimmed nails, hard pads without roughness, clean between the toes.
Rear end	Clean around the anus with no dried faeces, trim off some coat if there is a deposit. Faeces are mid-brown in colour (depends on food), slightly moist, with no mucus or blood in evidence.
Appetite	Puppy is hungry and keen to eat his dinner without hesitation.
General appearance	Growth and development is keeping apace with breed expectations.
Mental responses	Puppy is interested and stimulated by everything going on around him. Curious and investigative, keen to explore.
Activity levels	Puppy is running around full of life, bright and alert and ready to do anything.

● *Your puppy should exhibit joie de vivre, and be inquisitive and mischievous if he is in a healthy condition. A puppy that is listless, sleeping a lot and not enjoying exercise needs checking.*

Learning About The World

Different dog breeds exhibit behaviours which are natural to their breed because our ancestors bred them with those traits – gundogs retrieve for hunting, working dogs guard people and terriers dig to hunt prey. Consequently, you can expect dogs from particular groups to display behaviours that are associated with those characteristics. You should try to take advantage of these natural behaviours when socialising and training your puppy. **Socialisation** refers to the process of getting your puppy accustomed to the presence of other people and animals around him, while **habituation** refers to the process of getting him used to other places and unfamiliar objects in their different environments.

• *Rewarding good behaviour helps puppies to learn manners.*

everyday noises around their home and accept a repertoire of different household events. They have some idea of personal space in relation to toys, doing a wee, where to sleep and eat, or what they normally eat, but they need time to get used to this routine in their new home.

There may be other pets in the new household to which puppies need to be introduced if they are to grow up accepting their position in the family order. Basic training can start at this time; it involves learning how to behave with other people or other pets in the family, becoming familiar with the daily routine, learning to come when called, to sit for treats, accepting who is in charge and not to bite anyone with their sharp little teeth. Socialisation as the puppy becomes more adventurous should address their need to learn from experience and understand how to behave at home and in the wider community.

Socialisation

Most breeders will have started this process before a puppy leaves for his new home as socialisation starts at birth and progresses through different stages up to six months. While socialisation is important from early days, new owners must spend time following a process of socialisation continuously to produce a confident, well-behaved dog. Most 8-week-old puppies are ready to move on to new challenges; they are familiar with

Habituation

Gardens are usually the first place in which puppies learn about their environment, and they also learn where they can go and where they cannot. Outside the garden, habituation training must include travelling in a car, visiting the vet, or going to a groomer – these are all different environments about which a puppy must learn. Providing new stimulus is essential while your puppy is becoming familiar with you and your home to prevent him becoming nervous or fear-aggressive when he goes elsewhere. A puppy cannot g

• *Introduced early, puppies and kittens learn about each other in the right way and will respect one another's company.*

understand that is unacceptable to play-bite humans.

Puppies encourage and invite others to play, and learn to attract attention doing a play bow, or bringing toys. These actions also teach them how to interact, and help to develop and stimulate their minds. Encouraging puppies to play frequently during socialising helps them to grow up more intelligent, able to problem-solve, and to act more confidently when they find themselves in different situations. Encouraging play using toys filled with food treats is helpful for dogs who spend time alone; they can play to alleviate boredom and reduce separation anxiety problems. Providing toys can also direct a puppy's natural destructive urges onto items that can be easily and cheaply replaced.

When given plenty of stimulation through play, dogs develop quick and active minds. Using play in sequences

out until immunisations are complete, but you can carry him down the road to see the world outside the back garden, or visit a neighbour's garden to explore. However, while doing this, make sure that you prevent the puppy from doing things that you do not want him to do: i.e. climbing on furniture or going upstairs. This is all valuable early training.

Play

Play is important for puppies, starting at around two and half weeks. Puppies learn their life skills in play, and owners can take advantage of playtime to teach control of natural behaviours and desirable social skills before bad habits form. Barking may seem cute in puppies, but it is not so cute when it happens continuously for attention when the puppy grows up. Problem behaviours may occur, but if corrected early, they can be stopped. Play-biting is an example. Through play-biting with their littermates puppies learn how and when to inhibit their biting response, but owners must correct this consistently for the puppy to

● *Playing is good for learning, but make sure only toys are used!*

to elicit a response, and giving treats to reward good behaviour, helps them understand how to behave to earn a reward. Stimulus-response training or clicker training use similar methods, so the basics learned through play help to prepare puppies for their more formal training later on.

Training Your Puppy

Training should impact on four specific aspects of a puppy's life: his physical well-being, emotional state, intelligence and social confidence. To develop satisfactorily, puppies need to be habituated to different places, to learn how to socialise with different people and other animals, and to learn by association with different events how to respond in particular ways to various situations. The basis of training comes from practising behaviours that reinforce actions you want to encourage. Puppies learn by consequences: behaving one way gets a reward, behaving in another way results in a gruff '**No**'.

● *Lure and reward training demonstrating the movement for 'Sit'. The puppy follows the treat and drops into a sitting position.*

In time, they are conditioned to learn this association of positive reinforcement for good behaviour. Two methods of learning are often used for training:

Clicker training Puppies learn the exact moment that desired behaviours occur because it is 'marked' by the sound of a clicker, which is followed by a reward such as a treat. This is called positive reinforcement, and the puppy learns by association. For example, if a dog jumps up and is told to get down on four paws, the owner should click the moment it does so. In this way the puppy registers the desired behaviour. Clickers are ideal for close-work training, but are not so effective for distance work.

Lure and reward Food treats are used as reinforcement and held close to the puppy's nose. Desired responses can be stimulated by movement of the treat. For example, by passing a treat backwards over the puppy's head while saying 'Sit', the puppy can be encouraged to move into a Sit position from a Stand. He automatically sits, thus earning the reward. With patience puppies can be lured into sequences of movement which is the beginning of training tricks.

Training for canine activities

Well-trained dogs are a joy to be with. Owners who persevere with training may find that keeping dogs is so engrossing that they enjoy getting involved in canine activities such as agility, obedience, flyball, sledging and so on. However, this depends on the dog's physical make-up, the natural behaviours typical of the breed, and how much time owners are prepared to spend on achieving success. Owners must be single-minded, patient, confident and committed to regular practice. Some breeds need very sensitive training (gentle voice, calm, quiet but determined), while others may need slightly firmer treatment to ensure success (stronger voice tone, more assertive handling). Harsh methods (shouting, scolding, smacking) should never be used with any dog. They are always counter-productive and harm your relationship with your dog.

Exercise

All dogs need exercise, but different breeds need varying amounts. Most breeders give advice on this, but generally puppies need to start with gentle walking, which should gradually build up to two short walks daily. When old enough, one good walk daily should satisfy an adult, bearing in mind its size, energy levels and the amount of mental stimulation needed. By exercising correctly, your puppy's health improves, his mind is stimulated and emotional equilibrium maintained. Exercise also facilitates bonding through play, hunting behaviours and social meetings with other people and their dogs.

As a guide (when fully grown):

Small dogs need two short walks daily of around half an hour each.

Medium dogs need around an hour once a day.

Large breeds may need up to two hours (or more) of running and galloping, plus extra time for play.

Lifestyles:

Apartment dogs may need a short trot down the road every two to three hours, plus a longer walk to satisfy their size and energy requirements.

Dogs with small gardens may need two good hour-long runs as they will not be able to get as much exercise by playing around in the garden.

Large dogs with big gardens can burn off a lot of energy and may be happy with less, but they will often accept as much exercise as they can get.

Using this book

This book provides useful information for prospective owners to give them a general idea about a dog they may want to take on as a family pet. It does not offer details on breed standards, and owners wanting show puppies or a hunting breed for a specific purpose should consult Kennel Club standards or experts in those breeds. Readers should bear in mind that the descriptions of individual breeds refer to typical specimens, but the impact of background breeding, environmental influences, socialisation, quality of training, plus the health of the puppy's forebears may mean that individual dogs differ from these norms.

Anyone purchasing a puppy should research their chosen breed very carefully and make sure that they buy from reputable breeders. Where breeds are identified as being **Good with children** in the Character Traits box, the entry assumes that the dog has been introduced to, and socialised with, children properly. The table entry for **Ease of training** marks some breeds as Poor, but this trait can be positively influenced by dedicated training and the handling ability of individual owners. It is a general guideline, not an immutable fact. This guide aims to provide insight into the basics of a breed and identifies the raw material that lies within each puppy. Ultimately it is up to individual owners to guide and support their dog in the best way possible to develop its own unique potential.

● *Lots of breed information can be found online.*

Small dogs

Small dogs, from the dainty Chihuahua to little spaniels, are easier to keep in smaller homes or apartments. They still have lots of energy, intelligence and character, but they need less food and exercise to keep them satisfied. They also make good watch dogs. Some are not particularly suitable as family dogs unless trained well but, chosen carefully, owners will find much to love in these small breeds.

Chihuahua

Originating in South America, this sacred dog of the ancient Mexicans was pictured on ancient Toltec pyramids, and is said to have died alongside Aztec rulers to guide their souls to heaven and expiate their sins. The first modern specimens were found around 1850 in the Mexican state of Chihuahua and bred in the USA. Smallest of the toy breeds, the Chihuahua is lively and playful, loving affection and company. Graceful and compact with a saucy expression, he is alert and highly intelligent. Possessive of his owner, he loves being the centre of attention. Ideal in a small apartment, he enjoys daily walking and mental stimulation. Available in smooth and long coats, in a variety of attractive colours, he can sometimes be used as a fashion accessory because his small size will fit in handbags. Popularity brings with it a need to purchase from a reputable breeder who pays attention to health and temperament.

Colour choices?

Colour combinations and markings vary from solid to marked or splashed. Usual colours are: fawn/brown, brindle fawn/brown, silver fawn, silver grey, white, cream, chocolate, black and tan, and black. Merle (a marbled colour effect) is not allowed because there may be health problems.

How much grooming?

Both coats are manageable. Long coats take two years to grow so regular grooming is essential; a gentle daily brush to remove tangles is best. Smooth coats need grooming to brush out dead hair and usually shed more.

Do they make good pets?

Their small size makes them suitable for most family homes. Better with older children, they are not suitable for small children as their size makes them vulnerable. They enjoy being the centre of attention and like being part of small groups, but often attach themselves to individual members of the family.

● *These delicate dogs are very compact and make delightful companions for owners with smaller homes.*

What home suits them?

This breed can live in apartments, or small homes with gardens, in town or the country. Loving homes providing companionship, regular daily walks and play, with plenty to do makes for a happy little dog.

What sort of owner?

Chihuahuas are unsuitable for working owners, because they need lots of attention and stimulation. Their possessive nature means owners must give, and accept, plenty of affection. Suitable for the housebound, they exercise through play or the occasional walk, although they also enjoy outdoor pursuits with an active family.

How much exercise and stimulation?

Accepting of limited exercise, they also enjoy walking. Indoors, Chihuahuas exercise by playing with each other or their owner. Stimulation is good, because their minds are active and agile.

Friendly with other pets?

This breed can appear reserved with other pets unless socialised as a puppy. Generally, however, they prefer their own kind for company.

Is puppy training easy?

Chihuahuas are not easily trained but can learn the basics quite early on. A firm, consistent approach with gentle training techniques is preferable. Some are slow to become house-trained, but patience pays dividends.

Character Traits	Poor	Average	Good	Excellent
Attitude to other dogs				
Quietness				
Behaviour at home				
Guarding ability				
Good with children				
Ease of training				
Obedience to owner				

Time to maturity: 2 years
Male height: 15–22cm (6–8.5in)
Female height: 15–22cm (6-8.5in)
Weight: 0.5–3kg (1–6.5lb)
Average lifespan: 10–18 years

Special puppy care?

Keep them warm, as puppies are sensitive to cold. Puppy eyes need attention and cleaning, and daily grooming is needed especially for the longer coats. Owners should take care of the puppy's head during the first six months as some have an open molera (a gap in the bones) on top of the skull (similar to the fontanelle of human babies). Although low maintenance to feed, puppies need careful feeding at every growth stage.

Possible health problems?

Mostly healthy little dogs, they can suffer from slipping knee caps, epilepsy and heart problems. Due to their small size and sometimes picky eating habits, they may experience low blood sugar levels. Potential owners should buy from breeders with healthy stock who provide reports of any health checks.

What can we do together?

Ideal as companion dogs, and quite popular for showing. Some enjoy long walks and mini-agility.

Don't forget!

The Chihuahua's size can make them vulnerable to bad handling or being trodden on. Buy from a reputable breeder. Sometimes called teacup, pocket size, tiny toy, miniature or standard sizes, these names only increase their value and are not associated with the breed.

Small dogs

● *Smooth coat Chihuahuas have coats that are velvety to the touch. These puppies are about 10 weeks old.*

Pekingese

Other names: Lion Dog, Chinese Spaniel, Pelchie Dog

The Pekingese or Lion Dog is one of the oldest dog breeds. Pekingese were the royal dogs of China because they resembled the Chinese Guardian Lion statues that traditionally were placed in front of palaces and temples. They led highly privileged lives in the Imperial Court during the Tang Dynasty. The first five Pekingese came to Britain following the storming of the Imperial Summer Palace by British troops in 1860 and their offspring arrived in the USA not long after this. Pekingese are beautiful dogs with a superior manner and great personality, and they are completely devoted to their owners. Good mannered and dignified, they can be playful and sporty, but dislike being left out and can be stubborn. An imperious, but calm and good-natured companion dog, their health has been affected by breeders exaggerating certain features, such as the short, flat face. Coat care may prove difficult for busy modern families.

Colour choices?

Available colours are red, gold, sable, cream, white, black, black and tan and occasionally blue or slate grey, but all Pekingese must have a black muzzle, nose and lips. Albinos are unacceptable and may have health problems.

How much grooming?

Their double coat of long, straight, coarse hair over thick, soft fur loses a lot of hair very readily. Most Pekingese enjoy grooming, which must go right down to the skin using a bristle brush and comb. The neck mane and the profuse feathering behind the ears, under armpits, legs and tail need extra attention to prevent matting. Face folds need wiping daily, and bathing regularly is needed to maintain clean healthy coats. Pet owners may prefer a short clip for convenience, but even then regular brushing is still needed.

Do they make good pets?

Pekingese are good mannered and

● *This noble dog has royal bearing.*

make excellent pets, but tend to attach themselves to one person although they still appreciate being in a family. Better with older children, they do not always tolerate young children.

What home suits them?

Pekingese suit most locations, and adapt well to apartment living. They enjoy homes with gardens, and like to explore undergrowth.

What sort of owner?

Strong-willed and independent, Pekingese become very attached to their owner, who must return devotion, share a sense of humour and treat them with the respect their superiority deserves. Owners need plenty of time for companionship, and must accept that even as puppies, coats need plenty of grooming as Pekingese shed profusely. Long coats are unsuitable for the house-proud.

How much exercise and stimulation?

Pekingese tolerate very little exercise because of breathing difficulties and short legs. They are not athletic, so enjoy short daily strolls at a slow pace for constitutional purposes. Walking in hot weather is inadvisable because of overheating and breathing problems. Puppies gain most stimulation from spending time with their owner.

Friendly with other pets?

Rarely aggressive, Pekingese fit in better with other pets when socialised early. Puppies may indulge in boisterous play, but care

Character Traits	Poor	Average	Good	Excellent
Attitude to other dogs				
Quietness				
Behaviour at home				
Guarding ability				
Good with children				
Ease of training				
Obedience to owner				

Time to maturity: 2 years
Male height: 15–23cm (6–9in)
Female height: 15–23cm (6–9in)
Weight: 2.75–5.5kg (6–12lb)
Average lifespan: 12–14 years

is needed to prevent injury to their prominent eyes.

Is puppy training easy?

Temperamentally Pekingese are positive and self-opinionated and expect owners to train them only in 'appropriate' skills. Handlers must be firm but gentle in training and can expect intelligent and willing responses from a quick learner.

Special puppy care?

Puppy coat care is essential to prepare for an adult life involving plenty of grooming. Care is needed to prevent injury to young dogs by rough handling, particularly with their prominent eyes, long backs and short legs.

Possible health problems?

Pekingese are prone to breathing problems, overheating, heart, eye (tear gland infections and injuries) and back problems, and patella luxation (dislocating kneecaps). The folds on the face can become infected if not cleaned regularly. Puppy heart problems are usually successfully treated if detected early.

What can we do together?

Mainly a companion dog, Pekingese enjoy showing, and sometimes may be successful in competitive obedience (if not too energetic).

● *Cute and cuddly, and just 8 weeks old.*

Don't forget!

Pick up Pekingese carefully, supporting them front and back in the arms, so as not to hurt their backs.

Small dogs

Brussels Griffon

Other names: Griffon Bruxellois, Petit Brabançon, Griffon Belge

This bearded, gnome-like, and charmingly self-important little dog originated in the city of Brussels and developed from local street dogs. His personality and skills found favour in stables as a small terrier ideal for hunting vermin. In the late 19th century Belgian coachmen became fond of the Griffon, and they were soon accompanying travelling nobility as fearless little guard dogs. Queen Marie Henriette became a breeder of Griffons, and increased their popularity worldwide. The Griffon's facial expression and whiskers endow him with monkey-like features, which together with a loving, playful nature make for an entertaining companion. There are two distinct varieties – the wire-coated and the smooth-coated (Petit Brabançon). Griffons have virtually no vices, and are intelligent, obedient, easily managed and cared for. They can sometimes be shy, but are usually fearless guard dogs, affectionate companions and ideal for apartment living.

Colour choices?

Accepted colours are clear red, black or black and rich tan. The Griffon Belge is noted for its mixed red and black hair combination which is accepted in Europe and the USA, but not in the UK.

How much grooming?

A Griffon's wiry coat needs grooming with a firm brush and comb most days, and hand-stripping every two to three months to keep the coat looking good. Smooth-coated Griffons need brushing once a week using a hound glove. Their large eyes and the wrinkle above the nose needs cleaning daily, during which you should also check for lacerations which may cause infection.

Do they make good pets?

These little dogs tend to form a particularly strong bond with their owners, and are especially suitable for single or older people. They may not appreciate boisterous small children, but their tough and sturdy physique, together with a

● *The Griffon has an elfin, quizzical expression. He is a great character.*

delightful even temper, make them ideal pets for sensible families.

What home suits them?

Ideal for apartment dwellers because of their size and easy care, they really enjoy spending time at home cuddling up with their owner rather than going for a walk, although they still need exercise and stimulation. Their home matters little so long as their owner returns their affection. Griffons are vulnerable to overheating, and need a cool place in shade to rest in hot weather.

What sort of owner?

Griffons are not suitable for owners with small children because they can be jealous and demanding, and appreciate a quiet home life. A sensible owner willing to spend time on grooming and training without pampering their Griffon is best.

How much exercise and stimulation?

Griffons do enjoy long country walks, but also don't mind not going far. Mostly they need plenty of mental stimulation through lots of play and training.

Friendly with other pets?

Having originated as ratters, forming friendships with small household pets may be risky, but if well socialised from early puppy days, they usually do well with other cats and dogs.

Is puppy training easy?

Griffons can be emotionally sensitive, stubborn, wilful and easily

Character Traits	Poor	Average	Good	Excellent
Attitude to other dogs				
Quietness				
Behaviour at home				
Guarding ability				
Good with children				
Ease of training				
Obedience to owner				

Time to maturity: 2 years
Male height: 18–20cm (7–8in)
Female height: 18–20cm (7–8in)
Weight: 2.3–5kg (5–11lb)
Average lifespan: 10–15 years

● *Bearded and gnome-like, these 8-week-old Griffon puppies have bags of charm, and their big trusting eyes and jaunty, unspoilt urchin look is most appealing.*

Possible health problems?

Healthy and long-lived, Griffons can suffer from cleft palates, usually found post birthing, glaucoma and cataracts, patella luxation (dislocating kneecaps), heart murmurs and syringomyelia, a serious condition when fluid-filled cavities develop within the spinal cord.

Small dogs

What can we do together?

Despite their sometimes stubborn character, Griffons can do well at obedience and agility. Generally though, they just enjoy being companion pets.

Don't forget!

Never play roughly with Griffon puppies as they can be sensitive, and always encourage your puppy to lie down in the shade and give him plenty of cool, not ice cold, water on a very hot day.

bored, but while they are challenging to train, they learn quickly and with positive reward-based training, which includes some fun activities, can excel at agility or obedience trials.

Special puppy care?

Griffon puppies enjoy playing, but take care with their eyes which are easily injured. Overheating is a problem so puppies must be well protected from the heat of the sun.

Yorkshire Terrier

The Yorkie came from a mixed terrier background, and was bred for catching rats in the Yorkshire cotton mills. He rose to popularity in Victorian times to become an aristocratic lady's companion, reaching exalted heights when he became popular in fashionable Hollywood circles. Although small, he is always busy, bustling, lively and full of importance. Not a lapdog, he has a true terrier spirit, and is brave, dominant and strong-willed. Yorkies have a courageous personality but must be guided through puppyhood, because without proper training and socialising they can be aggressive towards larger dogs. Coat care is a must if he has been chosen to show, as he needs plenty of grooming to maintain his fine silky coat as a gleaming mantle fit for the show ring. There is a noticeable difference between a Yorkie bought for showing and one bought as a pet, both in size and coat.

Colour choices?

There are usually four colour combinations: blue and tan, blue and gold, black and tan, black and gold. Other colours are not acceptable and may carry health problems. Puppies are generally black with tan points, changing to dark steel blue several months later. Hair on the head, chest and lower legs should be rich bright tan, until the coat matures at around three years old. A white star marking is sometimes found on the chest.

How much grooming?

The long silky hair of show dogs is not seen on pets because it needs special care and tying in ribbons and tissue paper to prevent damage. Most owners trim the coat short and brush out tangles. The fringe over the eyes is tied back in a bow or trimmed neatly over the forehead. The coat is hypoallergenic because very little hair is shed, so needs regular brushing.

Do they make good pets?

Yorkies prefer older children and

● *The gleaming mantle of the Yorkie takes a lot of brushing to keep it looking good, and takes a long time to mature.*

make great family pets, but are particularly good companions for adults, being very loyal and loving. They are not suitable around toddlers or children who tease, and may snap if provoked.

What home suits them?

Yorkies enjoy pampered indoor life in a house or apartment, in the town or country. Needing very little space they fit in most homes quite well.

What sort of owner?

This breed demands regular attention and is very loving, appreciating owners with plenty of time who are devoted to their every need. Great fun when trained well, they enjoy being active and taking part in family life.

How much exercise and stimulation?

Puppies need short walks daily. As a sporting dog, they enjoy being out and about, so adults need a reasonable daily walk. Yorkies also enjoy hunting down rabbit holes or taking on the challenge of a bigger dog. Strict training may be necessary if he gets up to mischief!

Friendly with other pets?

Very amenable to other pets, particularly cats, if well socialised and raised with them. Bearing in mind the Yorkie ratting ancestry, small family pets such as mice, rats and hamsters may be at risk.

Character Traits	Poor	Average	Good	Excellent
Attitude to other dogs				
Quietness				
Behaviour at home				
Guarding ability				
Good with children				
Ease of training				
Obedience to owner				

Time to maturity: The coat can take up to 3 years to mature
Male height: 18–25cm (7–10in)
Female height: 18–25cm (7–10in)
Weight: Up to 3.2kg (7lb)
Average lifespan: 12–17 years

Is puppy training easy?

His dominant personality means he may bark at anything, and needs strict handling to behave as a companion dog. Intelligent and quick to learn, he can be distracted. High energy levels and enthusiasm mean he can be stubborn.

Special puppy care?

The puppy coat needs daily grooming from early on because it does not shed naturally. Training starts early with short walks to socialise him with other animals.

Possible health problems?

Although usually quite healthy, Yorkies can suffer from dislocating elbows or knees, Legg-Perthes disease of the hip joint, cataracts, epilepsy and heart problems. Choose breeders who check for health problems.

From workman's ratter to noble ladies companion, the Yorkie is a popular choice for a family pet. This one is 6 months old.

What can we do together?

Show dog and companion dog. With their boundless energy and enthusiasm Yorkies may excel at mini-agility.

Don't forget!

Yorkies can get bored easily so provide a range of toys that keep his mind active if he needs to be left alone for short periods.

Small dogs

Standard Dachshund

Other names: Teckel, Dackel, German Badgerhound

These charming little dogs are thought to have originated in various parts of the world, their pictures appearing in Egyptian temples, while clay models have been found in Peru, Mexico and other countries. More recently they have been linked to Germany, where a small short-legged dog was needed to hunt in confined forest areas. The meaning of the breed's name is 'badger dog' – the Standard Dachshund will hunt and burrow underground for badgers and other lar animals such as foxes, while the Miniature will hunt rabbits. When hunting, this breed tend to rely on scent for trailing the prey, hence they are considere hounds rather than terriers. Dachshunds are availab in three types of coat – smooth, long and wire-hair – and there is also a Miniature version available. The breed has a great personality, full of character can be very active; they make goo family pets, although they can b quite wilful and headstrong.

Colour choices?

The smooth and long-haired Dachshunds are red, black and tan, chocolate and tan, cream, dapple (merle), brindle and piebald (white on a base colour). Wire-haired Dachshunds are found in most colours. Some have a small white patch on the chest.

How much grooming?

Smooth-hairs are very easy care, needing only a good brush twice weekly. Long-hairs need daily grooming with a brush and comb. Wire-hairs are hand stripped from being puppies to achieve the correct wire texture. The choice of a wire-hair puppy benefits from expert advice: smoother coat (not fluffy coat) puppies usually develop the best adult wire-hair texture.

Do they make good pets?

Dachshunds make devoted, loyal and friendly pets, but occasionally they can be aggressive. They are courageous little dogs and very protective of their family. Their

● *Dachshunds are low slung, with short legs and loose skin. They were bred to hunt prey underground in deep holes.*

general demeanour and high intelligence make them excellent companions. Some show jealousy and if teased as youngsters may nip, but generally they are amenable to well-behaved children.

What home suits them?

The Dachshund's size makes it ideal for modern living in town or country, and it is suitable for apartment living providing they get adequate exercise.

What sort of owner?

Loving and full of character ev as puppies, they can be feisty ar stubborn. They need a strong-minded owner who will not allow them to develop bad habits, as we as a caring owner who understand their need for entertainment.

How much exercise and stimulation?

As puppies these sporting dogs enjoy walks of gradually increasing length, the regular exercise helping to prevent back problems from developing. They enjoy playing and jumping around, but take care with boisterous games because their long back is vulnerable to injury.

Friendly with other pets?

Very easygoing and sociable with other animals, but they do have a hunting instinct so need socialising early to live in harmony. They usually enjoy the companionship of another dog in the household.

Character Traits	Poor	Average	Good	Excellent
Attitude to other dogs		▓	▓	
Quietness		▓	▓	
Behaviour at home		▓		
Guarding ability		▓		
Good with children		▓		
Ease of training		▓		
Obedience to owner		▓		

Time to maturity: 2.5 years
Male height: 20–25cm (8–10in)
Female height: 20–25cm (8–10in)
Weight: 7–13kg (15–28lb)
Average lifespan: 12–13 years

Is puppy training easy?

Training is easier if the owner is firm and more determined than they are. Highly intelligent, smart and strong-willed, they take advantage if owners are not firm with training. Reward-based training with a positive and consistent approach is best. Bored and untrained puppies may become destructive.

Special puppy care?

Puppies should not go on long walks too early, play too roughly, or become obese from too many treats in training because they risk back problems later in adult life.

Puppies are prone to separation anxiety or chewing if left alone too long. Some are difficult to house-train, so more patience than usual is needed in this regard.

Possible health problems?

Back problems caused by slipped discs. Also elbow dysplasia , patella luxation (dislocating kneecaps), epilepsy, cataracts and progressive retinal atrophy. Blue, fawn and cream colours may suffer from alopecia (hair loss).

● *Despite their charm, these 7-week-old puppies could grow up to be very mischievous.*

What can we do together?

Great walking companion dogs when adult, and very good guard dogs.

Don't forget!

Take care of their backs when carrying them and don't let children play too roughly with them in case of back injury.

Small dogs

Maltese
Other names: Maltese Lion Dog, Cokie

For many centuries the Maltese, which as its name suggests came from the island of Malta, has wooed the hearts of ladies as a faithful companion and 'comforter'. It is one of the oldest of European Toy breeds, and was mentioned by Aristotle and other ancient Classical authors. To keep the breed small, it is said that they were dosed on spirits and kennelled in boxes. Their introduction to England came during the reign of Henry VII, and they were greatly fancied by the Elizabethan nobility. They made a formal debut in the 1860s when showing first started in England, closely followed by recognition in the United States in 1877. The long, soft and silky coat makes this a beautiful dog which is suitably complemented by his gentle, sweet nature and happy disposition. He is the ultimate in lapdogs, loving cuddles at home but also actively enjoying being out and about when walking with his owner.

Colour choices?
Always snow white with a black button nose, some have a slight lemon colouring which is still accepted for showing.

How much grooming?
Smart dogs with long silky coats and no undercoat, they demand a lot of attention to keep them looking good. Most pet owners keep a 'puppy trim' even for adults, but they still need grooming daily. Kept long, owners should use a bristle brush with the long coat on the head tied up on the forehead to keep it out of the eyes. The coat sheds very little, although it mats and tangles as it is hair not fur, and is suitable for people with allergies.

Do they make good pets?
These little dogs are most suited to families with older children who enjoy playing without being rough. They can be demanding and dependent on their owner, but are equally loving and good tempered with sensible families. Persistent barking can be a problem.

● *This sumptuous coat is beautiful but not very practical for pet owners.*

What home suits them?
Happy with city or country life, and ideal for apartments, they do well with plenty of company. They enjoy country walking or pavement walks, but the longer the coat, the more dirt they pick up and the more grooming is needed.

What sort of owner?
Cuddly companion dogs and comforters, they really appreciate owners who keep them close as they will suffer separation anxiety if left alone too long. They can be very lively and exuberant puppies, so play and owner companionship with plenty of attention is important to them, although they can become dependent if an owner is not firm, becoming quite spoilt if over-indulged.

How much exercise and stimulation?
Maltese enjoy good country walks with the stimulation of a good snuffle in the undergrowth, but a long coat may be a disadvantage. Mental stimulus is a must.

Friendly with other pets?
Providing they have been well socialised and raised with other pets, Maltese enjoy the company of other pets. They do have a hunting instinct so friendships with small household pets should be limited. Their small size and playful nature may place them at risk of injury around the house.

Is puppy training easy?
Maltese prefer gentle training, and are eager to learn and please their trainer. Often hard to house-train, they have a habit of barking which needs addressing early before it becomes an annoying habit.

Character Traits	Poor	Average	Good	Excellent
Attitude to other dogs				
Quietness				
Behaviour at home				
Guarding ability				
Good with children				
Ease of training				
Obedience to owner				

Time to maturity: 2 years
Male height: 20–25cm (8–10in)
Female height: 20–25cm (8–10in)
Weight: 3–4kg (6.5–9lb)
Average lifespan: 14 years

Special puppy care?

If the coat is left long, puppies need to get used to lots of grooming to remove knots and tangles, and also to allow eye cleansing to avoid eye problems.

Possible health problems?

Generally very healthy, Maltese can suffer from problems such as patella luxation (dislocating kneecaps), hypoglycaemia, teeth and gum weakness, and liver problems. Eye infections can develop and cause tear staining which marks the coat around the eyes.

Small dogs

What can we do together?

Long country walks are enjoyed, despite his small size, and surprisingly they do well in competitive obedience and agility.

Don't forget!

Maltese can become noisy barkers if left alone, so need training early to prevent the onset of separation anxiety.

● *Cuddly and affectionate, these smart puppies make delightful pets.*

Japanese Chin
Other names: Japanese Spaniel, Chin Chin

This stylish little aristocrat's roots stretch back to the Imperial Japanese courts around the 8th century AD, following their presentation there by Korean nobility, although even earlier records come from China where they featured on oriental pottery. A devoted Japanese emperor even declared them an object of worship. Subsequently, Chins appeared in the West after trade opened up in the mid-19th century. They caused so much interest that dog-napping became rife. Queen Victoria took an interest in breeding them and eventually they found their way to New York and the show ring in 1882. This affectionate, entertaining little dog has a great sense of humour and is very well mannered around his family. Seldom found far from his owner, to whom he will be devoted, he rarely barks and makes an ideal apartment dog. The Chin is an excellent companion pet, but firm training is essential to prevent him from becoming spoiled.

Colour choices?

Usually white with symmetrical black or red markings, with shades of red in varying intensity from deep red to lemon and brindle, and never tri-coloured. A white blaze on the head and face is particularly special.

How much grooming?

The long, profuse, single coat, without curls or waves, sheds like a human's. A brush and comb daily will keep it clean and smart, with careful grooming needed under the ears, on the legs and skirt and along the curved plumed tail. Chins have no coat odour, so need bathing only occasionally. Skin folds and eyes need regular attention, and moisture pockets in folds need wiping to prevent fungal infection.

Do they make good pets?

Chins are lively, alert, affectionate, gentle, well-mannered and devoted to their owners, from whom they demand love and attention. They can be wary of strangers and meet any advance with a snarl, but careful early socialising should prevent this.

● *Japanese Chins are affectionate, lively companions, and rarely forget a friend.*

What home suits them?

Ideal as clean apartment pets, Chins suit town or country life providing they spend time with their owners. Regular daily walks, playtime and plenty of owner contact are their main requirements.

What sort of owner?

Chins are very devoted, preferring owners who understand their need for emotional well-being and devote time to loving them as lap dogs. This breed suits non-working owners best as they do not enjoy being left alone for long.

How much exercise and stimulation?

Chins are relatively tough, energetic dogs, so exercise is good, but not necessarily for mile after mile. Not the brightest of dogs, but they enjoy learning because of their eagerness to please.

Friendly with other pets?

Chins are regarded as quite cat-like in nature but without the predatory streak, and they are usually friendly with other household pets. Larger dogs in the household may appear overbearing to Chins, but if they are gentle, there should be no problem.

Is puppy training easy?

Chins love to please their owner, and will enjoy learning, but not all tasks will be achieved successfully. Early puppy training and socialisation encourages a more emotionally balanced puppy.

Character Traits	Poor	Average	Good	Excellent
Attitude to other dogs				
Quietness				
Behaviour at home				
Guarding ability				
Good with children				
Ease of training				
Obedience to owner				

Time to maturity: 18 months
Male height: 20–28cm (8–11in)
Female height: 20–28cm (8–11in)
Weight: 7–9lb
Average lifespan: 9–10 years

Special puppy care?

Puppies need checking for signs of hypoglycaemia (low blood sugar levels), such as tremors, listlessness and a staggering gait. This can persist if puppies mature as low-weight adults. Care is needed with the puppy diet because of the risk of allergies as they grow.

Possible health problems?

A Chin's short face and muzzle can cause breathing difficulties and heart problems, and for the same reason they can suffer from overheating. Other problems are patella luxation (dislocating kneecaps), seasonal allergies and damage to the slightly bulging eyes from scratching or ulceration. Puppies can also suffer from hypoglycaemia. Diet is important because of their sensitivity to corn.

What can we do together?

Typically a very calm pet that was bred as a lap dog for companionship. Chins love to be loved and owners will not fail to be entertained by a performance of the 'Chin-spin' – rapid circles performed upright on hind legs while pawing with the front feet, and singing their 'wooo' noise. Great companions for the loving owner.

Don't forget!

Check that your puppy is being provided with the correct diet, and look out for signs of hypoglycaemia and overheating.

Small dogs

● *Ancestors of the Chin were very aristocratic and became quite used to being carried around in the sleeves of Oriental ladies' kimonos. This puppy is around 9 weeks old.*

Papillon
Other names: Butterfly Dog, Continental Toy Spaniel, Squirrel Spaniel

Well known in European royal courts early in the 15th century, this dainty dog was often depicted in early Renaissance paintings as a drop-eared spaniel variety, known as a 'Phalène'. Favoured by nobility as devoted lap dogs, they are thought to originate from Italy or Spain, and became popular because of their sweet temper, playful ways and dainty appearance. Modern Papillons have pricked ears, and the name

Papillon, meaning 'butterfly' in French, was chosen because the distinctive face markings, with its blaze of white, and the upstanding fringed ears resembled a butterfly. Although slender and dainty, the Papillon is relatively hardy, always ready for a game, but equally happy to be quiet and calm. They have an appealing personality and make energetic playmates for children. The Papillon's easy-care, silky coat keeps them warm in winter and cool in summer, and generally they are healthy and long-lived little dogs if cared for properly.

Colour choices?

Usually white with a blaze on the face, and symmetrical body markings in any colour except liver. Tri-colours are available, with black markings and tan spots. Distinctive coat markings are important only for show puppies.

How much grooming?

Caring for a Papillon's abundant, fine, silky coat is easier if it is brushed for a few minutes daily and tangles removed by combing them out gently. Trimming the hair on the paws, with regular attention to toe nails, and bathing monthly is also recommended.

Do they make good pets?

Papillons are happy, friendly, adventurous dogs. They are good-natured with children, and, if socialised early, also with strangers and other pets. Active owners with sensible, older children are best because although these are energetic dogs, they are small and dainty enough to be vulnerable to injury if not treated carefully.

● *Papillons have distinctive facial markings and large 'butterfly wing' ears.*

What home suits them?

Providing they accompany their owner all the time, they adapt beautifully to most homes, whether in city apartments or a country home and garden. Potential escape holes and low fences need special attention because they can squeeze through gaps and also jump well.

What sort of owner?

Mainly companion dogs, Papillons need owners who will give them plenty of attention and not leave them home alone. They are energetic, so active owners who enjoy walking are particularly suitable. Papillons prefer kindly, gentle owners or families who are sensitive to their needs, and who bring out their charming and endearing personality.

How much exercise and stimulation?

Much of this breed's exercise comes through play, but walking out regularly is necessary to provide socialisation and prevent behavioural problems. Unlike other toy breeds, Papillons enjoy long walks and agility is an ideal activity for them. They are intelligent, but need gentle consistent training to master obedience tasks.

Friendly with other pets?

Early socialisation is recommended, but they are rarely aggressive and handled carefully should pose no risk to other pets. Papillons are bossy and possessive, sometimes forgetting their small size around larger dogs, but keep this tendency in check through training and proper introductions. Breeders

Character Traits	Poor	Average	Good	Excellent
Attitude to other dogs				
Quietness				
Behaviour at home				
Guarding ability				
Good with children				
Ease of training				
Obedience to owner				

Time to maturity: 2 years
Male height: 20–28cm (8–11in)
Female height: 20–28cm (8–11in)
Weight: 4–4.5kg (9–10lb)
Average lifespan: 13–14 years

often recommend keeping two Papillons together as they play and exercise one another.

Is puppy training easy?

Papillons are considered one of the easiest toy breeds to train because they want to please. They are reasonably intelligent and give a good account of themselves in agility,

but owners should not expect too much. They need gentle regular training to succeed.

Special puppy care?

Papillons are unsuitable for rough and tumble lives, especially when puppies, and owners should give a little extra care in those early years. Puppies can be possessive about

food and toys and will benefit from firm handling in this respect. Papillons, especially puppies, are sensitive to cold, and should not be allowed to stay outside for long periods, or remain wet and cold after walks.

Small dogs

Possible health problems?

Quite hardy, but Papillons can suffer from luxating patellas (dislocating kneecaps), eye problems, allergies.

What can we do together?

Papillons have been successful in obedience, agility and tracking, but their main pleasure is in spending quality time as a companion dog.

Don't forget!

Papillons will not appreciate being cold and wet. Always buy from a reputable breeder.

● *These 10-week-old cuddly puppies will make delightful family pets if their owner is patient, kind and firm in training.*

Pomeranian
Other names: Pomeranian Loulou, Dwarf Spitz

This ball of fluff is the smallest of the spitz breeds; it is named after Pomerania, an old Prussian province in Central Europe. With a deep thick coat, bright eyes and bushy tail, they are descended from larger forebears who were sled dogs in Iceland and Lapland. Favoured by Queen Victoria, she bred and showed them, and is said to have reduced the original height by 50 per cent. They have become one of the USA's most popular toy dogs since their debut in 1890. This tiny dog may look like a fluffy decorative plaything, but they need plenty of time for proper grooming. With a huge personality for such a small dog, they are extrovert, bossy, very loyal and protective of their owner. Pomeranians are active and take a keen interest in everything around them, making an interesting pet with a great character. Generally they can be one of the more expensive toy dogs to buy.

Colour choices?
Pomeranians come in a wide colour choice which includes white, cream, orange, orange sable, wolf sable, red, brown, beaver, blue, black, and parti-colours – black and tan, brown and tan, spotted, and brindle. Evidence shows that merle colouring can produce health problems.

● *These sturdy dogs have an extrovert nature.*

How much grooming?
Their double coat needs daily grooming through the overlying long, harsh, straight and thick outer coat to the soft, thick, short undercoat, and frequent trimming. The coat knots and tangles easily and sheds constantly, so a stiff bristle brush is used. For showing, the coat needs shaping to look like a ball of fluff with protruding legs.

Do they make good pets?
Pomeranians are typically friendly and loyal to their owners and love their company, but they can be equally calm and independent if the owner takes time with training. They are unsuitable for busy families or those with young children, because of the attention and coat care required.

What home suits them?
Pomeranians adjust well to city living or country life. Their small size makes them ideal for apartments providing they are taken out regularly or spend time playing with their owner. They make very good companions for elderly people who are housebound.

What sort of owner?
Pomeranians develop a strong bond with their owner and can suffer from separation anxiety. They are affectionate, demand plenty of time and attention, and will be jealous and protective of their family. They are not suitable for owners who have no time for grooming, spending time in socialising or training, and may become tyrants if their training is neglected or the owner is over-indulgent and spoils them.

How much exercise and stimulation?
Despite their size, the sled-dog background makes them capable of walking some distance, but owners can satisfy them with romping and playing in the garden for exercise and stimulation.

Friendly with other pets?
Generally friendly and sociable with other pets, but unless trained and socialised as puppies, they can be aggressive or bullying to larger dogs. They enjoy a good chase.

Is puppy training easy?
These are intelligent dogs and

Character Traits	Poor	Average	Good	Excellent
Attitude to other dogs				
Quietness				
Behaviour at home				
Guarding ability				
Good with children				
Ease of training				
Obedience to owner				

Time to maturity: 2 years
Male height: 22–28cm (8.5–11in)
Female height: 22–28cm (8.5–11in)
Weight: 1.4–3kg (3–7lb)
Average lifespan: 12–15 years

learn quickly, benefiting from regular, patient and gentle training. Not the most obedient breed, they can be naughty if bored or lonely.

Special puppy care?

Take care of puppies around other household pets and small children, as they are vulnerable because of their small size. Discourage barking when young or this may become a difficult habit to break later. Puppies need to be trained to stand for grooming because the coat needs routine daily care, as it sheds continuously.

Possible health problems?

Patella luxation (dislocating kneecaps), tracheal (windpipe) collapse, black skin disease causing the hair to fall out, entropion (inward-turning eyelashes), Cushing's syndrome, hypothyroidism and cryptorchidism (undescended testes). Merle colours also suffer from deafness, skeletal and cardiac problems.

What can we do together?

Excellent guard, companion and show dog.

● *This 6-week-old ball of fluff will enjoy quite active play.*

Don't forget!

These little dogs have a big personality, and need time devoted to grooming, as well as firm training.

Small dogs

Norfolk Terrier and Norwich Terrier

In 1932 these two working terriers were so closely related that they were regularly interbred and recognised as one breed, the only distinction being their different ear carriage. They were ideal for hunting rabbit and vermin across East Anglia's wide areas of cultivation and woodlands and fields, and were favoured as mascots by Cambridge University undergraduates. By 1964, under pressure from breed enthusiasts, the two breeds were separated, distinguished by the Norfolk's drop ears and its slightly softer expression, as opposed to the Norwich's pricked ears. Both have friendly, good-natured characters, and a loveable disposition. Their compact size makes them adaptable to most situations, and they suit owners who like a less feisty terrier temperament. Busy, bustling and with a captivating outgoing personality, they make ideal family pets for owners who enjoy companionship, and like caring for dogs with easy grooming and walking requirements.

Colour choices?

Shades of red, black and tan, wheaten or grizzle (red and black hairs mixed). There should be no white markings.

How much grooming?

This harsh, wiry outer coat and soft, warm undercoat benefit from grooming twice a week – especially face and leg hair – using a bristle brush, steel comb or hound glove. Hand-stripping will be needed twice a year to remove dead hair and encourage new growth. Trimming or cutting the hair is not recommended by groomers as it spoils the hair texture.

Do they make good pets?

These are sociable, busy terriers who enjoy family activities and thrive on company. They will not appreciate being roughly handled by young children, but are tolerant of older children who treat them sensibly. They are exceptionally companionable and make excellent pets for most age groups.

● *Norfolk and Norwich Terriers are distinguished by their different ear carriage.*

What home suits them?

With plenty of exercise, these terriers settle happily in town or the country, providing their owner never leaves them alone for too long. For preference, they prefer country living, because it presents opportunities for hunting and snuffling around hedgerows. A garden with secure fencing is best.

What sort of owner?

An owner who appreciates an active, busy life, and allows time for playing and grooming will suit these energetic little dogs. They like their owner to be available most of the time because they do get lonely. Owners must not mind if they indulge in digging in the ground – a true terrier trait!

How much exercise and stimulation?

Bred for hunting, these terriers enjoy at least an hour walking every day. They can be adaptable and cope with shorter walks, but really they need stimulating activity at least a few times a week to stop them putting on weight and to provide valuable mental stimulation.

Friendly with other pets?

Assertive and energetic, but friendly with other household pets, they need early socialisation and to learn good manners while puppies to avoid problems later. They may be inclined to hunt small rodent pets or give chase to the neighbour's cat.

Character Traits	Poor	Average	Good	Excellent
Attitude to other dogs				
Quietness				
Behaviour at home				
Guarding ability				
Good with children				
Ease of training				
Obedience to owner				

Time to maturity: 2 years
Male height: 23–25cm(9–10in)
Female height: 23–25cm(9–10in)
Weight: 5–5.5kg (11–12lb)
Average lifespan: 13–14 years

Small dogs

Is puppy training easy?

Like any terrier they can be wilful and disobedient with a mind of their own. Both breeds need to start being trained as soon as possible, and benefit from firm, kind and reward-based training. Obedience is not their forte, but patient, conscientious owners will achieve a well-behaved dog.

Special puppy care?

Puppies do not appreciate rough play and are inclined to nip small children if they tease. Seeing how puppies can be assertive when very young should prompt owners to get on with training without delays and to make it consistent and regular.

Possible health problems?

Expect them to be hardy and healthy, but some suffer from eye problems, hip dysplasia (deformity), luxating patellas (dislocating kneecaps), allergies, heart defects and respiratory problems. Reputable breeders always check their stock for health problems, and US breeders record results on the open registry. Both Norfolks and Norwichs can have bad reactions to rabies vaccine.

What can we do together?

Hunting, Earthdog trials (not UK), agility and flyball competitions and they excel as companion pets.

Don't forget!

These terriers can appear hungry, but try not to overfeed them. Buy only from reputable breeders. The ears of the Norfolk need checking weekly to keep them clean.

● *Both these terriers enjoy life to the full, and have the character of big dogs in little dogs' bodies. This puppy is 12 weeks old.*

Havanese

Other names: Bichon Habanero, Havanese Silk Dog, Havaneser

This breed is the national dog of Cuba. It is descended from the Bichon and the now extinct Blanquito de la Habana. The Philippines also claim the breed, but it is likely they originated in the western Mediterranean and were taken overseas by Spanish Conquistadors. The most common colour, 'Havana Brown', inspired their name as they lived mainly in Cuba's capital city. By the 1950s they were almost extinct in Cuba, but a few specimens smuggled into the USA created an opportunity for the breed to become popular again. Their greatest popularity in modern times came in the 1990s, when they established a reputation for their lively, affectionate charm and suitability as an excellent children's playmate and family dog. These dogs make ideal companions for apartment or town living and require very little walking, but their beautiful coats do need plenty of grooming to keep them looking smart.

Colour choices?

Coat colours are white, cream, fawn, orange, red, brown, silver, black or blue. Colour can be solid, or with mixed markings, pied, brindle or parti-colours.

How much grooming?

Some Havanese have dense, curly coats which mat and tangle, needing more grooming; the correct, soft silky coat is less time-consuming. A soft bristle brush and wide-toothed comb is best, and coats should not be trimmed or stripped; pets can have shorter coats for convenience. Hair above the eyes can be trimmed, plaited or tied back. Paw-pad hair is trimmed to prevent slipping. Weekly ear cleaning with excess hair removed, and eye cleaning to remove tear stains is needed.

Do they make good pets?

These fun-loving characters are happy anywhere. Gentle with children and very much a family member, they are good watch-dogs, but never yappy. However, firm handling is important.

● *Good natures and sociability make these delightful pets for the right family.*

What home suits them?

Robust enough to live and exercise in the country, they make happy companions for city-dwelling flat owners. Very undemanding, they love human contact but are also happy with other pets.

What sort of owner?

Great companions for owners who spend time and lavish affection on them. Havanese can be left for short periods, but prefer attention and company. Owners must be attentive and conscientious about coat care and playtime.

How much exercise and stimulation?

Short walks two or three times a day around town are fine, but Havanese do enjoy long walks too. Their personality is lively and bright, so play, romps and learning new tricks are good for mental stimulation

Friendly with other pets?

This is the 'love people, love other pets' dog, although their ideal may be another Havanese. Some owners may have difficulty with breeding them if they are kept alone, as they prefer to be in breeding 'groups' rather than housed individually.

Is puppy training easy?

Always cheerful, Havanese enjoy showing off, and thrive on learning tricks. Puppies are more likely to retain obedience skills if learned young, and taught with a positive and sensitive approach.

Special puppy care?

Puppies must learn to let their coats be groomed daily and have their ears and eyes cleaned. Lighter coats may need more warmth in

Character Traits	Poor	Average	Good	Excellent
Attitude to other dogs				
Quietness				
Behaviour at home				
Guarding ability				
Good with children				
Ease of training				
Obedience to owner				

Time to maturity: 2 years
Male height: 20–30cm (8–12in)
Female height: 20–30cm (8–12in)
Weight: 3–6kg (7–13lb)
Average lifespan: 14–16 years

winter, so take care puppies keep warm. Teaching obedience early is essential to prevent bad habits that may persist to adulthood.

Possible health problems?

Havanese are particularly hardy with few inherited health problems reported. Most breeders participate in rigorous health testing for potential problems. They can, however, suffer from cataracts, retinal dysplasia, patella luxation (dislocating kneecaps), heart and liver disease.

Tear marks around the eyes can be caused by dietary allergies. Ears must be plucked and cleaned to prevent infections.

What can we do together?

Havanese will participate in flyball, dog agility, dancing with dogs and obedience trials. They also work as therapy dogs, and as hearing dogs for people with problems with deafness.

Small dogs

Don't forget!

The lighter coats are ideal for tropical weather, so some dogs may appreciate more warmth in colder weather.

● *Start your puppy training early to help this 10-week-old Havanese learn good manners from a young age.*

Bichon Frise
Other names: Tenerife Dog, Bichon Tenerife

Bichons originated in the Canary Isles in the 14th century, where they were reputed to descend from Water Spaniels or Barbets. Italian sailors befriended them as sailing companions. Bichons became favourites of Italian, French, and Spanish aristocracy, and were particularly popular at the court of the French king Francis I, and they were also greatly admired by King Henry III. Bichon-type dogs often appear in paintings of royal families from the past and they resemble the cuddly white ball of fluff with jet black eyes and nose that we see today. The breed later became popular as performing dogs in circuses. In the mid 1900s they established a place as popular show specimens esteemed for their glamorous looks. Today this lively and exuberant small dog loves long walks and makes a charming and entertaining family pet. Intelligent, but adaptable and very strong-willed, he does need firm training to be at his best.

Colour choices?
Usually white, especially show specimens, but apricot or grey are available. White puppies may have apricot shades or grey in immature coats, but this clears by 18 months.

How much grooming?
One of a group of breeds reputed to have hypoallergenic coats, Bichons need lots of care with a bristle brush and wide-toothed comb. Matted coats cause health problems, so daily brushing is essential. Trimming is needed four to six weekly, with bathing once a month. Continental owners prefer the natural curly look, whereas British and US owners like sculpted round trims, particularly for showing. Pet owners will find a puppy clip more manageable. The white coat needs attention around the eyes and mouth to prevent stains, and hair on the feet and muzzle must be trimmed tidily.

Do they make good pets?
Bichons love company, demanding attention in abundance. They are good natured, sensitive, affectionate

● *Little fluff-ball puppies will grow up to look just like adult Bichons.*

and well-mannered if trained properly, but their strong-minded attitude may make them household tyrants. With their high energy levels, they enjoy playing with sensible children and make charming family pets.

What home suits them?
The Bichon size is suitable for most dwellings, providing he has plenty of exercise, but his preference would be for a garden to play outdoors.

What sort of owner?
Owners must be willing to devote hours of attention which will be repaid in abundance. Not liking to be left alone, Bichons need an owner who is always around to groom them daily, play with them or go on long walks. Owners should [be careful] not to overindulge, or let bad habits and wilfulness take over.

How much exercise and stimulation?
Bichons enjoy long walks, and lots of exuberant playing. Their background as circus performers makes them eager for mental stimulation through learning tricks and obedience tasks.

Friendly with other pets?
Bichons get on well with other household pets, particularly cats and dogs. However, early puppy socialisation is important as this character enjoys being the centre of attention and other pets may find his playful nature too demanding.

Is puppy training easy?
Training should start early for this puppy and owners must be consistent. Bichons are strong-willed, stubborn and manipulative, so they can be challenging. Training needs to be imaginative using toys to attract attention and maintain interest.

Character Traits	Poor	Average	Good	Excellent
Attitude to other dogs				
Quietness				
Behaviour at home				
Guarding ability				
Good with children				
Ease of training				
Obedience to owner				

Time to maturity: 2–3 years
Male height: 23–30cm (9–12in)
Female height: 23–30cm (9–12in)
Weight: 3–5.5kg (7–12lb)
Average lifespan: 12–14 years

Special puppy care?

Puppies who fail to thrive or are underweight should be checked early for liver problems as later treatment is less effective. Bichon puppies take longer than most dogs to mature, so persistence with training is necessary. Use suitable shampoo according to age and coat type for bathing puppies.

Five little bundles of -week-old cuteness.

Possible health problems?

Very robust and healthy, they can suffer from dislocating kneecaps, hip dysplasia (deformity), haemophilia, eye, heart and liver problems.

What can we do together?

Mainly companions, Bichons will enjoy long walks, learning and performing tricks and showing.

Don't forget!

Firmness really counts with this breed, so early puppy training and socialising is a must. Don't overindulge this puppy as he could become a spoiled little character. It is recommended that all Bichons should have an annual eye test.

Small dogs

Lhasa Apso　*Other names: Abso Seng Kyi*

The Lhasa Apso, named after the sacred Tibetan city of Lhasa, is one of the most ancient of dog breeds. Thought to have been domesticated as long ago as 800 BC, Tibetan nobility and ancient Buddhist monks needed sentinel dogs to guard their homes and monasteries and the Lhasa proved ideal. The Dalai Lama was particularly possessive of Lhasas, presenting them only to the most important visitors, because the Lamas' souls were thought to be preserved in the Lhasa Apso. Consequently, the breed only made its debut in the Western world early in the 1900s. With a beautiful long flowing coat and a character encapsulated in the Tibetan name which means 'bearded lion sentinel dog', Lhasas are reputed to bring good luck. They are lively, independent, courageous, hardy dogs with assertive minds, who can be wilful and disobedient if untrained, but for their size and character they make ideal family pets.

Colour choices?
Golden or lion-like colours are preferred, so sable, honey, dark grey, slate, smoke, black, white, brown or parti-colours are all acceptable.

How much grooming?
A Lhasa's coat is long and beautiful, and owners need to provide thorough daily brushing with a firm brush and comb through the soft undercoat to the skin. Neglect can cause skin problems, excessive tangles and painful matting, so pet owners may prefer to give a puppy clip every six weeks and tie back the hair over the eyes. Lhasas do not enjoy bathing but coats need regular washing, with particular attention paid to the hair on the face and underbody.

Do they make good pets?
Lhasas make great pets because they are devoted and love to please their owners. They can be wilful, however, and may snap if treated roughly, and often find it hard if they are not the centre of attention. If trained and socialised well, they are

● *Always on the alert to warn of visitors.*

versatile, merry, loyal, affectionate and extremely devoted pets.

What home suits them?
This adaptable dog will live in towns or the country, but his lively spirit needs to be satisfied with a good daily walk or several shorter interesting outings. A garden to play in is ideal, or a large park close by for apartment dwellers.

What sort of owner?
With a high-maintenance coat, this dog is suitable only for owners with time to provide the necessary grooming care. Extremely loyal and devoted, these dogs want to please, and owners must devote time to training and socialising them.

How much exercise and stimulation?
Lhasas are hardy and lively by nature, so they tolerate plenty of exercise despite their small size. Stimulation is essential for their intelligent minds and they enjoy time spent with their owner.

Friendly with other pets?
Naturally wary and suspicious of strangers, including other dogs, males may be aggressive towards rivals. While they get on well with family pets if well socialised early on, cats will be chased and household pets belonging to other families may not be tolerated.

Is puppy training easy?
Lhasas need firm training because they are intelligent, alert, assertive characters and may try to be dominant. They love learning; owners who enjoy their respect, and who use fun, reward-based training, will achieve the best resu

Character Traits	Poor	Average	Good	Excellent
Attitude to other dogs				
Quietness				
Behaviour at home				
Guarding ability				
Good with children				
Ease of training				
Obedience to owner				

Time to maturity: 18 months
Male height: 23–28cm (9–11in)
Female height: 20–25cm (8–10in)
Weight: 6–7kg (13–15lb)
Average lifespan: 13–14 years

● *If you want a pair of Lhasas, don't choose two males or rivalry may develop between them.*

Small dogs

8-week-old puppies enjoy cuddling up together, or sharing a toy.

Special puppy care?

Habituate puppies to grooming and bathing early on. This ensures good coat quality, which will maintain health and prevent skin problems later. Take care to check kidney function in puppies as they can suffer from kidney problems when quite young. If the puppy seems off-colour, take advice from your vet.

Possible health problems?

Mainly eye problems, but skin problems occur if they are not groomed regularly, even if the coat is kept short. Some puppies suffer from juvenile kidney disease.

What can we do together?

Mainly companion dogs, but Lhasas will enjoy long walks with their owner. They make excellent show dogs but have high maintenance needs. Their keen hearing and deep bark make them good watch dogs

Don't forget!

Regular coat care is essential. Lhasas have big characters and need early training and socialising to prevent them from becoming spoilt.

Border Terrier

This tough little terrier derives from a mix of several terrier breeds, and he hails from the Border country between England and Scotland. The Border was specifically bred to be rugged, courageous, strong to tackle a fox or badger, and have abundant energy to keep up with horses during a day's hunting. Slightly longer legged, Borders are plucky and tireless, and have a reputation for being the most brave and powerful of hunting terriers. The breed excels in many features; they are agile, playful and friendly, and known for not being as aggressive as some terriers. His daily requirements are relatively low, but attention and stimulation for an energetic mind is essential. Borders hate being left alone at home when they are likely to be noisy, destructive and mischievous. Generally they are friendly and loving and make one of the best family pets with a reputation for being good with children.

Colour choices?
Red, wheaten, grizzle and tan, or blue and tan. There may be white markings on the chest.

How much grooming?
Borders have double coats, a harsh, dense and wiry outer coat which is weather- and dirt-resistant, and a short soft undercoat. Grooming twice weekly is ideal, using a palm brush to remove dead hairs and combing down to the skin. Hand-strip bi-monthly for showing, or twice yearly for pets. Occasional bathing may be necessary for dogs kept indoors.

Do they make good pets?
Borders' gentler personality makes them less feisty than other terriers, and their cheerful, friendly nature means that they bond well with sensible children. They enjoy owners who value their company and in return make loving pets.

What home suits them?
The breed's happy disposition makes it suitable for living in towns

• Traditionally these little dogs were tenacious and hostile, but today's Border is a most amiable dog. The otter-like head and strong legs are ideal for burrowing in the ground.

or the country, providing it is well exercised to maintain its health and well-being. They adapt well to both apartment living or the countryside, providing there is plenty of action. A secure garden is important as they are game for adventure and will seek to escape if life on the other side looks more interesting.

What sort of owner?
Borders are great for active families who enjoy being out and about, and who accept their fun-loving, lively character. Having time to spend playing, exercising and providing early basic training and socialisation should be an important consideration for owners.

How much exercise and stimulation?
These terriers were bred to hunt all day, so plenty of exercise is needed, particularly for dogs living in smaller premises. Stimulation is essential or they will find mischief and they may become destructive if bored or lonely.

Friendly with other pets?
Generally friendly with low aggression levels, but small household pets (rabbits, guinea pigs and mice) may be at risk from a Border with hunting instincts. Good socialisation and early training helps considerably.

Is puppy training easy?
Borders are not difficult to train, but can be stubborn and strong-willed so need firm handling. Puppies need training to respond to command early, before they develop independent minds and focus on other pursuits. Training should be firm and consistent. Hide-and-seek tasks and agility make ideal training.

Character Traits	Poor	Average	Good	Excellent
Attitude to other dogs				
Quietness				
Behaviour at home				
Guarding ability				
Good with children				
Ease of training				
Obedience to owner				

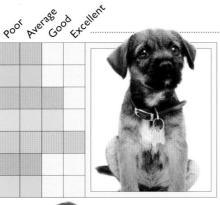

Time to maturity: 3 years
Male height: 25–28cm (10–11in)
Female height: 25–28cm (10–11in)
Weight: 5–7kg (11.5–15.5lb)
Average lifespan: 14 years

task-related activities appeal to their intelligence. They can jump to order and run fast, so agility-based activities will be fun. Earthdog trials (not in the UK) are a popular way of testing a Border's hunting abilities.

● *Puppies at 5 months are agile and playful.*

Special puppy care?

Puppies won't take kindly to being teased or treated badly, so children need supervising. Take care with small toys as they may be chewed or eaten as puppies respond to their natural hunting instinct for small prey.

Possible health problems?

Borders are usually a hardy breed but do have some genetic problems which include heart and eye problems, hip dysplasia, Legg-Perthes disease (malformation of the hip joint) and sometimes seizures.

What can we do together?

Learning tricks is not their forte, but

Don't forget!

Not a breed for leaving at home, puppies particularly may become destructive; they will benefit from plenty of exercise and play. Remember that these dogs will

● *Borders love watching their owner to tune into their emotions.*

go to ground in pursuit of interesting smells or game, so make sure when you walk there is no danger of them getting stuck down holes.

Small dogs

Early training to teach basic commands like 'Stay' is ideal.

Tibetan Spaniel

History tells us that Tibetan Spaniels were used to turn the prayer wheels used by the ancient orders of Tibetan monks. Although one of several sacred Tibetan breeds, this one was considered the monks' favourite. Originating in the Himalayas, they served the purpose of sitting guard high up on the monastery walls. Using their excellent vision, they could see intruders approaching and barked an alarm well in advance of other watchdogs. Tibetan Spaniels arrived in Britain around 1900, although they did not become popular in the United States until the 1960s. Noted for being a gentle breed, good natured and affectionate, they are calm, intelligent and relatively quiet by comparison with other dogs. With an excellent natural watchfulness, fuelled by a mistrust of strangers, they make good guard dogs, but are very unlikely to be aggressive. They need regular coat care but otherwise their needs can be fairly easily met by family pet owners.

Colour choices?

Several varieties of solid or multi-colours, but the usual colours are black, black and tan, red, gold, fawn, cream or white. Darker colours often have white markings on the paws.

How much grooming?

Tibetans have medium-length, silky, double coats, shorter on the face and legs and with feathering on the ears, toes and tail. They need brushing daily to maintain health and coat hygiene; grooming with a soft brush and comb is best. Bathing once a month is usually sufficient.

Do they make good pets?

These dogs have great personalities and make excellent pets. They have an outgoing nature and are quite strong physically for a small breed. They enjoy a full life, either running around playing, or sitting quietly indoors with the family. Take care, especially when with young children, as their gentle nature is sensitive to rough play, and their size makes them vulnerable to injury.

● *Coat feathering takes a long time to grow and may not develop for months.*

What home suits them?

Tibetan Spaniels are very adaptable and capable of adapting well to most household environments. They enjoy homes with a garden where they can run around, but providing they are walked daily, they will settle equally well in town apartment or countryside locations.

What sort of owner?

Tibetans need owners who understand them and appreciate them for what they are: gentle little dogs who have long been closely associated with Buddhism. Owners must also pay attention to regular coat care and walking.

How much exercise and stimulation?

These little dogs enjoy daily exercise and mental stimulation, because they are very positive and outgoing temperamentally. Suitable habituation and socialisation helps overcome distrust of strangers, and spending time meeting people should always form part of early puppy activities.

Friendly with other pets?

Kind and gentle, these little dogs get on well and enjoy the company of other household pets, and particularly have no problem with cats, although early socialisation with all pets as puppies is still needed.

Is puppy training easy?

Training is very easy. It should be gentle and reward-based as they respond well to kindness. With the delightful temperament Tibetans are unlikely to take over their household, but generally need guidance in learning what behaviours an owner will find preferable and what is not allowed

Character Traits	Poor	Average	Good	Excellent
Attitude to other dogs				
Quietness				
Behaviour at home				
Guarding ability				
Good with children				
Ease of training				
Obedience to owner				

Time to maturity: 18 months
Male height: 25–28 cm (10–11 in)
Female height: 24–27cm (9.5–10.5in)
Weight: 4–7kg (9–15.5lb)
Average lifespan: 11–12 years

Special puppy care?

Although small dogs, they are full of life and think they are bigger than they are! Puppies can be vulnerable because of their size. Training must be gentle and sensitive, particularly for puppies in the early stages. A puppy's failure to thrive needs prompt investigation as it could indicate signs of liver problems.

Possible health problems?

Like many breeds Tibetans have problems with their eyes (progressive retinal atrophy causing blindness), allergies and liver shunt (a blood supply abnormality that causes problems with filtering out waste in the body and becomes evident in puppies or young dogs).

What can we do together?

Tibetans are great as family pets, or for single owners who want a companionable little dog for going out strolling. They make good watchdogs too.

Don't forget!

Liver shunt is inherited, so remember to ask if tests have been done on relatives and if the puppy's parents are healthy when buying one. Their small size and sensitive nature should be respected, particularly if they are handled by small children.

● *This silky coat of this 5-month-old puppy is best groomed by daily brushing using a soft brush. Coat feathering takes a long time to grow.*

Small dogs

Pug

One of the oldest of the short faced (brachycephalic) breeds, the Pug originated in China as a tiny Mastiff dog and was bred as a lap dog during the Shang Dynasty. The name 'Pug' is believed to mean 'monkey face', although in Latin 'pugnus' means fist, which notes the round fist-shape of the head. Travelling west in the 16th century with Dutch East India Company traders, they become favourites with Dutch, French and Italian nobility, and from there came to England where they became popular in the 18th century. This is one of the few breeds retaining its original looks with its coil tail, button ears, round black-muzzled head and wizened little face. The vertical wrinkle or 'prince mark' on the Pug's head is highly favoured. Low maintenance, this breed is neat, obedient and companionable. The Pug's fortunes have dipped and risen over the years, but appear to be blossoming again.

Colour choices?

The smooth glossy coat is silver, fawn, apricot or black with well defined markings. The dark mask appears on the muzzle and ears of lighter colours, with a thumb mark or diamond shape on the head, and a black 'trace' line down the back from head to tail.

How much grooming?

Grooming is needed several times a week, using a hound glove or chamois cloth to remove shedding hair that may be abundant. Facial wrinkles need gentle cleansing to keep them dry and prevent infection, and eyes need checking as they are sensitive to dust and injury.

Do they make good pets?

Pugs make excellent family pets, joining in and enjoying playing with children, providing they are gentle. Their good nature and even temper allows bonding with any household and they can become an essential member of any family.

What home suits them?

The Pug is clean and companionable and suits most homes because they are robust for country living, but small and neat for apartments. This breed is gregarious, and will want to be around people and not shut away on their own.

● *Busy and curious, Pugs have personality plus and make very appealing family pets.*

What sort of owner?

Pugs sense their owner's mood, and may be quiet and docile or energetic and active. Owners may find this personality demanding, but they are affectionate little dogs and are happy to follow the owner's lifestyle, providing it does not involve long walks and they do not work away from home.

How much exercise and stimulation?

Pugs need exercise to avoid obesity, so a good walk daily and time to play is usually sufficient. Keeping them active and stimulated maintains their health.

Friendly with other pets?

A good breed to mix with other household pets as they do not have specific natural behaviours likely to cause a problem. Their bulging eyes can be vulnerable to injury by cats. Other pets may find their characteristic snorting and grunting disconcerting.

Is puppy training easy?

Pugs need firm training early on to develop their potential as good-natured adults. They train reasonably easily but are strong-minded, so may not always be obedient. Persistence is needed.

Character Traits	Poor	Average	Good	Excellent
Attitude to other dogs			●	
Quietness		●		
Behaviour at home			●	
Guarding ability	●			
Good with children			●	
Ease of training		●		
Obedience to owner		●		

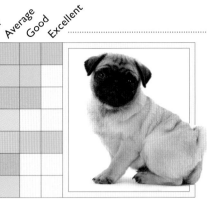

Time to maturity: 2 years
Male height: 25–28cm (10–11in)
Female height: 25–28cm (10–11in)
Weight: 6.5–8kg (14–18lb)
Average lifespan: 11–12 years

These pups are about 9 weeks old.

throat can shorten episodes of breathing problems. Hip dysplasia, Legg Perthes disease (a hip problem), luxating patella (dislocating kneecap), Pug dog encephalitis affecting puppies from six months to 7 years, hemivertebrae (congenital spinal deformity), obesity, heat sensitivity. The Pug's bulging eyes can be prone to injury.

Small dogs

What can we do together?

Pugs have been known to do obedience, fly ball, agility and provide support for disabled owners or hearing dog owners.

● *With their flat face, bulging eyes and great charm, the Pug will appeal to milies who enjoy quieter, less active lives.*

Special puppy care?

Encourage your puppy to allow cleaning the face wrinkles and eyes when very young as this needs to be done regularly. Overheating should be avoided. Incorrect feeding can cause flatulence so the diet needs attention to get it right. Pugs can be hard to house-train, so need patience and understanding.

Possible health problems?

Snuffling, snorting, breathing difficulty caused by respiratory problems or pharyngeal gag reflex (elongated palate) – massaging the

Don't forget!

Pugs do not tolerate overheating and must be kept cool on a hot day. Take care with the wrinkles around the face and avoid injury to their protruding eyes.

Scottish Terrier *Other names: Aberdeen Terrier*

These terriers hail from the Highlands of Scotland, although controversy rages about their exact ancestry and correct name. However, these dour, serious and sharp-natured terriers have a long history in the farming communities of the Scottish Highlands where they were also used as fine little hunting dogs, despite their small size. Today's Scotties are so synonymous with their heritage that they often appear in advertisements for many Scottish products. Reserved and often unfriendly to strangers, as family dogs they make ideal companions enjoying family life and time spent with close friends. By nature very territorial, some may be inclined to take over households, but in the main they are kind dogs with a lively, playful and sensitive temperament, and devoted to their owners. Scotties settle well in any home from an apartment to a country farm house, and can adapt well to a variety of lifestyles.

Colour choices?
Nearly always black, but Scotties can also be wheaten (pale straw colour), or brindle.

How much grooming?
Scotties typically have hard, wiry, waterproof outer coats with soft, thick undercoats, and longer coat on the beard, legs and under the body. Professional grooming is needed three to four times a year for hand-stripping and clipping, but owners must be conscientious about daily brushing with a hard bristle brush and combing through the longer hair on the face and lower body to keep the coat in good order.

Do they make good pets?
Strong-willed, hardy and courageous, Scotties can be feisty by nature, and have strong hunting instincts. They respect and form strong, loyal bonds with their owners and make good family pets with sensible children, although they avoid young children who may be rough. Scotties seldom bark, but their territorial nature is excellent for guarding.

Small but perfectly formed.

● *A true Highlander, with bags of charm.*

What home suits them?
Scotties suit town or country, but apartment dwellers should provide good daily walks to release their abundant energy. Gardeners beware, this is an enthusiastic digger – they burrow under fences if the world outside seems more interesting. Secure, high fencing is essential, and in the country their hunting instinct may become evident.

What sort of owner?
Scotties are proud and stubborn, their strong personalities on occasions appearing quite obstinate, but owners who handle them firmly and understand and work with this disposition to guide good behaviour will be well rewarded. These dogs also like owners who give them plenty of company and provide the necessary regular coat care.

How much exercise and stimulation?
Full of energy, Scotties were bred to hunt, and a lot of exercise and stimulation will be needed. Scotties are intelligent and playful as puppies and time spent bonding through play usually pays dividends in successful training.

Character Traits	Poor	Average	Good	Excellent
Attitude to other dogs				
Quietness				
Behaviour at home				
Guarding ability				
Good with children				
Ease of training				
Obedience to owner				

Time to maturity: 2.5 years
Male height: 25–28 cm (10–11in)
Female height: 25–28 cm (10–11in)
Weight: 8.5–10.5kg (19–23lb)
Average lifespan: 13–14 years

Friendly with other pets?

Scotties expect to rule any household, but with early socialisation they nearly always get on well with other family pets, although small pets may be at risk because of their inherent hunting instincts.

Is puppy training easy?

Training is difficult for owners who do not engender respect and bond sensibly with their Scottie puppy. They are stubborn and may only cooperate on their own terms, so early socialisation is essential. Training must be firm, consistent and sensitive, but always kind.

Special puppy care?

This breed really does need early socialising. Try to buy from a reputable breeder who starts this process early. Avoid any puppy stress, such as situations when they are lonely or frightened, as this could cause health problems.

Possible health problems?

Scotties have a few health problems ranging from flea allergy, cranio-mandibular osteopathy (a disease of the lower jaw), von Willebrand disease (a blood coagulation abnormality), hypothyroidism (low levels of thyroid hormone), Scotty cramp (an inherited problem related to stress) and a higher incidence of cancer than other breeds.

Small dogs

What can we do together?

Scotties enjoy hunting and country pursuits, and have proved successful in the show ring, but otherwise they make excellent companion dogs for the right kind of owner.

Don't forget!

This dog has a strong personality that requires plenty of socialising, and training can be difficult, so owners also need to be strong personalities to handle them.

● *Even at 12 weeks this Scottie is devoted, playful and sensitive. Scotties will appeal to families seeking a dog with an honest nature.*

Miniature Pinscher

Miniature Pinschers hailed from Germany several centuries ago. Their exact origins are unknown but they probably developed from indigenous German terrier types.

Celebrated as the 'King of Toys', Pinschers are particularly admired for an elegant high-stepping gait and a smart, clean, dainty body. Often considered the most soundly built of toy breeds, the Pinscher's solid, muscular body can cope with high activity levels when needed. Their fearless nature and readiness to take on all-comers, coupled with high energy and inquisitiveness, make them enthusiastic watch dogs, as well as loving and entertaining companions. Without adequate training, Pinschers become tyrants because they are strong-willed and dominant, despite looking small and fragile. They make ideal pets for experienced owners who understand proper socialising and training. But the Pinscher's character has lots of 'pep', and so it is not an ideal choice for novices.

Colour choices?

Solid red or stag red, black, chocolate or blue, or any of these colours with well defined tan markings. Slight white markings on the chest are allowed but not considered desirable.

How much grooming?

Regular brushing once a week will remove dead hair and dander, with a soft cloth polish to finish. This and the occasional bath are all the grooming that is needed.

Do they make good pets?

Pinschers are assertive, outgoing, intelligent and active and they make ideal pets for experienced owners who know how to deal with an ultra big character. This is not a particularly good pet for novice owners. Always busy, they are excellent watch dogs, but will be wary of strangers to their home until they get to know them. This breed does not enjoy rough handling by small children and may nip if upset, so it is not the best dog for families with young children.

● *Adult Min Pins (left) could be mistaken for their cousin, the German Pinscher (right), but will obviously not grow as big.*

What home suits them?

The Pinschers' compact size make them ideal for apartment living but they are equally at home in the country. However, an intelligent and inquisitive mind may cause them to seek diversion in the outside world, so a fenced-in yard is essential. Warm homes suit them better because their smooth coat is not thick enough to withstand lower temperatures.

What sort of owner?

Pinschers are best suited to experienced owners, who will appreciate this dog's fearless spirit and strong personality with its 'big dog' attitude. Owners who work away from home for long periods are not ideal for this breed.

How much exercise and stimulation?

Plenty of socialising and training in regular short sessions is needed, along with firmness, gentle handling and patience, to prevent them from becoming tyrants in their own home. As adults, Pinschers enjoy longish walks with their owner.

Friendly with other pets?

Towards their own household, Pinschers are free from aggression and very friendly if socialised early. Very much a house dog now, they were originally used for rat hunting so very small pets may be at some risk around the home.

Is puppy training easy?

Pinschers need firm, consistent training, or they can start behaving badly. Training should be fun as

Character Traits	Poor	Average	Good	Excellent
Attitude to other dogs				
Quietness				
Behaviour at home				
Guarding ability				
Good with children				
Ease of training				
Obedience to owner				

Time to maturity: 18 months
Male height: 25–30cm (10–12in)
Female height: 25–28cm (10–11in)
Weight: 3.5–4.5kg (8 –10lb)
Average lifespan: 12–13 years

they quickly become bored and have a short attention span. Generally amenable to discipline, training needs to be consistent and firm. Go with short training sessions and use plenty of rewards to maintain a focus on learning.

Special puppy care?

Pinschers have rather fine, fragile-looking bodies. They are quite sturdy, but do take care when playing with puppies as they are vulnerable to injury. Puppies (particularly) and adults need protection from the cold.

Possible health problems?

Usually a very healthy breed with patella luxation (dislocating kneecaps) being the main reported problem.

What can we do together?

They have a reputation as good companion dogs, and agility is possible for the owner who can train well and get the best out of their Pinscher. They make an ideal show dog.

Don't forget!

Training is essential for this breed because they can be very animated and have a fearless spirit.

● *Early training, socialisation and firm patient handling are essential for the first year to support outgoing personalities and develop good manners. With the right owner this is a great family dog.*

Small dogs

Adolescent puppies at 9 months enjoy playing, but can also be assertive.

Shih Tzu

Other names: Shi Xi Quan, Chrysanthemum Dog, Tibetan Lion Dog

The Shih Tzu is associated with the ancient Tibetan religion of Lamaism. With a flowing mane of hair, he is said to have been able to turn into a lion and was depicted in pictures with Manjusri, the Lamaist god of learning. Tibet's spiritual leader, the Dalai Lama, presented them to Manchu emperors living in Imperial China. The last empress in China had Shih Tzus until the early 1900s, although they were not seen elsewhere until 1930. This is a courageous little dog, with a big personality, who is noted for his rather arrogant posture. An excellent guard dog, he has a gentle, affectionate and intelligent temperament making him a good family dog. The rich abundant head coat has led to the name of 'Chrysanthemum dog', and he needs plenty of time grooming to keep it looking good. The American and European standards show distinct variations in type.

Colour choices?

Various shades of solid colours in gold, white, brown and liver are available or combinations of black, grey, silver, white and brindle. Parti-colour dogs can be gold with a black mask, black and white, liver and white, brindle and white, or grey and white. Parti-colours with a white flare on the forehead and white markings on the tail are particularly popular.

How much grooming?

Grooming is a big commitment, and needs daily attention. A good brushing right down to the skin is essential with a regular fortnightly bath. Many pet owners prefer the coat trimmed to a 'puppy clip' every six weeks even when adult, but they still need daily grooming.

Do they make good pets?

Shih Tzus are lively, active and independent, needing plenty of love and attention. They have a wilful charm and character, which makes them a favourite family pet, but the grooming may be too much for

● *Shih Tzus have beautiful coats but this often proves impractical for a pet, because of the grooming required.*

some families. They make a great companion and affectionate playmate, and will want to be involved in all family activities.

What home suits them?

An ideal city dog, this breed adapts to town or country living. Apartment living necessitates a walk to a park several times a day. They are usually happiest with a house and garden and joining in regular family outings.

What sort of owner?

Playful and companionable, they need someone willing to spend time enjoying their company and who will groom daily to keep them in the best of health and condition. They can become tyrants if allowed, so need an owner who is firm with training and makes time for socialisation.

How much exercise and stimulation?

Shih Tzus enjoy long walks and playing in the garden, but are equally happy with several short daily walks. This breed needs entertaining to keep them stimulated or they will find their own ways of making mischief.

Friendly with other pets?

Generally friendly with other pets but they do need time and good handling to become well socialised.

Is puppy training easy?

This is a strong-minded breed, and quite outgoing, so puppies need firm, consistent but kind handling in training. Not the most obedient of breeds, so a more playful approach in training would suit them better.

Character Traits	Poor	Average	Good	Excellent
Attitude to other dogs				
Quietness				
Behaviour at home				
Guarding ability				
Good with children				
Ease of training				
Obedience to owner				

Time to maturity: 2 years
Male height: 25cm (10in)
Female height: 25cm (10in)
Weight: 4.5–8kg (10–17lb)
Average lifespan: 10–16 years

● *The 3-month-old puppy will soon begin to be groomed and trimmed in the lighter style seen on his adult companion.*

Special puppy care?

This breed does not tolerate heat well, so take care not to overheat them. Regular baths and eye checks are needed and the hair needs to be kept out of the eyes. Puppies can be difficult to house-train, so patience is needed.

Possible health problems?

Shih Tzus can suffer from liver problems, hypothyroidism (a reduced level of thyroid hormone) and intervertebral disc disease. Breathing problems due to the shape of the head may need surgery later.

Small dogs

What can we do together?

These dogs are very good as children's playmates, or a companion dog for adults, and they make excellent guard dogs.

Don't forget!

The Shih Tzu coat needs plenty of grooming, maybe as much as 30 minutes daily, and frequent baths. Pet owners may want to trim the coat every six weeks, so consider the cost implied by this.

Pembroke and **Cardigan Welsh Corgis**

Popular folklore tells of woodland fairies giving Corgis to Welsh farmers. Fairy warriors were reputed to have ridden them around on the hills, so leaving the saddle marking that is visible on their backs. Considered the oldest breed in Britain, hill farmers interbred them over many years until they separated into two breeds in 1934. Pembroke Corgis are the most common, possibly because they became popular in the 20th century with the British Royal Family. The Cardigan is believed to have moved into the Welsh hills with the Celts, while Pembroke Corgis originated among Flemish weavers. Differences are subtle: the Pembroke is slightly smaller and longer bodied, with a naturally shorter tail. Whatever their background they have striking similarities, both performing the same tasks of herding cattle, ponies, sheep, pigs, and even geese and hunting rabbits or vermin. More recently they have been used as drug search or rescue dogs.

Colour choices?

White is limited and never predominates on either breed, only marking the chest, head and foreface as a blaze, and white feet. Most colours are acceptable for Cardigans, but Pembrokes should be red, sable, fawn, or tri-colour (black, tan and white).

How much grooming?

Both breeds have easy care double coats, and need grooming regularly each week into the undercoat, or daily when undergoing their twice-yearly moult. The slightly thicker, harsher coat of adult Cardigans does better with a stiffer brush.

Do they make good pets?

Welsh Corgis make excellent pets when raised with children – they are fun-loving, confident and even-tempered. Puppies are excitable, so need supervision with young children, but generally they have an excellent reputation for being good family pets. Wary of strangers, they make excellent guard dogs.

● In the foreground a Pembroke Corgi and her pup, while behind sits a Cardigan Corgi. The Cardigan's head has more of a foxy look than the Pembroke's.

What home suits them?

Better suited to country homes because of their farming background, Corgis need plenty of walking or somewhere to run loose. They can fit into town life if owners walk them regularly in a park allowing them a good run around to burn off energy.

What sort of owner?

Corgis are loyal, affectionate and friendly, but need sensible owners; Pembrokes particularly are inclined to heel-nip to round up the family. These are active, strong-minded breeds, so owners must be prepared to spend time from the start walking and playing, while maintaining a firm early training regime.

How much exercise and stimulation?

Gradually building up to longer walks with some running and active play is appreciated. Their active minds need variety to stimulate them, as they can quickly become bored.

Friendly with other pets?

Early socialisation within households prevents dominance developing among other males. Their background as vermin hunters may place other small pets at risk. Otherwise, early socialisation and suitable introductions creates the right environment in which they are generally friendly with other pets.

Character Traits	Poor	Average	Good	Excellent
Attitude to other dogs				
Quietness				
Behaviour at home				
Guarding ability				
Good with children				
Ease of training				
Obedience to owner				

Time to maturity: 2 years
M/F height: Cardigans c.30cm (12in)
 Pembrokes 25–30cm (10–12in)
Weight: 14kg (30lb) and 13kg (28lb)
Average lifespan: 12–14 years

Is puppy training easy?

Approached with intelligence and firmness Corgi puppies are easy to train. They do not enjoy repetitive training, but usually comply with plenty of reward-based training techniques. More complex activities are suggested as training progresses and later they enjoy activities in which owners can participate.

Special puppy care?

Training puppies not to nip should start early to prevent bad habits forming. Young dogs need reward-based training to motivate them. They can have a tendency to obesity if overfed, which often causes back problems later in life.

Possible health problems?

Corgis, particularly Cardigans, are a healthy breed with few inherited problems, but long backs and short legs may make them prone to back problems such as canine degenerative myelopathy or intervertebral disc problems. Some suffer from hip malformation (dysplasia), von Willebrand's disease (a blood-clotting disorder), and inherited eye problems (progressive retinal atrophy). Pembrokes may also suffer from epilepsy.

Small dogs

● *Two Pembroke Corgi puppies at just 9 weeks of age. This breed has a working ancestry as a hunting and farm dog, and so it relishes having tasks to do.*

What can we do together?

Corgis are intelligent and with the benefit of their herding background can take part in dog agility, herding trials, tracking events, obedience competitions, flyball and showing.

Don't forget!

These breeds need training early on to prevent them developing bad habits like nipping. Take care not to give too many treats to puppies because of the risk of obesity.

West Highland White Terrier

Poltalloch Terrier, Roseneath Terrier

Commonly known as the 'Westie', the origins of this terrier are not clear. Some stories suggest it descends from Spanish dogs that arrived when a Spanish Armada ship was wrecked on the Scottish coast in 1588. Others credit the 16th Laird of Poltalloch, who around 1900 wanted to produce a strain of white hunting dogs to avoid them being mistaken for foxes and shot in error. He developed the Poltalloch terrier which was renamed the West Highland White in 1908. The breed quickly found recognition in Britain and the United States. Westies are a family's dream of a four-legged playmate with a great sense of fun that endears them to any family. Reasonably good as a watchdog, Westies are lively and merry, and great characters, but can turn on the dignity in the blink of an eye. They are also rustic, courageous, independent, sometimes stubborn, but all in all an affectionate dog who is good with children.

Colour choices?

Only pure white is available, although some puppies appear more cream-coloured than white.

How much grooming?

Westies have weatherproof, straight topcoats over short, thick, soft undercoats, which shed continuously and need grooming with a bristle brush and combing to remove tangles and dead hair. Professional grooming is needed every three or four months for bathing and hand-stripping, when coats may be sculpted for showing or left shaggy. Hair on the face and ears needs trimming, and ears and eyes should be cleaned regularly. If well cared for, Westies don't tend to smell quite so 'doggy'.

Do they make good pets?

Charming, fun-loving, playful, family dogs, Westies are happy to join in anything. They don't like being handled roughly but make the best of companions for sensible children. Tremendous house dogs, they are alert and protective of their family.

● *Not quite ready to leave home, at 7 weeks, puppies are still dependent on their mother for love and protection.*

What home suits them?

Intelligent and inquisitive, Westies particularly enjoy country living and long family rambles, but they are equally happy in town if they get a good daily walk with time to explore the local area.

What sort of owner?

Frequently a one-person dog and often a good choice for single or active older people, they are tremendous family dogs, despite their sometimes bossy terrier nature. Westies make great companions for sensible owners who allow them the leeway for some self-expression and accept their cheeky, affectionate, playful character, but are also firm with training and consistent about providing regular grooming.

How much exercise and stimulation?

Westies' hunting background makes them active and energetic and they really do enjoy long country walks, but are equally happy romping in their garden. Town-dwelling Westies will need two or three decent walks every day, and preferably somewhere to explore off-lead in safety.

Friendly with other pets?

Westie puppies need early socialising with other pets as their strong hunting instinct may put small pets at risk. Generally, expect reasonable relationships after early introductions, but supervise the behaviour of puppies carefully.

Character Traits	Poor	Average	Good	Excellent
Attitude to other dogs				
Quietness				
Behaviour at home				
Guarding ability				
Good with children				
Ease of training				
Obedience to owner				

Time to maturity: 2 years
Male height: 25–30cm (10–12in)
Female height: 23–28cm (9–11in)
Weight: 6–10 kg (13–22lb)
Average lifespan: 10–18 years

Is puppy training easy?

Westies can be wilful and stubborn, and training should start early to establish who is in charge. Short reward-based sessions, involving fun activities and new challenges to sustain interest, are best. They are unlikely obedience champions, but do make well-behaved family pets if treated with a firm, kind approach. Some may be possessive of food and toys, so train carefully to prevent this becoming an issue.

This litter of 7-week-old puppies looks cute, but they also can be mischievous!

Special puppy care?

Training must start early or you can expect a puppy's bossy nature to assert itself and take control. Coat care is needed early on, as this helps to promote bonding and establishes who is in charge. Check and clean ears regularly.

Possible health problems?

Generally robust and healthy, Westies can suffer from inherited skin disorders (hyperplastic dermatosis), white dog shaker syndrome and globoid cell leukodystrophy – both inherited

Learning to submit is part of growing up.

neurological disorders that puppies may suffer up to 30 weeks – Legg-Perthes disease (hip problems) and Westie jaw (a bone overgrowth).

What can we do together?

These dogs make brilliant companion dogs, as well as great family pets who will get along well with children in the household.

Don't forget!

Buy only from reputable breeders, never from puppy farmers, to avoid risks of health problems or the consequences of poor early care. Training, socialising and grooming should start early!

Cavalier King Charles Spaniel *Other names: English Toy Spaniel*

In the reign of King Charles II the English toy spaniel was brought to the UK from France, where it was used for sporting purposes. The king became so devoted to them as his soulmates and companions, he called them King Charles Spaniels. Today's Cavalier originated as a separate breed from those dogs; it is a little larger, with a slightly different head shape, although very similar. Although Cavaliers were only recognised in 1945, they are one of the most popular toy breeds, and loved all over the world. Considered a lap dog, Cavaliers make ideal family dogs because of their size, gentle nature, good manners, ease of handling, relatively low maintenance and loving and affectionate nature. This breed is sociable, and enjoys family life and playing with children; they hate being left out. Their sporting background lends them to long walks while their size makes them good companions for older people.

Colour choices?

There are four colour choices: black and tan, ruby (solid red – there should be no white markings) chestnut markings on white (known as Blenheim), and tri-colour (white with black and tan markings).

How much grooming?

Coats are long and silky with only a slight wave, and require brushing every few days with a slicker brush and comb, with special attention to combing ear, feet, leg and tail feathering. Ears need checking and cleaning regularly.

Do they make good pets?

Exceptionally good as they are sweet-natured, easy to handle, mix well with all ages, and are patient, eager to please, kind and affectionate. They are not good guard dogs because they enjoy company and are rarely shy.

What home suits them?

Cavaliers are very versatile and will live in towns or the country,

● *This dam will use play opportunities to teach her puppies some manners and social skills before they leave home.*

providing they have some form of daily exercise including a vigorous walk. Puppy walking should be carefully graded to prevent damage to young bones. Off-lead they have poor road sense and may be distracted by scent trailing.

What sort of owner?

Owners must include their Cavalier in family social activities, as they are fun-loving and gregarious. These dogs adapt well and fit into family life or life with single or elderly owners, and do not enjoy being left alone. They will adore owners who dote on them, enjoying time spent either in active pursuits or just cuddling together.

How much exercise and stimulation?

The breed's sporting ancestry encourages Cavaliers to enjoy walking off their almost boundless energy. They are active and enthusiastic about walking and following a scent, but a good walk and play session in the local park should suffice. Country walking is always enjoyed but take care not to over-walk an enthusiastic puppy.

Friendly with other pets?

Very friendly with household pets, this breed enjoys living with his own kind and other smaller or larger animals. Small pets may be seen as game for chasing or playing, but early puppy socialisation will encourage respect and tolerant friendship.

Is puppy training easy?

Cavaliers are always eager to please, so training is welcomed. However, start early as they are

Character Traits	Poor	Average	Good	Excellent
Attitude to other dogs			██	
Quietness		██		
Behaviour at home			██	
Guarding ability	██			
Good with children				██
Ease of training		██		
Obedience to owner		██		

Time to maturity: 2 years
Male height: 25–32cm (10–12.5in)
Female height: 25–32cm (10–12.5in)
Weight: 5.5–8kg (12–18lb)
Average lifespan: 9–14 years

not overly intelligent, so patience and time are needed for success. It is unlikely they will star in agility competition or obedience.

Special puppy care?
Keep an eye on puppies for symptoms of early onset heart disease, and also 'air scratching' (the dog scratches with his hind leg in mid-air) or spinal scoliosis (curvature of the spine) as these could be indicators of syringomyelia (see below). Puppies are very playful, so make sure that they are not treated roughly.

Possible health problems?
This breed has potential for visual (cataracts, retinal dysplasia) and hearing problems, patella luxation (dislocating kneecaps), mitral valve problems, and some inherit a serious neurological condition called syringomyelia in which fluid-filled cavities develop within the spinal cord. Check that your breeder tests for syringomyelia.

What can we do together?
Not being the brightest pups on the block, walking, good companionship and cuddling are the things they excel at.

- 6 weeks old and nearly ready for a new home.

Don't forget!
Breeding protocols recommend Cavaliers should be medically checked for heart problems before being bred from, so take care to buy from a reputable breeder who has tested their breeding stock.

Small dogs

Cairn Terrier

One of the oldest of the Scottish terriers, this breed originated in the Isle of Skye and Western Highlands early in the 15th century. A small and compact working terrier, Cairns hunted in rocky crags and fells where rabbits and foxes lived. It is from this skill of hunting in 'cairns' (outcrops of rock and stone) that the breed gained its name. The Cairn temperament is excellent for a family dog and they do not usually display aggressive tendencies, although they do make good guard dogs. This breed adapts well to wherever his owner lives, but they are most at home with country rather than town living, because they enjoy an active life and will happily walk for miles. Cairns are merry, lively pets and good family companions, particularly for children. Cairns respond well to firm training and usually do well for owners who want either a companion or a dog to show, or even both.

Colour choices?

Red, sandy, grey, brindled or nearly black to blend with the colour of heather or bracken in the native Highlands are the usual colours.

How much grooming?

The Cairn's double, weather-resistant coat requires less grooming than other terriers, and brushing two or three times a week is sufficient. Bathing is needed every six to eight weeks. Professional help to hand-strip the coat may be needed, but owners can easily learn this technique if they want to. Early training to accept brushing and hand-stripping is sensible.

Do they make good pets?

Cairns are good guard dogs and also good pets for families, although some may prefer bonding with just one person. This breed loves children although puppies do not appreciate rough treatment.

What home suits them?

This puppy adapts to wherever his owner lives, although he prefers the

● With patience and fun training, some Cairns can learn tricks that will delight and amuse their owner.

country to the town because adult Cairns like plenty of walking.

What sort of owner?

Cairns love owners who spend time on outings or long country walks. Owners need to be firm with their puppy, making sure they are in charge and not the Cairn! This lively and intelligent breed is a dog to test his owner's limits because of his natural instincts for hunting, if these are not curbed while young.

How much exercise and stimulation?

Cairns will take as much exercise as they are given, although puppy walking should be gradually built up to avoid straining growing bones and tendons. Games, play and training will stimulate his mind.

Friendly with other pets?

Generally Cairns get on well with other pets, although careful supervision is needed around smaller ones – rabbits and guinea pigs – because of the Cairn's natural hunting instinct. Some may take exception to cats if not socialised well as puppies.

Is puppy training easy?

Training should be fun and reward-based to encourage this merry little dog to learn well. Owners must keep sessions short and interesting to maintain their focus. Not the ideal dog for obedience, although firmness and consistency

● These 6-week-old puppies have a lot of growth and change ahead of them.

Character Traits	Poor	Average	Good	Excellent
Attitude to other dogs				
Quietness				
Behaviour at home				
Guarding ability				
Good with children				
Ease of training				
Obedience to owner				

Time to maturity: 18 months
Male height: 28–30.5cm (11–12in)
Female height: 28–30.5cm (11–12in)
Weight: 6–8kg (13–18lb)
Average lifespan: 12–14 years

bring rewards for patient owners. Training Cairns not to chase squirrels, cats and rabbits is essential as the instinct to hunt will take over at any opportunity.

Special puppy care?

Cairns enjoy long walks, but they should not be introduced too early or health problems may occur later. Some puppies have a tendency to bark but early remedial work should reduce any such problems.

Training must start early as puppies can be wilful and stubborn if not firmly handled. Take care with puppies who enjoy playing because they may be vulnerable to injury.

Possible health problems?

Generally a healthy breed, there are some health problems such as eye problems, Krabbe disease (a disorder of the nervous system), Legg-Perthes disease (malformation of the hip

joint) and von Willebrand disease (affecting the blood). Some also suffer from hip dysplasia and patella luxation (dislocating kneecaps).

What can we do together?

Cairns make useful hunting dogs as well as good family companions.

Don't forget!

This little dog needs careful training and handling while a puppy for him to grow into a great little family dog.

Chinese Crested

Other names: Crested Chinese Hairless, Powder Puff

Archaeologists have found 10,000-year-old remains of the Crested, and believe they originated in Africa. Early examples were unknown outside China until 1880, when they appeared in the United States and the UK. Cresteds were not seen in Europe until the 1970s, so are relative newcomers on the continent. Although seemingly two different breeds, the Crested can either come in hairless or coated 'powder puff' form and both can appear in one litter. Hairless looks as you would expect, but they have a 'crest' of hair on the head and ears, 'socks' on the feet and a 'plume' tail. The hairless body is soft, humanlike and warm, without a 'doggy' smell. Powder puffs have long, soft, silky, double 'veil' coats, with very little moult; both are ideal for allergy sufferers. Although pretty, they are famous for winning ugly dog competitions, but they make delightful pets because of their gentle, affectionate nature and adaptability for apartment living.

Colour choices?

Any combination of colours are available, the skin often being spotted or dappled; base skin colours are blue, lilac, gold or pink. Spotted puppies are born pink developing spots in the early weeks of life, the colours showing a seasonal darkening in summer and lightening in winter.

It takes a lot of time to prepare an adult powder puff for showing, but their beauty makes it worthwhile.

How much grooming?

Hairless puppies need their skin cleansed and creamed daily and after bathing, the use of oil-free moisturising cream to prevent dryness, and sun cream in summer is recommended. If neglected, their skin is susceptible to acne and blackheads; hair on other parts needs regular brushing to remove tangles. Powder puffs' long hair needs daily grooming with a soft bristle brush to remove shedding coat which does not moult.

Do they make good pets?

Cresteds make lively, alert, energetic pets, but this graceful, dainty dog may find boisterous, noisy families too much. They love playing with sensible children and being cuddled, but need the family to respect their sweet, honest nature. Sociable and affectionate, they expect these qualities in abundance from their owner

What home suits them?

Cresteds must live indoors because they are sensitive to cold and heat. Adaptable to most types of home – apartments, town or country homes – their kind, loving nature yearns for constant family company.

What sort of owner?

Owners must appreciate that they need to spend time playing and carrying out daily skin care or brushing their Crested. These dogs want to spend time with an affectionate and sociable owner or family, and do not like being left alone.

How much exercise and stimulation?

While this breed enjoys long walks, they are happy to fit in with owners who enjoy only short walks or outings, but they still need plenty of stimulation with suitable play activity.

Friendly with other pets?

Chinese Cresteds are very friendly with other family pets if introduced and socialised properly while a pup. They are gentle companions, lacking any hunting instinct, so other family pets are not likely to be at risk.

Is puppy training easy?

Crested puppies need firm, gentle and consistent training. They do have a mind of their own, and can be stubborn, but early training will pay dividends. As a breed they have the potential to be tyrants, but this is avoided if they are trained early.

Character Traits	Poor	Average	Good	Excellent
Attitude to other dogs	■	■	■	
Quietness	■	■		
Behaviour at home	■	■	■	
Guarding ability	■			
Good with children	■	■	■	
Ease of training	■	■		
Obedience to owner	■	■		

Time to maturity: 2 years
Male height: 28–33cm (11–13in)
Female height: 23–30cm (9–12in)
Weight: 4.5–5.5kg (10–12lb)
Average lifespan: 12–14 years

Special puppy care?

Never overwalk this puppy as they can suffer dislocation of the kneecaps early on. The hairless types are susceptible to extremes of temperature, so puppies need to be protected from heat and cold.

Possible health problems?

Cresteds are a very healthy breed, but a few have developed a progressive movement disorder (canine multiple system degeneration) and may succumb by six months. Some also suffer patella luxation (dislocating kneecaps) quite early. Other conditions include eye problems or skin allergies. Some are allergic to the use of lanolin in daily creaming regimes.

What can we do together?

These affectionate little dogs, if trained well, make really good companions and playmates.

Don't forget!

Check out the breeder's heath check regime, and take care that young puppies are not overwhelmed by a busy family.

Small dogs

● This 6-week-old litter includes three hairless puppies and one powder puff.

French Bulldog

This breed developed in France from the unwanted by-products of the English bull baiting sport that was outlawed in 1835. These smaller bulldog versions were bred as easy-care companion dogs. Suitable for city life, the diminutive, short-coated, sweet tempered, comical, bat-eared little dogs became popular with French aristocracy and fashionable Parisiennes. Crossing the Atlantic, they were soon sought after in the United States by influential families where their popularity grew and grew. Frenchies make excellent family pets, taking an active part in family life. The breed is often likened to a sweet-natured clown who loves to entertain his owner to whom he is devoted. Ideal for apartments, he is a handy compact size, lively without being too boisterous, low maintenance and quiet (he does not bark), but still a good guard dog. Not built for active life, he loves company and being part of all that is going on.

Colour choices?
Narrow choice in colour of mainly brindle or fawn with only a small amount of white on the head, or pied – white with brindle markings – or entirely white.

How much grooming?
This is a low-shed coat although it will moult at certain times of the year, so a regular weekly brush will suffice, with a daily brush when moulting is happening. The eyes and head folds of skin need to be wiped daily. Bathing needs to be done about once a month.

Do they make good pets?
Frenchies make very good pets, being good-natured and fun-loving. Sensible families will take care not to allow him to overheat and won't be too active with him.

What home suits them?
Ideal for city homes, the Frenchie settles especially well in apartments. Their compact size suits smaller homes, and low-maintenance care and limited walking requirement

● *Very devoted to their owners, Frenchies soon find their niche in family life.*

often appeal to city dwellers. They cannot live outdoors because their breathing problems make it difficult to regulate their body to achieve an even temperature.

What sort of owner?
These dogs appreciate the sort of owner who will want to take their Frenchie to work with them. Someone who will appreciate their affectionate and gentle nature and enjoy their company is ideal, valuing and being entertained by their sociable nature. They love an owner who will give them plenty of love and attention in return.

How much exercise and stimulation?
Due to their short foreheads and associated breathing difficulties, they do not need active walking for more than a short distance; a short walk once or twice a day should suffice. They do, however, need plenty of socialising to stimulate their active and intelligent minds. Overheating when exercising is a danger because of their breathing problems. Play is essential for their well-being but it should not be too strenuous.

Friendly with other pets?
It is important to socialise this breed well as they can be very possessive of their owner and territorial around the home. They do get on well with other pets if introduced and socialised properly from early puppyhood.

Is puppy training easy?
Treating training sessions as fun times to enjoy together will contribute to their learning obedience a whole lot quicker.

Character Traits	Poor	Average	Good	Excellent
Attitude to other dogs			▓	
Quietness			▓	
Behaviour at home				▓
Guarding ability		▓		
Good with children			▓	
Ease of training		▓		
Obedience to owner			▓	

Time to maturity: 2 years
Male height: 28–33cm (11–13in)
Female height: 28–33cm (11–13in)
Weight: 11–12.5kg (24–28lb)
Average lifespan: 11–12 years

They are fun-loving so need to be treated appropriately; generally they tend to be fairly easy to train.

Special puppy care?

Keep the eyes and head folds clean and try to accustom puppies to this regular attention.

Possible health problems?

Compromised airways causing respiratory collapse. Chondrodysplasia (spinal disc disease), eye problems including cherry eye, juvenile cataracts, corneal ulcers, retinal fold dysplasia, thyroid problems.

What can we do together?

This breed make great companions and some have done well in obedience trials.

● *The ears of 8-week-old puppies look too large, but they soon grow into them and achieve the correct proportions.*

Don't forget!

This breed does not appreciate extremes of temperature due to their restricted airways. Some airlines will not accept Frenchies as passengers due to experience of fatalities from breathing problems while they were airborne.

Small dogs

Italian Greyhound

This delightful 'miniature greyhound' is thought to be one of the oldest breeds in history. Well known during the Roman Empire and the Middle Ages, they later found favour with nobility in the Italian Renaissance and appeared in many famous paintings of that time. The Italian Greyhound came to England around the 17th century as a companion to royalty, and remained popular in royal circles well into Victorian times. His debut in the United States, however, did not occur until the 19th century. His popularity declined during the Second World War. He has changed little since his origins as the smallest of the sighthounds, although modern breeding has produced a much sturdier dog, capable of being more than just a companion animal. As puppies, their dainty physique requires more care while they mature than other breeds, and they need plenty of gentle training or may lack confidence. They make delightful family pets in the right home.

Colour choices?
Recognised colours are shades of fawn, white, cream, blue, black, and fawn/white pied.

How much grooming?
Italian Greyhounds have very easy coat care: the short, fine, sleek-as-satin coat needs gentle brushing over to remove the small amount of hair shed. An occasional bath or wipe with a damp cloth to polish will usually suffice, as these dogs are virtually odourless. Dental cleaning is essential as they can suffer periodontal disease, but brushing daily will prevent teeth problems.

Do they make good pets?
This breed make delightful pets as they are intelligent, loving, merry and very playful. Preferring a quieter life, Italian Greyhounds may suit older or childless couples but can also make super pets for families with considerate children.

What home suits them?
This dog likes space to be active and lively, and his slim, compact build

This breed has a long and distinguished history.

● *Delicate to look at, but bold and speedy, this dog needs plenty of exercise to use up its surplus energy.*

suits apartment or town living, providing he has ample opportunity for exercise and play. Owners in apartments should guard against the risk of the dog jumping over the balcony railing inadvertently.

What sort of owner?
Italian Greyhounds need quiet, considerate owners who will be happy to indulge their need for warmth, comfort, affection and plenty of company.

How much exercise and stimulation?
Despite his fragile appearance, Italian Greyhounds are capable of speeds up to 40kph (25mph), so need space to burn off this energy, but without the risk of injury. Generally quiet and reserved, firm but gentle handling is needed as they can be timid, and need socialising and stimulation to prevent any lack of confidence. Early training and stimulation, with plenty of variety, is essential because of their short attention span.

Friendly with other pets?
Always prepared to be friendly with other pets, some care is needed as his sighthound origins might encourage chasing cats and small animals. For this reason this breed needs to be kept on a lead in open areas where he might otherwise be tempted to give chase.

Is puppy training easy?
Italian Greyhounds need short, sharp, regular training sessions with plenty of encouraging praise and

Character Traits	Poor	Average	Good	Excellent
Attitude to other dogs				
Quietness				
Behaviour at home				
Guarding ability				
Good with children				
Ease of training				
Obedience to owner				

Time to maturity: 2 years
Male height: 32–38cm (12.5–15in)
Female height: 32–38cm (12.5–15in)
Weight: Up to 5kg (11lb)
Average lifespan: 13–14 years

titbits to maintain their concentration. Patience is essential as they are not inclined towards obedience.

Special puppy care?

Puppies tend to be lively and athletic, and their high level of activity may cause the risk of broken bones, so puppies should not overexert themselves. Try to get into the habit of cleaning their teeth daily from an early age to help prevent the onset of tooth decay and gum problems.

Possible health problems?

As with many breeds, these little dogs can develop eye, orthopaedic, liver and thyroid problems. Also Legg-Perthes disease (malformation of the hip joint), epilepsy, auto-immune haemolytic anaemia and hair loss can occur in some colour ranges.

A loving companion, even from this early age.

What can we do together?

Lure coursing, agility and great companionship are the usual reasons why people love having these dogs around.

Small dogs

● Caring owners who indulge this 6-week-old puppy's need for extra warmth, and provide plenty of play, exercise and training, will suit him well.

Don't forget!

Fragile bones can easily be broken in active puppies, and they need a coat to keep them warm in cold weather. As the long, thin head is the same width as his neck, a 'martingale style' harness is best to prevent strangling or slipping out of the leash.

Miniature Schnauzer

Miniature Schnauzers are smaller versions of Standard Schnauzers bred 500 years ago in the German provinces of Württemburg and Bavaria. The Miniature has proved more popular in the USA and Europe, perhaps because its smaller size suits apartment living. It also has a less powerful and dominant nature compared to the larger types. Miniatures conform to the same basic breed standard as the bigger sizes, and were also used as vermin hunters and guards for farms, factories or homes. Created in the 19th century, Miniature Schnauzers have been popular with American families only since around 1920, and even later in Britain – the 1960s. Robust, active and intelligent, Miniature Schnauzers are sometim described as 'a terrier without the attitude', and they make an ideal family pet who enjoys compan and is content to be a loyal and affectionate companion. These Schnauzers are particularly quic to learn and are ideal for obedience trials or agili

Colour choices?

Black, pepper and salt, black and silver, with dark masks and no white markings. White and parti-colour Schnauzers have been bred, but they are only accepted in Europe, not in the United States and Great Britain.

How much grooming?

These are high-maintenance coats, and need hand-stripping preferably about every eight weeks, which retains the wiry top coat and protects the soft, warm undercoat. Puppy owners may prefer trimming for convenience. Starting daily as puppies, a stiff brush through the coat is needed, and the whiskers and legs should be combed. The beard needs washing after meals. Bathing will be needed around every four to six weeks.

Do they make good pets?

This breed can be energetic and bossy, but is not usually aggressive. This is a versatile dog and matches perfectly with single and inexperienced owners, or families

● Always on the look out for mischief, and opportunities to be a bossy boots!

with young children. Miniature Schnauzers are obedient and devoted to their owners, and their size often suits modern living better than larger breeds.

What home suits them?

This Schnauzer, unlike the larger versions, will adapt to life in apartments or small homes with gardens, providing there are good places for walking.

What sort of owner?

Miniature Schnauzers have a lively, live-to-please personality. Owners must be responsive to their lovir nature, but also be firm and kind, and not allow the to become bossy. They should nev be left at home by working owner as they become bored and lonely and could be destructive.

How much exercise and stimulation?

Puppies need gently increasing exercise levels, with short activity sessions and play times until they mature, when they will need arour an hour's walk daily. Like most dog Schnauzers do not like being confined indoors alone, and need t be stimulated to prevent boredom Either take them with you on famil outings or make sure they are not left alone for too long. They can be task-orientated, so teaching them t fetch the newspaper or slippers is something they will readily learn.

Friendly with other pets?

Usually good natured, they need introducing to other family pets as

Character Traits	Poor	Average	Good	Excellent
Attitude to other dogs				
Quietness				
Behaviour at home				
Guarding ability				
Good with children				
Ease of training				
Obedience to owner				

Time to maturity: 2.5 years
Male height: 33–36cm (13–14in)
Female height: 30–33cm (12–13in)
Weight: 6–7kg (13–15lb)
Average lifespan: 13–14 years

puppies, and supervising while learning how to behave. Male dogs may try to be dominant with other dogs, but early socialising will help.

Is puppy training easy?
These dogs are fun to train, and plenty of rewards encourages quick learning. Owners will be well rewarded if they use a firm, calm and confident approach.

Special puppy care?
Puppies need less walking initially, gradually building up more time. Try to incorporate play into training, as it makes obedience more fun. Schnauzers are good guard dogs, but can bark a lot, so dealing with this issue early may prevent problems later.

Possible health problems?
Schnauzers may suffer from hypothyroidism (lack of thyroid hormone), haemophilia and von Willebrand's disease (both

● At 12 weeks, these puppies are old enough to learn how to behave for grooming. The coat will need hand-stripping later on.

Daily brushing through the coat is enough for now,

blood disorders), Legg-Perthes disease (degeneration of the hip joint), epilepsy, eye problems (cataracts, progressive retinal atrophy), skin and digestive disorders and liver shunt.

Small dogs

What can we do together?
Devoted, loyal companions, their love of learning often makes them successful in obedience competition and agility trials.

Don't forget!
Buy only from reputable breeders who do health checks on their stock, particularly eye testing.

Parson Russell Terrier

Other names: Jack Russell, Russell Terriers

The original terrier was developed by Parson Jack Russell of Devon in the 1800s for hunting, and had to be sturdy enough to keep up with horses over some distance. Once the prey went to ground, this lively and rustic little fellow's job was to dig underground, courageously face up to the quarry and flush it out for the hunters. Parson Russell Terriers are recognised in most parts of the world, but there are other terriers bred from the same source. Recognition in 1990 of the longer-legged version now named the Parson Russell Terrier standardised the breed into a dog more closely resembling the original type. The non-registered versions, known as Jack Russell Terriers, are not officially recognised, and have slightly different physical proportions with shorter legs. However, their similar characteristics and uses as working terriers make them equally suitable as companion pets.

● *Somewhat longer legged than the Jack, this adult Parson more closely resembles the original type.*

Colour choices?

Usually white with black and/or tan patches, or solid white sometimes with dark ticking.

How much grooming?

These terriers have harsh, dense double coats in three different combinations: rough, smooth and broken coated (rough and smooth combined), which can occur in the same litter. Rough coats need hand-stripping, but puppy owners may prefer to trim as puppies may not stand still for stripping. Rough and broken coats benefit from weekly tidying, and 'raking' with a rubber curry comb. Although clean by habit, regular brushing is preferable to bathing. Check ears and between paws for grass seeds that may have worked their way into the coat after walking through long grass.

Do they make good pets?

Friendly and outgoing, these make affectionate pets. Rough handling is not appreciated, but they are kind and attentive if treated well, and good with children.

What home suits them?

Mainly country lovers, these dogs will also fit into apartment life but need a daily programme of outings to stimulate their active minds. Homes with a large garden for play and activity are ideal.

What sort of owner?

An owner who provides regular exercise and plenty of attention is essential. Puppies left alone for too long are likely to want to escape in search of adventure and mischief. Parson Russell Terriers are best suited to active owners who enjoy walking in the country and who are happy to involve their dog in family activities.

How much exercise and stimulation?

By nature they appreciate working the field all day, using their abundant energy and tenacious skills, so plenty of exercise and stimulation is needed, although this should be carefully graded for puppies. Boredom will encourage them to find their own way of exercising their energy and intelligent minds.

Friendly with other pets?

These terriers have a natural instinct for hunting or chasing, and can be aggressive or predatory with other pets unless well socialised early on. Other smaller household pets may be at risk as they are by nature hunters of small animals.

Is puppy training easy?

The natural spirit of this terrier can make them either easy or difficult to train as puppies, depending on the owner. Training needs to be firm, patient, consistent and respecting of their independent spirit. Some are harder to train than others, but patient owners will be rewarded.

Character Traits	Poor	Average	Good	Excellent
Attitude to other dogs	■			
Quietness		■		
Behaviour at home			■	
Guarding ability			■	
Good with children			■	
Ease of training			■	
Obedience to owner			■	

Time to maturity: 18 months–2 years
Male height: ideal 36cm (14in)
Female height: ideal 33cm (13in)
Weight: 5.5–6.35kg (12–14lb)
Average lifespan: 13–16 years

Special puppy care?

A pet puppy with a rough coat is better trimmed rather than hand-stripped. Otherwise they are easy to care for, requiring few baths, some grooming and sensible nutrition. With high energy levels it may be tempting to overwalk puppies, but short walks and active play are better, gradually extending to longer walks.

● *These 6-week-old Jack Russell puppies will make super pets with the same disposition as their cousins, the Parson Russell Terrier.*

Possible health problems?

Generally a healthy and hardy breed, but they may suffer from eye problems such as cataracts, primary lens luxation (the lens slips out of position), also deafness, patella luxation (dislocating kneecaps), Legg Perthes disease (degeneration of the head of the femur) and von Willebrand disease (a blood-clotting disorder).

Small dogs

What can we do together?

These terriers do well at agility, earth dog trials (not allowed in the UK), obedience and hunting.

Don't forget!

Puppies need firm handling to prevent their independent spirit from taking over family life and ruling the roost. This breed's extrovert character is its most important feature, but it needs training to become the ideal pet. Only Parson Russell Terriers can be officially registered with the Kennel Club.

Beagle

A happy little dog popular in America since 1840, this is an old English breed that is one of the smallest of the hounds. These dogs are excellent scent hounds and they were bred by the Elizabethans for hunting. Called 'singing hounds', the yeomen of the time walked on foot behind small packs hunting hares and rabbits. In the 1860s they became popular for 'beagling', and later found a place in Field Trials. They have a strong hunting instinct and will go scent tracking, often disregarding the owner's call to return. Many are used for working purposes, their ability to scent being utilised for drug and bomb detection. Beagles make fine all-round additions to most families, being good companions and adaptable to most lifestyles and activities, as well as smart show dogs. His tail-wagging and ear-flapping enthusiasm for life make him a popular choice for a family.

Colour choices?

Usually black, tan and white (tricolour) is the most common, but also lemon and white, red/tan and white or occasionally mottled. The short, slightly curved tail (the stern) is white-tipped. The position of colour markings is relevant when choosing a puppy for showing.

● Beagles easily put on weight, so keep an eye on rations.

How much grooming?

This short, dense and weatherproof coat, sometimes produces a pungent 'doggy' smell. Easy to care for, it needs regular brushing to keep clean and smart. Grooming with a hound glove or stiff hairbrush removes dead hair which sheds profusely. Regular attention is needed to keep the large floppy ears clean and infection-free.

Do they make good pets?

This versatile, energetic hound is merry, brave and intelligent. His affectionate, good-natured manner and gentle disposition make him a great family pet. Sometimes too bouncy and mouthy for small children, he is quite mischievous as a puppy, but well-trained mature Beagles adore children.

What home suits them?

Beagles generally prefer the country, but they are happy in the city with a securely fenced garden. Regular daily walks to let off steam discourage escape artists from finding their own amusement. This is not a suitable breed for apartments for this reason.

What sort of owner?

Beagles love people and fit in well with most age groups. They love playing rough and tumble, and are usually good natured and affectionate with everyone. Owners may need to be more easy-going and tolerant of their mischievous ways as strict training is not appreciated. They are not suitable for working owners because they enjoy company so much.

How much exercise and stimulation?

An intelligent energetic dog, so exercise and stimulation with plenty of play sessions is essential. Beagles enjoy a good country walk but also enjoy town walks with plenty of activity to satisfy their natural instincts. Some make their own exercise regime if bored, and may run for miles in pursuit of an interesting scent.

Friendly with other pets?

Beagles generally get on well with most other household pets, but enjoy a chase if encouraged.

Is puppy training easy?

Intelligent and single-minded, this breed needs moderate firmness in training. Mostly obedient, but a good scent is distracting, so a good recall is essential. Training should start early, using reward-based

Character Traits	Poor	Average	Good	Excellent
Attitude to other dogs				
Quietness				
Behaviour at home				
Guarding ability				
Good with children				
Ease of training				
Obedience to owner				

Time to maturity: 2 to 4 years
Male height: 33–40cm (13–16in)
Female height: Marginally smaller
Weight: 8.2–16kg (18–35lb)
Average lifespan: 10–13 years

techniques, but train sparingly and with plenty of patience as they can be stubborn.

Special puppy care?

Don't overdo rewards in training as they can be greedy – even puppies! The large floppy ears need careful cleaning to keep them dry and infection-free. Starting ear care early trains them to accept such care later.

Possible health problems?

Physically they are a healthy breed, although they can run to obesity. They are usually free of most health defects although epilepsy, ear infections, eye problems and 'Beagle pain syndrome' (usually in puppies) can sometimes occur.

What can we do together?

Great walking companion, good show dogs, suitable for Field Trials.

Small dogs

Don't forget!

This dog is bred for hunting and following scent; he will be tempted to go off alone, particularly if he gets bored and finds a way out of the garden.

● *Just 4 weeks old, these Beagle puppies will rapidly grow into sturdy and compact hounds.*

American Cocker Spaniel
Other names: Cocker Spaniel (USA)

English Cocker Spaniels arrived in the USA on the *Mayflower* in 1620, but it was not until later in the 1880s when they were introduced as gundogs that the American Cocker developed. Quick to nurture their natural ability for hunting, American sportsmen trained them to flush out and retrieve woodcock. Boldness and a willingness to please charmed owners and won them a proud hunting heritage. The modern conformation of American Cockers is more compact than the English Cocker, slightly heavier with a squarer, more domed head and shorter back and legs. His distinguished looks and thick silky coat have repeatedly won the breed popularity as proficient and smart show dogs. This is a most beautiful dog, but the consequence of fame is the high-maintenance required to keep them looking the part. This little dog's glamorous appearance is unsuitable for working, so life for him tends to be as a companion and show dog.

Colour choices?
A variety of colours are available in three main groups: black, black and tan, solid colours other than black – brown, liver, red, golden, sable, cream, silver; and parti-colours which are white with distinct patches of solid colours, including roan. Some merle colours are produced but these are not recognised.

How much grooming?
This breed will keep owners busy with coat care every day. They need dedicated care for coat maintenance, which will be time-consuming and costly because professional assistance is required, even for short coats. Daily brushing and combing through the luxuriant coat with especial attention to feathering on ears, legs and underside is a must. Bathing is needed, if not twice a month, then at least once.

Do they make good pets?
This easy-going, good-natured, merry little dog is an eye-catching

● *A fine specimen of an adult, this dog aims to impress in the show ring.*

charmer, loving his family, joining in all activities and one of the family for outings. They make gentle playmates for children who take care not to be rough.

What home suits them?
This is an active breed, so countryside locations are appreciated. However, town houses with gardens and walking space are fine too. Apartment living with access to park walks may be acceptable with the right owner.

What sort of owner?
Not recommended for owners ou at work, these dogs enjoy family company, or an older person who gives the time necessary for long walks, training and essential grooming. They are very responsive to an affectionate owner, but need firm handling.

How much exercise and stimulation?
Plenty of walking will suit then fine, together with play and stimulation as they are an active intelligent breed.

Friendly with other pets?
Always friendly with other dogs an cats, they do have a hunting instinc so socialisation from an early age necessary.

Is puppy training easy?
Essentially bred from a working or hunting line, American Cockers ar extremely bright, quick to learn an eager to please, but they can be stubborn. Firm, gentle handling is ideal with suitable rewards and no

Character Traits	Poor	Average	Good	Excellent
Attitude to other dogs				
Quietness				
Behaviour at home				
Guarding ability				
Good with children				
Ease of training				
Obedience to owner				

Time to maturity: 4 years
Male height: 34–39cm (13.5–15.5in)
Female height: 34–37cm (13.5–14.5in)
Weight: 11–14 kg (24–30lb)
Average lifespan: 10–11 years

10 weeks old and very cute.

harsh tones. Games that test their intelligence and draw on their background as retrievers are ideal to include in puppy training schedules.

● *He will be eager to please.*

Special puppy care?

Start brushing and combing as soon as possible, as puppies need to learn patience to stand still long enough for grooming. Training should not be harsh, but fun and playful, exercising the dog's bright and happy nature to develop a good foundation of learning.

Possible health problems?

American Cockers can suffer from many different conditions: cancer, liver disease, heart problems, glucose deficiency problems, epilepsy, eye problems (progressive retinal atrophy, glaucoma and cataracts), haemolytic anaemia, patella luxation (dislocating kneecaps), hip malformation (dysplasia), as well as a tendency to ear infections and skin allergies.

What can we do together?

Ideal as a companion dog, they also make excellent show specimens for owners with plenty of time to spend on the coat.

Don't forget!

This breed is not for the faint-hearted when it comes to coat care. Attention to grooming is a must, and if professional attention is sought, it is likely to be costly if required on a regular basis.

Tibetan Terrier
Other names: Chrysanthemum Dog, Phassa Terrier, Dhokhi Apso

As the name suggests, this breed comes from the high Tibetan mountains where they were very much more than just temple dogs, but also used for farming work as well. Tibetans are hardy dogs and were frequently used to herd livestock and accompany caravans from place to place. Their long, thick, water-resistant coats proved ideal for coping with harsh weather conditions. Bred in the West from two dogs given as a gift to a British doctor by a Tibetan princess in 1920, they are now a popular breed around the world. Tibetan Terriers are classic shaggy dogs, solid and robust, with a happy temperament. Medium-sized, with glamorous coats, they are not true terriers, although they do have the same energy, intelligence, spirit and stubborn streak. They can be distrustful of strangers, which makes them good watchdogs, but as a family dog they are very appealing, and are gentle with children and devoted to their family.

Colour choices?
Many including black, grey, gold, cream, white, parti-colours and tri-colours. Chocolate and liver are not acceptable in the show ring.

How much grooming?
Tibetans have soft, warm, thick undercoats with a topcoat rather like human hair. The coat needs daily attention to remove tangles and dead hair, using a good bristle brush and a comb. Take particular care around nine months when the puppy coat sheds and the adult coat grows. Face hair needs wiping after meals. Some owners prefer to opt for short puppy clips, although daily brushing will still be needed, and bathing once a month.

Do they make good pets?
Tibetans are delightful, compact family pets with an outgoing nature. Rarely nervous, they fit easily into most homes and family life. They demand attention, and if treated well, happily go with the flow. They are good tempered without vices, if occasionally sharp, but have a

● *This terrier is a distinctly shaggy dog and the coat needs regular grooming.*

reputation for being amenable and affectionate companions.

What home suits them?
Home is where the heart is, and with family for company, they are always happy, adapting well to town or country homes.

What sort of owner?
Owners must be equally loving and need to spend time returning affection; they cannot expect sole devotion, however, because Tibetans love all members of their family. Owners should be willing to include their Tibetan in all family activities.

How much exercise and stimulation?
Tibetans have plenty of energy and enjoy as much exercise and stimulation as their owner has time for. They will, however, accept shorter or longer walks according to the circumstances, and are an ideal size for sensible children to take out.

Friendly with other pets?
Other household pets may not appreciate this puppy's exuberant friendly nature, so early socialising is important for teaching good behaviour. They must learn manners and how to treat other animals with respect. Some can be jealous, which may be hard for other pets.

Is puppy training easy?
Perhaps not the best 'first' dog for novice families – some are strong-willed, but they usually want to

Character Traits	Poor	Average	Good	Excellent
Attitude to other dogs				
Quietness				
Behaviour at home				
Guarding ability				
Good with children				
Ease of training				
Obedience to owner				

Time to maturity: 2 years
Male height: UK 35–41cm (14–16in), US less than 43cm (17in)
Female height: Slightly smaller
Weight: 8–13.5kg (18–30lb)
Average lifespan: 13–14 years

● It takes time for coats to grow long, but experience of grooming is essential for a puppy.

● This 3-month-old puppy should prove to be a quick learner.

Small dogs

please. Intelligent and quick to learn, puppies need early training that adopts a sensible and consistent approach to curb their bouncy nature. Advanced training often brings out the best in them.

Special puppy care?

If left alone, these exuberant puppies can be hyperactive and noisy, so time spent on early training and socialising is advised. Puppies must not over-exercise, and the length of walks should be built up slowly to allow bones and joints to mature properly.

Possible health problems?

Tibetans are fairly robust but still have health problems such as hip dysplasia (malformation of the hip sockets), patella luxation (dislocating kneecaps), eye problems, hernias and heart murmurs, and an inherited condition, canine neuronal ceroid lipofuscinosis, which affects the nervous system. Some are allergic to dairy products and certain grain foods, so take care with puppy diets.

What can we do together?

This breed enjoys lots of activities, such as obedience, flyball, showing, tracking and even participating in non-competitive herding trials.

Don't forget!

Being firm but kind will pay with this puppy. Check that breeders have done health checks on all their stock before buying.

Fox Terrier (Smooth and Wire)

Fox Terriers are classic British dogs and one of the most ancient breeds in the British Isles. Originally developed for fox hunting, these terriers would unhesitatingly go to earth to drag foxes out for the hunt. The breed arrived in America around 1875, and at intervals both coat types have swapped the lead in the popularity stakes. Fox Terriers became famous in the music industry as the HMV (His Master's Voice) record logo features one, and some won enviable army service commendations, but now they are most often associated with Snowy, the cartoon companion of Tintin. These dogs are inquisitive and mischievous, shouldering their way into the limelight. With their jaunty disposition, Fox Terriers are entertaining characters: cheerful, gay and sociable family dogs for either town or country families, and also vigilant watchdogs. They still have a strong hunting instinct, so other pets may not fare so well when sharing a home with them.

Colour choices?
Solid white, or predominantly white with tan, black or black and tan markings; other colours are not permitted. Fox Terriers are noted for their coloured 'saddle' on the back.

How much grooming?
The smooth coat needs brushing twice a week to remove dead hair and dander. Wire coats, which feel a bit like coconut matting, require daily attention, using a stiff brush and wide-toothed comb. Wire coats also need hand-stripping; pet owners may prefer trimming but this can change the texture of the coat. Both coats benefit from occasional bathing.

Do they make good pets?
Fox Terriers are fast, active and energetic, with a true terrier personality and temperament, being courageous, bold and game for a scrap. They are considered one of the most affectionate terriers, and prized for being family-orientated and gentle with children. In the right home they make excellent pets.

Adult wires need daily grooming.

Smooth coats need less maintenance.

What home suits them?
Fox Terriers were bred to hunt and run, and while they adapt to city life, with energy levels this high they will need long daily walks. Ideally, the better option is a country life with long active walks and a garden to explore.

What sort of owner?
Their fast, active, strong personalities need firm, strong-minded owners, who enjoy plenty of walking, to keep them under control and avoid clashes of personality with others. Owners w become devoted to this great, fun-loving character but he will demand constant attention.

How much exercise and stimulation?
Fox Terriers love plenty of exercise and have loads of energy. They nee stimulation for their intelligent, activ minds, with task-orientated activitie to maintain interest. Playing in the garden is not enough as they become nervous or aggressive without exercise and stimulation.

Friendly with other pets?
Early puppy socialisation is essentia although they may still be unfriendl to other pets or dogs. Fox Terriers have strong hunting instincts so sm household pets are at some risk, an cats may be chased.

Is puppy training easy?
With good handling this dog does well, but owners must be firm and

Character Traits	Poor	Average	Good	Excellent
Attitude to other dogs	▓			
Quietness		▓		
Behaviour at home			▓	
Guarding ability			▓	
Good with children		▓		
Ease of training			▓	
Obedience to owner			▓	

Time to maturity: 2 years
Male height: 36–41cm (14–16in)
Female height: Slightly less
Weight: 7–9.5kg (15–21lb)
Average lifespan: 13–14 years

● *Tiny puppies need weaning before they can leave their mother.*

Small dogs

● *Socialisation will be essential training for this puppy at 6 months old.*

consistent. Training should be task-orientated and fun, and consist of regular short sessions because they have low boredom thresholds. Positive, reward-based training to maintain interest helps. Training a good recall is essential as they are independent thinkers and will happily head off on their own missions!

Special puppy care?

Puppies are likely to be energetic, so exercise with care and establish boundaries for playtimes to prevent damage to growing bones. Terriers have an instinct for digging, so it helps to train puppies not to do so.

Possible health problems?

Usually a healthy breed and frequently long-lived, Fox Terriers can get Legg-Perthes disease of the hip joint and von Willebrand's disease (a blood-clotting disorder). Skin allergies also affect some, but care with diet can improve or prevent this.

What can we do together?

Lots of walking; these companionable dogs are great pets and good watchdogs for the home.

Don't forget!

Given the opportunity Fox Terriers are great car and bicycle chasers. Sensible diet helps to prevent skin problems. Socialisation is essential to prevent dog-related aggression or other unwanted behaviours.

Shetland Sheepdog

Other names: Sheltie, Miniature Collie, Shetland Collie

Charming, quick-witted, nimble little dogs, they hail from the Shetland Isles off the north coast of Scotland. The stern, rugged and weather-beaten environment produced a working breed needing a dense coat and a Lilliputian size; perfect for herding in rocky, storm-swept pastures or guarding crofters' cottages and flocks for well over a century. Today's breed is thought to have developed from crossing the original Shetland Collie with Greenland's whale fishermen's 'Yakki' dogs, together with Scandinavian fishermen's spitz dogs. The breed went relatively unnoticed until the early 1900s when English and US dog fanciers took an interest. From its origins as a general farm dog and sheep herder, this loyal and affectionate dog shows similarities with the Rough Collie in terms of his elegance and popularity as an obedient and loyal family member. This is an active dog, affectionate, devoted to his owner, and a wonderful companion to live with.

Colour choices?
The commonest colours are shades of sable – mahogany sable, shaded sable and sable merle, also tri-coloured (black, gold and white), blue merle, and sometimes black and white, or black with tan. All colours have white markings on the collar and chest, legs, tail tip, and a forehead blaze.

How much grooming?
A Sheltie has a double coat with long, rough, water-repellent guard hairs lying over a soft thick undercoat, which retains coolness in summer and warmth in winter. Moulting in spring and autumn, the hair is gently teased out in clumps and combed. Daily use of a stiff brush and comb to penetrate through both coats to remove dead hair and tangles is necessary. The soft hair around the hind legs (the skirt), inside the thighs and armpits is particularly susceptible to tangles. Bathing more than once a month is not recommended.

Do they make good pets?
Shelties make wonderful pets, but

● *Adult Shelties have profuse double coats. Prospective owners must be prepared for lots of grooming.*

dislike noisy households or boisterous children, so may react badly and nip in chaotic or busy homes. They are affectionate and gentle and easy for family members to train, but can be vocal, which may not suit all families.

What home suits them?
Country or town life suits them equally, providing their need for exercise and freedom in open spaces is met. Country life is preferable as they love open space.

Expect Shelties to be reserved but not fearful with strangers.

What sort of owner?
Shelties are unsuitable for working owners, as they are affectionate, sensitive dogs who are intensely loyal to their owners and so will miss their company if they go out to work. Owners should be prepared to spend time on grooming and exercise, and be gentle and sensitive with training.

How much exercise and stimulation?
Active, intelligent little dogs they enjoy long walks and garden romps. They can be noise-sensitive so walk venues should be chosen with this in mind, as they may bolt if startled. Early socialisation to prevent nervousness and low stress levels at home, with high levels of stimulation are important.

Friendly with other pets?
Most Shelties get on well with other pets; however, they enjoy a chase if encouraged.

Character Traits	Poor	Average	Good	Excellent
Attitude to other dogs				
Quietness				
Behaviour at home				
Guarding ability				
Good with children				
Ease of training				
Obedience to owner				

Time to maturity: 2 years
Male height: 36–41cm (14–16in)
Female height: 36–41cm (14–16in)
Weight: 5–14kg (11–31lb)
Average lifespan: 12–13 years

Is puppy training easy?

Highly intelligent and retaining lots of original characteristics, Shelties can be vocal and excitable, but they like to please and work hard for sensitive owners. Responding well to encouragement and reward-based training, they dislike harshness or scolding, which makes them sensitive.

Special puppy care?

It is important that this breed is socialised early, as their natural shyness could develop into nervousness. Puppies should learn to accept handling as their thick coats need grooming daily.

Possible health problems?

Deafness in puppies from merle parentage. Progressive retinal atrophy (PRA), Collie eye anomaly (CEA), von Willebrand's disease of the blood, heart problems, hypothyroidism, epilepsy, hip dysplasia, patella luxation (dislocation) and skin allergies. Many of these can be checked from parental blood tests.

What can we do together?

Shelties make excellent companions and train well for obedience, agility, flyball, showing, tracking and herding.

Small dogs

Don't forget!

They are sensitive and dislike loud noises or busy households with boisterous children. Regular coat care is a necessity.

● *Just a few weeks old and absolutely irresistible.*

Boston Terrier

Other names: Boston Bull, Boston Bull Terrier, Boxwood American Gentleman

The Boston Terrier is the result of all-American breeding, and the first non-sporting dog produced exclusively in the USA in around the 1870s. Originating from bull and terrier specimens crossed with French Bulldogs, the modern breed does not reflect either the rat-catching tenacity or fighting-dog tendencies of the bull breeds or the querulous terrier nature that his name suggests. The Boston Terrier has captivated people's hearts and his early fighting background has been replaced with courtesy and irresistible charm. His gentle, happy-go-lucky disposition and the ability to win hearts with his good nature has earned him the title of the 'American gentleman'. A compact little dog, he fits well into city life in an apartment, and makes a delightful companion for most age groups. His ease of training, low-maintenance care and lack of demand for regular walking makes him a favourite for modern lifestyle.

Colour choices?

Colour is important and markings should be even and specifically placed on show puppies. Usually brindle or black over the body, every dog carries a 'shirt' with a handsome white blaze on the face, collar, breast, forelegs and the hind legs below the hocks.

How much grooming?

The coat is short, smooth and lustrous with the advantage of minimal shedding; brushing once a week should suffice. The face and eyes need to be wiped over and cleaned more regularly.

Do they make good pets?

An intelligent and affectionate little dog, his good nature and low maintenance makes him an excellent companion dog for a modern lifestyle. Bostons make firm friends and good playmates for children in a family, but equally will enjoy life in a more sedentary situation. He demands company and attention and will be unhappy if left alone too long.

The Boston is a very good natured companion.

● *Like other short-faced breeds, Bostons can suffer breathing problems.*

What home suits them?

The Boston Terrier, as the name suggests, is a city dog, and fits well into apartments or house and small garden situations. He does not require much walking and so he fits in to a modern city lifestyle very readily. He prefers homes where there is someone around for company most of the time.

What sort of owner?

This breed is happiest with an owner prepared to give plenty of love and attention. He makes an ideal companion for older people who appreciate his gentle, courteous disposition, but can also be lively and sociable within younger, more active families.

How much exercise and stimulation?

Bostons do not enjoy excessive walking and would rather be carried, but will want to go everywhere with their owners. They should walk at least a short distance daily to maintain good health and to stimulate and socialise them outside their home. Regular playtime in the garden or home will exercise their intelligent and active minds.

Friendly with other pets?

Early socialisation is always necessary, but they are a friendly breed who fit in well with most other household pets. Some males may show inter-male aggression.

Character Traits	Poor	Average	Good	Excellent
Attitude to other dogs				
Quietness				
Behaviour at home				
Guarding ability				
Good with children				
Ease of training				
Obedience to owner				

Time to maturity: 2 years
Male height: 38–43cm (15–17in)
Female height: 38–43cm (15–17in)
Weight: 4.5–11.5kg (10–25lb)
Average lifespan: 11–13 years

Is puppy training easy?

Training can be easy if the owner appeals to this highly intelligent mind, making training more like fun than serious work. Bostons are stubborn, so a firm and consistent approach is needed to bring out the best in this character. Tricks and obedience tasks will be well received if owners show patience and consistency in their training.

Special puppy care?

Most puppies are delivered by caesarean section because of the head's shape and size, so smaller puppies may need continued nurturing. Avoid extremes of heat or cold, and take care to provide correct nutrition from early on as Bostons can suffer from flatulence.

Possible health problems?

Breathing problems associated with the short face. Cataracts (affecting puppies or adults) and other eye problems, usually checked in the litter. Also luxating patellas (dislocating kneecaps), deafness, heart murmurs and allergies.

What can we do together?

Great companion dogs, some do really well in obedience, or for showing.

Don't forget!

Feed puppies correctly from the start, or they will produce a lot of wind! This breed does enjoy very hot or very cold weather.

Take care that eyes do not get injured during boisterous play.

Good socialisation overcomes nervousness.

● *At 6 weeks old play gives this puppy the confidence to enjoy life.*

English Cocker Spaniel *Other names: Cocker Spaniel (UK)*

An old English breed, this spaniel's ancestors have been used for hunting wildfowl since the 14th century. The UK officially recognised the breed in 1892, at which time some were exported to France and the United States where their skills for 'cocking' (hunting woodcock) were developed. Cockers are the best known of spaniels and popular all over the world. As gundogs, working strains are smaller and stocky, and not bred to the same standard but recognised for their working ability; they are trained to flush, drive and retrieve the game. For family pets, the merry little Cocker with his non-stop wagging tail is full of life, exuberant, good-natured, affectionate and gentle. Devoted to his family, he is a faithful companion, but strong-willed and independent. With their outgoing personality and working ability, Cockers can be trained as hearing dogs, to provide support for disabled people and as police search dogs.

Colour choices?

There are a wide variety of colours to choose from: black, liver, red, golden, sable, silver, black and tan, black and white, liver and white, tri-colours (black, tan and white) and roan (solid colour patches and white with ticked areas) colours – blue, liver, orange, and lemon, but never all white. White on solid colours is not allowed except as a small patch on the chest. Working Cockers can come in any colour, there is no restriction.

How much grooming?

The Cocker's thick silky coat needs grooming with a brush and comb daily, with particular attention paid to the feathering around the ears, legs, chest and underside. It should be bathed about once a month. The long ears should be checked regularly as they can become dirty.

Do they make good pets?

The Cocker is a most charming pet, with his constantly wagging tail he really is a 'merry Cocker'. Exuberant, active, playful, affectionate and

● Maturity is reached by two years as these handsome dogs show; feathering on their bodies is already grown.

gentle, he appeals to all age groups. Cockers are particularly family-orientated, but do not like rough treatment from children.

What home suits them?

Apartment living is possible but it may be a little small; generally they suit a town or country home with garden space for playing and long walks on the doorstep.

What sort of owner?

Any sensible and responsible owner will suit this breed; someone who includes their dog in family activities and takes care of his physical needs. Best suited to an owner who spends time training and enjoys his learning development from puppy to adult.

How much exercise and stimulation?

Cockers can become frustrated and obese without adequate amounts of exercise, so plenty of walks are needed. It is best to start puppies on short walks initially and build up to long walks with playtime sessions. Highly intelligent, this breed needs mental stimulation from training.

Friendly with other pets?

Good with other animals, although their hunting instincts may surface if a chase is available.

Is puppy training easy?

This breed's intelligence makes training a pleasure, but it must start early before bad habits form. Cockers can be strong-willed and independent, but harnessing this

Character Traits	Poor	Average	Good	Excellent
Attitude to other dogs				
Quietness				
Behaviour at home				
Guarding ability				
Good with children				
Ease of training				
Obedience to owner				

Time to maturity: 2 years
Male height: 39–41cm (15.5–16in)
Female height: 38–39cm (15–15.5in)
Weight: 13–14.5kg (29–32lb)
Average lifespan: 11–12 years

trait through firm but gentle training as a puppy moulds them into excellent family companions.

Special puppy care?

Training needs to start early or an owner's commands may be disregarded in favour of their own activities. Frustration can cause destructive behaviour so make sure a puppy cannot be injured if he chews. Check ears regularly as they become painful if allowed to get dirty.

Possible health problems?

Usually quite healthy, but they do have their share of eye problems (progressive retinal atrophy), deafness, kidney disease, heart problems and dislocating kneecaps. At one time solid colours, mainly reds, had a problem with rage syndrome, but this has largely disappeared.

What can we do together?

Small dogs

Cockers (and owners!) will enjoy agility, flyball, obedience competitions, walking and games that involve retrieving.

Don't forget!

Make sure ears are checked and cleaned regularly as these can become smelly and painful. Firm but gentle training will prevent this puppy from getting the upper hand.

● *Affectionate and gentle, at 8 weeks old this puppy is ready for a loving family.*

Bedlington Terrier

Other names: Rothbury Terrier, Rodbery Terrier, Gypsy Dog

This lamb-like dog has a lion's heart and was originally bred by miners in the 13th century in Northumberland, England to clear coal mines of rats. As well as a reputation for ratting, the Bedlington, named after the village where it originated, was famed for his speed and became known as the 'miner's racehorse' in field racing. His speed, agility and hunting skills also made him an attractive dog for poachers. The breed was not recognised in England until the early 1870s and was unknown in the United States until the 20th century, but it quickly became popular as a show dog and loyal family companion. Tractable and devoted to their owner, Bedlingtons make loving pets. The roached back and soft, linty wool coat with ear fringes and topknot is distinctive because of its shade of blue. This delicate-looking dog is nevertheless a game terrier, not inclined to fight but quite capable of looking after himself.

Colour choices?

Mainly blue, but also liver or fawn (sandy) with or without tan markings. Topknots in adult dogs should be lighter coloured than the shade of the main coat.

How much grooming?

Expert groomers need to do the first coat clipping, thereafter pet owners should brush this low-shedding coat with a wide-toothed comb and slicker brush regularly to remove dead hair. The coat may need to be professionally clipped two or three times a year into a 'pet clip' suitable for easy maintenance; for show puppies the coat is sculpted into a specific style, which can be rather difficult for novices to achieve.

Do they make good pets?

Charming and loyal pets, Bedlingtons are very friendly but also make good guard dogs; they tend to attach themselves to a family or one member of a family. Calmer and less boisterous than other terriers, they are

● *Adult Bedlingtons usually get on well when kept in pairs. They may look a bit delicate, but they are feisty terriers.*

affectionate, good-natured pets with mild manners, and normally play gently with children.

What home suits them?

Owners prepared to give them an outlet for their high energy levels will find them suitable for apartment living, but homes with space and access to good walks are best. Bedlingtons should not be left home alone, as they can be destructive when bored and will find their own entertainment.

What sort of owner?

This breed needs owners who return affection and loyalty, and devote time to releasing high energy levels through exercise. A conscientious owner prepared to allocate regular time for grooming and training is necessary.

How much exercise and stimulation?

Bedlingtons need a daily walk, grading the distance and timing for puppies and progressing to longer walks as they mature. A bored Bedlington could be destructive and aggressive so mental stimulation is essential as they have active, intelligent minds as well as the normal physical needs.

Friendly with other pets?

Bedlingtons need to be well socialised as puppies to get on with other household pets, and there may be gender issues between males. Households with small pets should take care because of their natural instinct for hunting rats and small vermin.

Character Traits	Poor	Average	Good	Excellent
Attitude to other dogs		■		
Quietness			■	
Behaviour at home			■	
Guarding ability		■		
Good with children			■	
Ease of training			■	
Obedience to owner			■	

Time to maturity: 2 years
Male height: c.42cm (16.5in)
Female height: c.39cm (15.5in)
Weight: 8–10.5kg (17–23lb)
Average lifespan: 13–14 years

Is puppy training easy?

Always eager to please, this breed does really well with firm but gentle training, and can be trained for a wide variety of activities that owners may enjoy.

Special puppy care?

Puppy coats must be clipped close to the skin by a professional for easy care. Plenty of early socialising is essential to ensure puppies fit into a home with other pets.

Possible health problems?

Health problems reported have been heart murmur, eye problems and copper toxicosis (the inability of the body to eliminate copper – this disease has almost been eradicated in the USA); for breeders, reproductive problems have caused concern too.

What can we do together?

Owners can participate in several activities, such as agility, Earthdog trials (not in the UK), obedience, showing and other performing tasks. Working Bedlingtons need to express their natural ability for hunting.

Don't forget!

Only buy from reputable breeders who provide evidence of DNA testing or liver biopsy results proving that the puppy's parents are unaffected by copper toxicosis. This is not an easy breed for novice groomers wanting to show.

● *Puppies can appear scruffy by 16 weeks old, and need trimming to bring out their good looks.*

The thoughtful look may signal some mischief!

Small dogs

Medium dogs

Medium-sized breeds
offer the best of
both worlds and
are often very popular as family companions. They are
an ideal size for handling, and not too big for the
average home. There are a number of possible choices:
from the low-maintenance coats of Bulldogs and
Dalmatians to fluffy Chows and Soft-coated Wheaten
Terriers, with plenty of coat types in between!

Bulldog
Other names: English Bulldog

The first references to the Bulldog in literature come from around the 1500s when their use for bull baiting, a popular sport of the times, is described. Characterised as a 'compressed Hercules', the Bulldog's longer-legged and more agile 19th-century gladiator ancestors were also used for fighting. The more modern version of this very British dog has been bred to have a very sturdy body, massive chest, loose wrinkled skin and pendulous flews. Distinctive features are the Bulldog's short broad face with the lower jaw jutting forwards and a foreshortened upper jaw, bowed legs and a naturally short tail. Sadly, breed exaggerations have caused significant health problems as well as difficulties with whelping caused by the size of the head. Carefully bred, Bulldogs are happy characters, strong-minded but affectionate and humorous. Not ideal for novice owners, but experienced owners will find a soulmate in the calm, quiet nature of this excellent character.

Colour choices?
Most colours are available, although usually solid red, fawn, white, brindle (often waves or colour stripes), with/without black masks and muzzles, or piebald (white with another colour).

How much grooming?
Coats are short, flat and sleek needing minimal care. Weekly brushing with a hound glove and bristle brush removes dead hair. Facial wrinkles, particularly the 'rope' wrinkle over the nose, need cleaning daily with a dry cloth to remove dampness and prevent sores or eczema from developing.

Do they make good pets?
Despite their fierce looks, Bulldogs make excellent companions, with no vicious or aggressive tendencies. They have affectionate demeanours and a calm, dignified presence. Particularly noted for their kind temperament and patient nature, they get on well with children, other dogs and pets, although they are boisterous and mischievous puppies.

● *This 3-week-old puppy still has lots to learn from his mother.*

What home suits them?
A Bulldog's home is where his heart is, with his owner. Adaptable to towns or the country, they do need space for a daily walk. Shady gardens are best as Bulldogs feel the heat badly.

What sort of owner?
These puppies are devoted to their owner, and are affectionate around the family. Ideal for owners who want to walk for some exercise, but not too far, this dog is an individual and needs to spend time in his owner's company. Firm handling is best as Bulldogs are physically strong, like their own way and are unlikely to be obedience stars.

How much exercise and stimulation?
Bulldogs are content as couch potatoes, but need two half-hour daily walks to keep fit. Their short legs, heavy bodies and breathing problems do not make long walks a favourite pastime. Bulldogs need to go at a steady pace on all walks and should avoid hot or humid weather. Stimulating a Bulldog's mind in active and interesting ways is a good idea too.

Friendly with other pets?
Bulldogs are very good natured and get on well with other family pets, although there may be dominance issues between males.

Is puppy training easy?
Strong-minded, obstinate and with no interest in obedience, this can be a difficult dog to train. They are sensible, and reward-based training

Character Traits	Poor	Average	Good	Excellent
Attitude to other dogs				
Quietness				
Behaviour at home				
Guarding ability				
Good with children				
Ease of training				
Obedience to owner				

Time to maturity: 2.5–3 years
Male height: 30–36cm (12–14in)
Female height: 30–36cm (12–14in)
Weight: 22–25kg (49–55lb)
Average lifespan: 8–12 years

is a big motivator for good behaviour. Firm, patient handling is best; harsh training gets nowhere. Owners must be patient, positive and confident in demeanour.

Special puppy care?

Socialisation should start early with regular walking to avoid puppies getting used to a couch-potato life. Teeth cleaning and daily wiping of facial folds will accustom puppies to these necessary procedures.

Possible health problems?

Not the most robust breed because of over-exaggeration of features through their breeding, Bulldogs can suffer from cardiac defects, cancer, hip dysplasia (malformation), elbow and patella dislocations, vertebral deformities, interdigital cysts, dental, skin and eye problems. Their short 'screw' tail can be malformed causing bowel problems, and they suffer badly from overheating.

What can we do together?

Good companions and guard dogs. Some have attempted obedience and agility, although not many!

Don't forget!

It is important to buy from reputable breeders only.

Medium dogs

● *8 weeks old and ready for a play.*

Basset Hound

Bassets are an ancient French breed originating from 16th-century St Hubert hounds. Used as pack hounds for hunting because of their excellent scenting ability, noblemen used to follow them on foot. Short-legged and low-slung for use in heavy cover ('basset' means 'rather low' in French), their endurance, courage and ability to trail and flush out game such as roe deer, wolf, fox and bear was remarkable.

Introduced into Britain and the United States in the late 19th century, modern breeding has not been always to their advantage, with some exaggerated features developing. They are, however, delightful family dogs with peaceful, mild dispositions and good natures. Despite short legs, they love an active life; exercise is necessary, as is training as they are stubborn to recall if they find a good scent. Bassets deserve their rise in popularity and their placid, affectionate and gentle nature makes them prized as family companion dogs.

Colour choices?

Usually black, tan and white tri-colour, or tan and white bi-colour. White tips to tails and a white face blaze.

● Adult Bassets' long ears need care to prevent injury or infection.

How much grooming?

A Basset's long, smooth, short coat is easy maintenance, but sheds constantly so needs brushing twice weekly with a stiff brush and hound glove. Their long pendent ears, designed to sweep up scent, need checking and cleaning frequently. The folds of supple, elastic, hanging skin should be dried to avoid the problem of sores developing.

Do they make good pets?

These gentle, friendly, non-aggressive dogs make excellent pets. Great companions, Bassets love people and are gentle with children and other pets. Powerful dogs, they are stubborn, and are unsuitable for lead walking by children or elderly people who may not be strong enough. Bassets use affectionate, murmuring whines to gain attention and 'talk' to their owners.

What home suits them?

Although short-legged, Bassets are big dogs and benefit from larger homes with gardens. Long country walks daily are preferred, but they adapt to apartment life providing they have company. Solitude is not appreciated, and Bassets will tell the world about this using a deep, melodious bark, which may upset neighbours by its persistence.

What sort of owner?

Suitable for tolerant owners only, Bassets drool, shed hair, smell strongly doggy and, because they are low-slung, bring lots of dirt of into the home. Owners should be patient and appreciate their placid nature, independent character and occasional stubbornness.

How much exercise and stimulation?

Plenty of exercise is needed for adult Bassets, but take care with puppies as over-exercise could cause back problems. Puppies should have gradually increasing exercise time from six months old, preferably provided in shorter walks several times a day, with time for off-lead running and plenty of active play.

Friendly with other pets?

Bassets are non-aggressive dogs and well disposed to other household pets. They are hunting dogs and have a hunting instinct, however, so early socialisation and introductions to smaller house-hold pets will be advantageous.

Is puppy training easy?

Bassets' strong will and stubbornness is legendary, and firm training is a must. Teaching a good recall is the most important objective, but this breed is not good at obedience, so anything else learned is a bonus.

Character Traits	Poor	Average	Good	Excellent
Attitude to other dogs			■	
Quietness			■	
Behaviour at home			■	
Guarding ability	■			
Good with children				■
Ease of training		■		
Obedience to owner		■		

Time to maturity: 2 years
Male height: 33–38cm (13–15cm)
Female height: 28–36cm (11–14in)
Weight: 18–30kg (40–66lb)
Average lifespan: 10–12 years

Special puppy care?

Never over-exercise a puppy and introduce recall training early to avoid problems later. Avoid overfeeding as obesity causes back problems. Walking too soon after meals can cause gastric problems – wait at least an hour before you go for a walk.

Possible health problems?

Physical exaggerations in breeding have caused eye problems, hip and elbow dysplasia (malformation), dermatitis in skin wrinkles and ear infections. Bassets also suffer from gastric torsion (bloat), weight problems, arthritis, cancer, cardiac problems, von Willebrand's disease (blood coagulation abnormality)

● *9 weeks, and already sporting long ears and the soulful looks of a friendly, confident puppy.*

Medium dogs

and hypothyroidism (insufficient levels of thyroid hormone).

What can we do together?

Companion dogs mainly, but small game hunting is available in organised clubs.

Don't forget!

Only buy from reputable breeders because of the health issues in this breed. Highly sociable, Bassets enjoy company, and should not be left alone as they will pine.

● *At 8 weeks old this Basset puppy is ready for a world of new experiences coming his way.*

Staffordshire Bull Terrier

This dog's ancestors came from 19th-century Staffordshire, and were bred by crossing Old English Bulldogs and various terriers to produce a dog with strength, tenacity, quick-wittedness and agility. The Staffie's wide body, sturdy physique and calculated aggression made them ideal candidates for bull baiting and later for the sport of rat killing. When bull baiting was banned, the fiercest of them, being highly prized for level headedness and courage, were used for dog fighting until that too was banned in Britain in 1835. Now the other attributes began to be prized – friendly, docile and ideal companions for owners, they soon found a place in people's hearts. Formal breed recognition in Britain came in 1935 and in the USA in 1974. Although they still hold an inherent grudge against other dogs, they are obedient, good-natured and well-respected family dogs. They are often called the 'nanny' dog because of the trust placed in them to look after young children.

Colour choices?

Colours can be solid red, fawn, black, blue, and brindle or any of these with white.

How much grooming?

This dog's smooth, short coat is easy care, and shines beautifully if brushed with a bristle brush or hound glove for a few minutes daily. An occasional bath is all that may be needed on top of this.

Do they make good pets?

Staffies are faithful, gentle and affectionate, and wholly devoted to their owners. These are brilliant family dogs, trustworthy and fond of children, with a great sense of fun and puppies love playing games of chase and fetch.

What home suits them?

Although Staffies are muscular, powerful and athletic, they can adapt to most homes providing they get plenty of exercise. A garden or open space nearby that can accommodate off-lead play and long walks is desirable though.

● *Well-trained adults make great pets.*

What sort of owner?

These dogs are unsuitable for the housebound or elderly, but ideal for owners who live alone wanting close companionship, or families with children. They are devoted, loyal dogs and deserve the right owner who will appreciate their unswerving loyalty. Owners must commit to regular exercise, constant companionship and entertainment. Staffies have got into the wrong hands and developed a bad impression, but with the right owner they thoroughly deserve their fine reputation as excellent family dogs.

How much exercise and stimulation?

Staffies are an athletic, powerful breed needing plenty of exercise and space for uninhibited play to keep them in condition as they mature. Highly intelligent, they also need mental stimulation, but some of this will come from playing.

Friendly with other pets?

All puppies need socialising and careful introductions to other household pets, and Staffies are not averse to scrapping, so there may well be confrontations with other dogs. Owners may need to walk them in quieter places or keep them on the lead. Proper socialising within the first weeks of arrival should settle puppies into family life, but they still need careful supervision until they know their place.

● *Hold youngsters like this 4-week-old pup, cupped safely in both hands.*

Character Traits	Poor	Average	Good	Excellent
Attitude to other dogs				
Quietness				
Behaviour at home				
Guarding ability				
Good with children				
Ease of training				
Obedience to owner				

Time to maturity: 2 years
Male height: 36–41cm (14–16in)
Female height: 36–41cm (14–16in)
Weight: 11–17kg (24–38lb)
Average lifespan: 11–12 years

● *The best of friends at 6 weeks, but early socialisation will be needed to prevent dominance issues between these two puppies later on.*

breed thrives on plenty of energetic exercise, this should not be introduced too early to allow young bones and joints to mature.

Possible health problems?

Staffies can suffer from eye problems (cataracts, distichiasis, ocular lens problem), kidney stones and metabolic disorders (causing behavioural changes and dementia symptoms), as well as being at higher risk of tumours (mastocytoma).

Medium dogs

What can we do together?

Staffies are primarily good guard dogs, affectionate pets and wonderful playmates or family walking companions.

Is puppy training easy?

Staffies are very intelligent, but can be stubborn if they are trained harshly. Firmness and consistency with praise, rewards and encouragement will work best; responding with anger and reprimands will not achieve the desired goal of good behaviour.

Special puppy care?

Puppies need socialising from the start if problems with other pets are to be avoided. Although this

Don't forget!

This is a breed that happily takes on bigger dogs so they may need walking on the lead in open spaces. They need an attentive owner to maintain them as an even-tempered, reliable companion.

Shiba Inu

Other names: Shiba Ken, Little Brushwood Dog

This ancient Japanese breed came from Honshu Island, and in 1937 it was honoured as a 'Natural Monument' of Japan. Shiba Inu literally means 'small dog', and their size and agile movement was ideal for hunting and flushing out small game in mountainous terrain and wild shrub land. Some speculate that 'Shiba' means 'brushwood' in recognition of their red colour, which is similar to that of the wild shrubs. Frequently crossed with other breeds, today's dog is one of the most popular breeds in Japan. Shibas are fastidiously clean, grooming their coats by licking like a cat, and particularly easy to house-train. If they are upset, startled or excited, they respond with high-pitched screaming rather than barking. They do not tolerate other dogs well, and are better in homes without children. This good-natured dog with its 'spirited boldness' can be reserved towards strangers, but is a loving and affectionate pet for owners who earn their respect.

Colour choices?

Colours are usually light red, sesame (red with black tips to hair), red sesame, black sesame, black and tan, brindle, or light grey. White is not considered acceptable. Cream, buff or grey hair should be on the sides of the muzzle, cheeks, under the jaw, chest, under the body, under the tail and on insides of the legs.

How much grooming?

A Shiba's naturally waterproof, double coat consists of stiff, straight hair with a soft, thick undercoat, with some parts, like the tail, thicker. Although Shibas tend to be clean dogs, daily brushing is needed, particularly when the coat is shedding, and they need occasional bathing to keep them clean.

Do they make good pets?

Normal behaviour is lively, alert and independent; they make good pets with the right owner because they are good-natured and dignified with a natural appealing beauty. Expect them to be reserved with strangers, but loyal and affectionate to owners.

● *Bold even at 8 weeks, puppies must learn manners before leaving home.*

What home suits them?

Shibas adapt well to life as house dogs, but as they have such energy for long walks or playtime, they do better in country homes with a garden where they can run.

What sort of owner?

Shiba owners will need to earn this breed's respect and be ready to take frequent, long, daily walks to enjoy this companionable dog. They should be firm and attentive to the Shiba's need for training, exercise, grooming and loving family companionship.

How much exercise and stimulation?

A Shiba's robust and naturally independent disposition, as well as its ancestry as a hunting dog, mean exercise is essential. They are also intelligent, so stimulation should be provided either by long walks or play. Daily exercise helps to maintain good health

Friendly with other pets?

Shibas have a strong prey drive and can be aggressive to other dogs, although usually this is between females. Although Shibas tend to do better in homes without other household pets, they often get on well with cats if raised together from youngsters and well socialised to get along together.

Is puppy training easy?

Training needs to be with firm, but gentle handling. If other household pets are kept, training a Shiba to accept them must begin early.

Character Traits	Poor	Average	Good	Excellent
Attitude to other dogs	■			
Quietness			■	
Behaviour at home			■	
Guarding ability				■
Good with children	■			
Ease of training		■		
Obedience to owner		■		

Time to maturity: 2 years
Male height: 36–43cm (14–16.5in)
Female height: 34–41cm (13.5–16in)
Weight: 7–11kg (15.5–24lb)
Average lifespan: 12–15 years

Special puppy care?

Shibas should not be walked too far or too long as puppies to allow time for joint and bone growth. As joint and bone problems can be a problem for these puppies, regular health checks should be made to watch for this as they mature. Start grooming early to establish a regular brushing routine.

Possible health problems?

This breed does not suffer from many inherited problems; however, they can be affected by allergies, eye problems, hip dysplasia (malformation of the hip sockets), and luxating patellas (dislocating kneecaps). Joint problems are likely to occur in puppies and young dogs, which should be regularly checked.

What can we do together?

Shibas make good guard dogs, but owners may also enjoy hunting for birds and small game with them. Otherwise they make very companionable pets.

Don't forget!

This dog is unsuitable for novice owners and not likely to fit into a household with other pets or children very easily.

● Shiba puppies (even from 8 weeks) are quick to learn clean toileting habits if put outside at regular intervals.

Medium dogs

Nova Scotia Duck Tolling Retriever

Tollers are the smallest of the retrievers. The breed became the provincial dog of Nova Scotia in 1955, where it first developed early in the 19th century. The Canadian Kennel Club registered them from 1945. The name Toller relates to the dog's ability for 'tolling', which is to trick and lure geese and ducks to approach them at the water's edge. The curious birds come over to investigate the disturbance on the shore and so put themselves within gunshot range. The Toller then retrieves the bird and returns to his owner. They have an appealing fox-like appearance and outgoing personality, but can be destructive when bored, or if left alone too long. They benefit from plenty of exercise to keep them stimulated. Tollers are intelligent, high-energy dogs, and although very affectionate as family pets and patient with children, they have a strong retrieving drive and are happiest when they work.

Colour choices?

Any shade of red from red-gold to copper with lighter coloured feathering on the underside, the backs of the legs and under the tail. White markings are acceptable only on the chest, feet, tip of the tail and a face blaze.

How much grooming?

Regular grooming with a comb and firm bristle brush removes seasonal shedding and mud and undergrowth debris from the longer hair on the body, and feathering on tail and backs of legs. Tollers love swimming and have double coats with natural oils that make the coat water repellent. Only bath them very occasionally or you risk washing out these oils. Check between toes as their webbed feet may pick up debris causing infection.

Do they make good pets?

Tollers are natural retrievers and love to play games. They are excellent family pets and get on with everyone, as well as other household pets. They are patient

● Adults normally get on well together.

and friendly with children, but may not be suitable as guard dogs as they only give a warning bark.

What home suits them?

Tollers are a high-energy breed and confining them to apartments or small gardens without adequate activity or amusement can cause them to turn destructive. Ideally a reasonable amount of space and company is needed.

What sort of owner?

Strong-willed and sometimes difficult to train, Tollers need owners who demonstrate good leadership and encourage them to behave well. Owners will need to enjoy retrieving games and generally take part in activities that appeal to their natural behaviours.

How much exercise and stimulation?

Tollers have plenty of energy and great endurance. They need long, brisk, daily walks with extra physical activities such as running after a ball or stick, and swimming, to provide them with sufficient exercise and mental stimulation.

Friendly with other pets?

Small pets may be at risk of being 'retrieved' but generally Tollers are friendly with other household pets.

Is puppy training easy?

If Tollers learn as puppies that their owner is in charge, they are likely to be quite easy to train. They can be strong-willed, and need firm, but kind, training to establish obedience and good habits. Training that draws on their natural behaviours is best: for example, recalls can best be taught by using their natural ability to retrieve.

Character Traits	Poor	Average	Good	Excellent
Attitude to other dogs				
Quietness				
Behaviour at home				
Guarding ability				
Good with children				
Ease of training				
Obedience to owner				

Time to maturity: 2 years
Male height: 43–55cm (17–21.5 in)
Female height: 43–55cm (17–21.5 in)
Weight: 17–25kg (37–55lb)
Average lifespan: 10–13 years

● *Submission in play is typical of a puppy with a low dominance trait and is an ideal sign in young puppies being chosen for a family.*

Medium dogs

Special puppy care?

Teach puppies basic skills in obedience as this will be a major benefit in controlling this strong-minded character. Tollers are very active, and owners should take care that they do not over-exercise them to avoid injuries.

Possible health problems?

With increasing popularity and a limited gene pool, Tollers are increasingly developing health issues. These include Addison's disease (a hormonal disorder), hip dysplasia (malformation), progressive retinal atrophy, thyroid and autoimmune problems. Cancer is presently the highest cause of death in this breed.

What can we do together?

Tollers are excellent at canine activities such as agility and obedience, and hunting.

Don't forget!

Tollers are dogs with natural behaviours developed for hunting and retrieving. With only a limited gene pool to draw upon, owners should make sure they buy only from experienced and reputable breeders.

● *This puppy is the ideal age (16 weeks) for learning who is boss in his life, and for training to control his strong willed nature. Starting with a 'Sit' and using treats for rewards should work well, or try clicker training.*

Welsh Springer Spaniel

Other names: Welsh Springer, Welsh Starter

In the early 18th century Welsh Springers were bred in the Welsh valleys for their ability to follow scent to 'spring' rabbits, birds and game – especially woodcock – from undergrowth and flush them out for hunters with falcons and later guns. The breed was first recognised in Britain in 1902 and the USA in 1906, although it then declined and was reintroduced to America in 1923. A Welsh Springer's attractive red and white coat distinguishes it from black and white English Springers. Unlike other working gundogs, size is no different between working and pet strains. Welsh Springers will readily involve themselves in their owner's life and activities. They have a kindly disposition, and show no aggression or nervousness and suit family life well because they thrive on human companionship. They are high spirited, affectionate, intelligent and perceptive, but can be a challenge to train.

Colour choices?

The Welsh Springer Spaniel's most distinguishing feature is its coat – rich red markings on a white background, and any pattern is acceptable. White areas may be flecked with red ticking.

How much grooming?

This thick, straight, silky coat will need regular grooming to remove tangles and debris from the undergrowth. Special attention is needed when brushing through the thicker feathered parts of the body: the backs of legs, chest, underbody, ears and tail. Ears need to be checked and cleaned regularly.

Do they make good pets?

Welsh Springers are conveniently sized, have companionable personalities and make sensible pets. They are active, loyal and affectionate, bold and friendly and make excellent housedogs. Although very good natured, they are independent, strong-willed and sometimes stubborn, so need firm handling to keep them compliant.

● *An adult and two half-grown puppies. These attractive dogs have lots of energy.*

What home suits them?

Not suited to apartment living, this breed suits country life best, with a garden and lots of places to exercise. This is a breed that owners will enjoy taking out on long country walks when adult, so you need space available close by.

What sort of owner?

Welsh Springers have a reputation for being friendly, merry and demonstrative with all family members. They get on well with children, are kind, gentle and never aggressive. They need owners who handle them kindly but firmly, because they are strong-willed. Owners should be active and provide plenty of walking, and activities appealing to their high-energy activity levels.

How much exercise and stimulation?

These are active, hard-working dogs built for endurance. High spirited with boundless energy, they need plenty of exercise. They are well suited to running in mountainous terrain and particularly like water. They were bred for an active outside life and lots of stimulation will help their mental well-being.

Friendly with other pets?

A Welsh Springer's kindly disposition is accepting of other household pets, and they generally react to them with a friendly, playful attitude.

Is puppy training easy?

This breed can be challenging to train, and is easily bored. Training is

Character Traits	Poor	Average	Good	Excellent
Attitude to other dogs				
Quietness				
Behaviour at home				
Guarding ability				
Good with children				
Ease of training				
Obedience to owner				

Time to maturity: 2 years
Male height: 46–48cm (18–19in)
Female height: 43–46 cm (17–18in)
Weight: 16–20kg (35–45lb)
Average lifespan: 12–15 years

essential to mould them into sociable dogs, and it should be firm, gentle and patient to achieve the best results. Puppies can be headstrong, but with good training they will be extremely obedient.

Special puppy care?

Welsh Springers can have a tendency for over-exercising as puppies, so exercise should be graded to allow for bone and joint growth to prevent injuries. Puppies and adults can suffer from separation anxiety; training should start early to prevent this problem developing later in life.

Possible health problems?

Small numbers of Welsh Springers suffer from seizures, hip dysplasia (malformation of the hip sockets), eye problems (entropion and glaucoma) and they are prone to ear infections. Breeders and owners are encouraged to check for these problems.

What can we do together?

These are very versatile dogs and are often involved with showing, agility, obedience and heelwork to music. They are trained as therapy and hearing dogs, and work as gundogs. In Britain there are opportunities for competing in Field Trials to maintain the breed's traditional purpose.

Don't forget!

Without sufficient exercise Welsh Springers will become hyperactive, so exercise and stimulation are essential for this energetic breed.

● At 1 year old this puppy is finding his feet. He will respond to firm, patient handling to achieve good results in training.

Happy to oblige with a Sit!

Medium dogs

Welsh Springers are ideal working dogs as well as making good family pets.

Soft-coated Wheaten Terrier

This happy, lively breed originated as Irish crofters' dogs used for guarding, herding livestock and hunting vermin. Breed recognition in Ireland came in 1937, in Britain in 1943 and in the USA in 1973. They have energetic, intelligent, cheerful characters and gregarious natures, and relate well to people, especially children, but their exuberant, sometimes stubborn and occasionally dominant nature makes training essential. Puppies look quite different from their parents, without their distinctive, soft, flowing coat, until maturity at around two. The softly waved, silky hair, reflecting the colour of ripening wheat, needs regular attention to maintain its non-shedding properties without matting. Wheatens are less feisty than most terriers, devoted to their owners, with bags of character, and always willing to join in family events, because they enjoy being the centre of attention. Carefully trained they make exceptional family pets.

Colour choices?

Puppies are black or dark brown when born, shading white by 18 months, before darkening to honey colours with black muzzle, ears and other points or clear wheaten – like ripening wheat.

How much grooming?

The loosely waved, but never curly, coat needs daily grooming with a pin brush and wide-tooth comb to prevent the non-shedding coat tangling. Sometimes trimmed short, especially round the eyes to help vision, Wheatens are never stripped as hair regrowth will be orange-coloured. Grooming daily between 12 and 24 months is essential as adult coats grow. Ears need regular checks for plucking and cleaning.

Do they make good pets?

Not for quieter families, they are 'big' characters, but easy to live with when trained well and delightful companions. Wheatens are mischievous, may learn bad habits though rarely aggressive, and jump up for kissing and affection. Their

● *This adult Wheaten's coat is trimmed, not stripped, to present a neat outline.*

loyal, playful nature and happy exuberance delights young and old, and they make excellent pets.

What home suits them?

Wheatens appreciate town or country living with good walks nearby. They love travel and adjust to changes well. Adaptable to most homes, ideally owners should have a garden where they can play and explore. Secure fencing is needed as they may escape if bored.

What sort of owner?

Wheaten owners should be gentle, firm and consistent with discipline, but equally appreciate an exuberant and extrovert nature. Owners need to adopt positive and sensitive approaches to training, must take regular walks and provide suitable toys to prevent boredom. Wheatens enjoy digging, so are not ideal choices for keen gardeners.

How much exercise and stimulation?

Puppies will need around 15 minutes twice daily, gradually building up time and distance; hour-long walks and occasionally more are needed for adults. A consistent firm approach taken early on is best, because they are highly intelligent, quick to problem solve and may take advantage. Mental stimulation using canine toys or activities is ideal.

Friendly with other pets?

Early introductions are essential for good relations with other family pets as their lively, inquisitive and bouncy nature may not be

Character Traits	Poor	Average	Good	Excellent
Attitude to other dogs				
Quietness				
Behaviour at home				
Guarding ability				
Good with children				
Ease of training				
Obedience to owner				

Time to maturity: 2.5 years
Male height: 46–49.5cm (18–19.5in)
Female height: Slightly less
Weight: 16–21.5kg (35–45lb)
Average lifespan: 12–14 years

appreciated. Small animals may be at risk from their typical terrier prey drive. Wheatens are often kept in pairs, although very occasionally this can lead to rivalry and jealousy.

s puppy training easy?

Firm, patient, reward-based, fun training is best; harsh training methods are ineffective. Ideally play-learning suits Wheatens rather than formal training, because life is for fun not obedience.

pecial puppy care?

Digestive problems caused by feeding puppies incorrect diets can occur. Puppies need early gentle persuasion, so they do not dictate their owner's life.

Possible health problems?

Wheatens are generally healthy dogs, but can suffer from eye, liver and kidney problems, and hip dysplasia (malformation of the hip sockets). Health-checked stock is recommended.

● *Irish-bred puppies have less coat than shaggier English-bred Wheatens.*

At 5 months this puppy is already growing a longer coat.

Medium dogs

Dietary and allergy problems occur if diets are wrong. Some are intolerant of anaesthetics.

What can we do together?

Wheatens are good guard dogs, enjoy long walks, agility or obedience, working as therapy dogs, and make amusing companion dogs.

Don't forget!

Wheatens are a handful unless properly trained and supervised. Coat care and checking ears is essential.

Chinese Shar-Pei *Other names: Chinese Fighting Dog*

Known for their distinctive face and body wrinkles and a blue-black tongue, this ancient Chinese breed originated 2000 years ago during the Han Dynasty. The breed was mainly used for temple or herd guarding, fighting and hunting boar. The Shar Pei's bristly 'horse coat' is a distinctive feature and the name literally translates as 'sand skin'. Its favour declined with Chinese peasant farmers when China increased its dog tax, but it was saved from near extinction by breeders in Hong Kong and the USA in the 1970s. Numbers increased and interest soon developed in Europe. It hippo-like head, bristly fur and heavily wrinkled skin give it an eccentric appearance. The Shar Pei's calm personality, however, means it is sought after by dog fanciers and families alike, its reputation as a fighting dog long gone. Despite the scowling expression, these are intelligent, affectionate and playful dogs who make great companions and family members.

Colour choices?
Black, chocolate, isabella (light fawn), blue, red, sable, red-fawn, apricot, and cream in solid colours are acceptable, while spotted ('flowered coats') or black and tan are not. Some have darker shading on the back and the ears, with lighter shaded underbody.

How much grooming?
There are three different coat types: horse, brush and bear coats, although bear coats are only found in China. Horse coat is prickly, rough and stands off the skin, brush coats are smoother and longer. Both coats are low maintenance but need brushing with a hound glove or stiff bristle brush, separating folds and penetrating to the skin, once weekly. Moulting occurs twice yearly, and brushing should increase to remove the shed. Ears need cleaning regularly using cotton swabs.

Do they make good pets?
Shar Peis are reserved and aloof with strangers, but especially good with children and happiest living

● *A Shar-Pei puppy at 7 weeks starting to develop the wrinkles so distinctive of its parent (left).*

with families. They seldom bark but when they do, it is with good reason. Overall, they are devoted, loyal and affectionate, and capable of calm companionship, making excellent pets if well trained and socialised early.

What home suits them?
These puppies appreciate homes with gardens for playing and running, but either town or country living suits them provided there are good walks and family company.

What sort of owner?
Shar Peis need owners with firm and sensitive leadership, with time for training, exercise and mental stimulation. These dogs are not ideal for novice owners because they are strong-minded.

How much exercise and stimulation?
Shar Peis are adaptable and enjoy long or short walks, although any exercise in hot weather should be avoided. Shar Peis are highly intelligent and enjoy the stimulation of two daily walks. Active play each day also provides exercise and benefits their health.

Friendly with other pets?
Early socialisation is important as puppies develop their natural guarding senses; usually they are good with other dogs, although inter-male aggression may occur. Shar Peis are fine with family cats but have strong chase instincts so beware of neighbours' cats and farm livestock.

Is puppy training easy?
Strong-minded and independent dogs, they are amenable and intelligent for training to high

Character Traits	Poor	Average	Good	Excellent
Attitude to other dogs				
Quietness				
Behaviour at home				
Guarding ability				
Good with children				
Ease of training				
Obedience to owner				

Time to maturity: 2–3 years
Male height: 46–51cm (18–20in)
Female height: 46–51cm (18–20in)
Weight: 18–25kg (40–55lb)
Average lifespan: 10–12 years

standards of obedience. Firm, gentle training and early socialisation will prevent aggressive traits or other behaviours. Repetition causes boredom and Shar Peis learn best with varied training sessions to maintain interest, and owners who foster mutual respect.

Special puppy care?
Shar Peis' suspicion of strangers needs addressing when young to prevent this causing territorial and protective behaviour. Puppies may need special attention to their diets.

Possible health problems?
Their popularity has caused problems with breeders exaggerating excessive wrinkles and skin folds. They also suffer from allergy-induced skin infections, recurring familial Shar Pei fever (swollen hock syndrome), amyloidosis (kidney problems), eye problems (entropion, ectropion, blocked tear ducts), low levels of thyroid hormone, Vitamin B12 deficiency, gastric torsion and chronic ear problems.

Medium dogs

What can we do together?
Obedience, agility, herding and tracking events.

Don't forget!
Be careful to buy only from reputable breeders who address potential health issues.

● Puppies at 8 weeks look cute, cuddly, and playful, but they are old enough to go out into the big wide world to start learning good manners.

Australian Cattle Dog
Other names: Blue or Red Heeler, Queensland Heeler

This breed really embodies a whole cocktail of qualities derived from other dogs combined to make one species. Its historical antecedents include the Smithfield (now extinct), the Dingo, Collie, Kelpie and Bull Terrier. Australian Cattle Dogs were bred to drive cattle over long distances in the harsh terrain of the outback. They are also called Heelers because their method of driving cattle is to nip at their heels, without causing injury. Courageous, intelligent, dynamic, always alert and extremely hard-working, this is an active dog that will need plenty of exercise. They rarely bark and when they do it sounds like the hooting of owls. This breed is not meant for the city, but will prosper in the countryside, particularly when doing what it does best – herding livestock. Very loyal and protective of their owners, they are devoted to their families but will always need an active working life to be happy.

Colour choices?

Born white, puppies colour up as they mature. Adult colouring is brown (red) or black (blue) hairs evenly distributed in white hair. Blue colouring is blue, blue mottled or speckled, with or without black, tan and white markings. Red colouring is speckled with solid red markings. Symmetrical markings of solid colours are preferred in dogs bred for showing. Chocolate and cream colours occur occasionally.

● A strong muscular breed which benefits from plenty of working activity, but also enjoys canine sports with his owner.

How much grooming?

Easy to groom and keep clean, ACDs have little doggy odour. Coats moult once yearly, but daily brushing and occasional bathing, particularly when shedding, works well. Attention to nails, ears and teeth keeps this puppy healthy.

Do they make good pets?

ACDs are very devoted to their owners, and love being part of the family. Highly protective, loyal and wary of strangers, they are quick to respond to their owner's emotions. They are happy, playful, affectionate dogs but can develop undesirable habits such as chewing, nipping, barking, digging and chasing which need training to prevent.

What home suits them?

Country homes, farms or estates are best, with plenty of space to run and expend their large amounts of energy. A securely fenced garden is necessary as they like to wander.

What sort of owner?

They are very protective and never far from their owner's side. Owners should train their dog not to be possessive to prevent problems. Training is essential with children around, as play and active movements may encourage nipping and herding behaviour.

How much exercise and stimulation?

This breed has high energy levels, sharp intelligence and an independent spirit. Plenty of exercise is needed and preferably a 'job' or herding activity that engages mind and body. Lack of space or activity encourages mischief and bad behaviour.

Friendly with other pets?

ACDs introduced as puppies respond well to other family dogs or those that they come to know. However, this breed does not enjoy living as a pack and natural aggression amongst them is a strong possibility, while a pecking order is established.

Is puppy training easy?

Well-structured training with rewards, challenging activities to

Character Traits	Poor	Average	Good	Excellent
Attitude to other dogs				
Quietness				
Behaviour at home				
Guarding ability				
Good with children				
Ease of training				
Obedience to owner				

Time to maturity: 2 years
Male height: 46–51cm (18–20in)
Female height: 43–48cm (17–19in)
Weight: 20–28kg (44–62lb)
Average lifespan: 11–14 years

create interest, and purposeful tasks are best. Training must be consistent, and never repetitive or boring; it is a good idea to use games and lots of encouragement to assist training.

Special puppy care?
Puppies will need careful training to prevent them developing bad habits. Close supervision and mental stimulation will also be needed from the start as boredom may cause puppies to be mischievous and badly behaved.

Possible health problems?
This robust, hardy breed may suffer from deafness, eye problems (blindness) or accidental injury brought about by its highly energetic and active lifestyle.

What can we do together?
Owners will enjoy their ACD if they enjoy active sports events. Structured activities such as non-competitive herding tests, agility and rally obedience, or any other athletic or endurance competitions, are popular. These dogs are also used as assistance dogs and in the armed services.

Don't forget!
Training to avoid the puppy developing its natural habit of herding and nipping will be needed from the start. These puppies need plenty of activity from early on, but don't let them over-exert and damage young bones and joints.

Medium dogs

● *Puppies like this at 11 weeks need to grow into their pricked ears!*

● *Symmetrical markings are preferred for show specimens, but any colour or marking is suitable for pets.*

Border Collie

Borders have been the shepherd's working partner for centuries, arriving in the British Isles with the Vikings. Used for herding sheep in the border regions between England, Scotland and Wales, Borders are incredibly intelligent and very trainable. Guided to obey their owner's whistles, they group, separate and herd sheep to order over hillside terrains or can take the initiative to bring flocks safely home.

Colour choices?

Usually Borders are bi-colour – white with either brown, black or red (the most common); or tri-colours – black, brown/tan and white. They can also be red or blue merle (marbled colour on white), sable; brindle and some are solid black or brown.

How much grooming?

Borders either have thick, double, long coats which are soft, silky and shed; or smooth coats needing less attention. Keeping thicker coats in good condition needs more regular grooming with attention to feathering on legs, tail and around the head. Check ears once a week to keep them clean. Bathing may be needed occasionally, although regular grooming should suffice.

Do they make good pets?

These dogs need to be on the go, working and herding or undertaking meaningful activities, which is what they are happiest doing. They are devoted and affectionate pets, but perhaps not for busy families.

● *A lovely group of mother, father (right) and their 6-week-old puppies.*

What home suits them?

This is an active, energetic dog and country homes with plenty of space and an enclosed garden with secure fencing are best. These are not ideal town dogs, and definitely not suited to homes that cannot offer them enough exercise or activity.

What sort of owner?

These dogs were used to spending long working days with only their owner for company. Owners will need to be active, keen on long walks and intensive training, or happy to be involved in energetic activities that interest their Border.

Borders work patiently with a hypnotic trance-like attention. This breed really is the canine Einstein, excelling at many activities and it is used in the services for search and rescue or police work. Borders need early socialisation, intense training and sensitive handling to reach their true potential. Committed owners who work their minds will find them exemplary dogs, very rewarding and highly responsive, but they must be prepared to commit time and attention to them. This is not a dog for a novice owner.

Definitely not a dog for novice owners, and nor is a Border suitable for owners who don't appreciate the pleasures of exercise.

How much exercise and stimulation?

Borders need plenty of exercise and mental stimulation to keep them happy. Daily activity with play, training and supervised exercise and company are best. If these are not provided for them, they can become thoroughly neurotic, aggressive and territorial.

Friendly with other pets?

Early socialisation is recommended so they get on well with other pets but their instinct to herd may be a problem for smaller pets. Training and socialisation around farm livestock for country-living dogs is also recommended.

Is puppy training easy?

Borders are very trainable, but need to be trained in the right way by an owner who keeps one step ahead of their response to different

Character Traits	Poor	Average	Good	Excellent
Attitude to other dogs				
Quietness				
Behaviour at home				
Guarding ability				
Good with children				
Ease of training				
Obedience to owner				

Time to maturity: 2 years
Male height: 46–53cm (18–21in)
Female height: Slightly less
Weight: 14–22kg (30–49lb)
Average lifespan: 12–14 years

situations. Highly intelligent and very quick to learn, they can be sensitive and need sensitive, responsive training to do well.

Special puppy care?

Good socialisation is essential or this puppy may become neurotic. Some may find their own entertainment, and because they are motion-sensitive may develop a habit of chasing moving vehicles, which should be curbed.

● Lovely puppies, but not the best choice for inexperienced owners.

Possible health problems?

Generally very hardy, Borders can suffer from hip and elbow malformation, eye problems (collie eye anomaly), epilepsy, deafness and hypothyroidism (lack of thyroid hormone). Some merle-coated dogs may have eye or hearing problems.

What can we do together?

Energetic owners will enjoy a variety of activities with their Border such as flyball, competitive obedience, agility and sheepdog trialling/herding.

Don't forget!

This is a breed only for owners willing to lead an active life, and not for novices.

Medium dogs

This beautiful lilac colour is becoming quite popular.

With unlimited energy, training must start soon for these 8-week-old puppies.

Whippet

This graceful, slender little sighthound was 'the poor man's racehorse', bred by miners in the north of England a little over a century ago. Trained to run like a 'scared spirit', Whippets can achieve speeds of 56kph (35mph), and love the sprint to a finish line. As excellent runners they entertained their owners by competing in coursing, racing and hunting hare for the pot.

Recognition of the breed came in Britain in 1888 and in the USA in 1890. Whippets are ideal companion pets, because they are quiet, very home loving, affectionate couch potatoes, and appreciative of their creature comforts – warmth and a good bed. Their medium size makes them ideal for most types of homes, and their undemanding sweet natures and easy-care coat makes them an excellent choice for most families. Whippets' exercise requirements are very reasonable and they develop an excellent rapport with children and adults.

Colour choices?
Whippets are available in several colours from solid black to solid white, or red, fawn, cream, brindle or blue, with spots, blazes and parti-colours.

How much grooming?
A Whippet's short, smooth coat is excellent for families who do not want to commit to regular daily grooming. Occasional use of a rubber hound glove, finishing with a silk cloth or chamois leather, will keep coats looking good. Whippet coats are quite thin and not weatherproof, so take care to keep them warm in cold weather.

Do they make good pets?
These are quiet, affectionate, gentle dogs which love children and make excellent family pets. Puppies are mischievous at first and demand lots of attention, but eventually they mature and grow into sensible dogs. They are quite adaptable to varying amounts of exercise.

What home suits them?
Whippets enjoy active country lives

● *These graceful and elegant dogs are well respected for their speed. This young adult still retains his inborn hunting instinct and may head off after an interesting scent when out walking.*

but can live quite happily in a town environment. If well exercised, they will adapt to living in apartments, but homes with gardens or space to run off-lead are best.

What sort of owner?
A Whippet's calm, loyal and friendly character may suit active older people, although families with children for playmates are ideal. Owners who enjoy active lifestyles will enjoy a Whippet's sweet and good-natured companionship.

How much exercise and stimulation?
Whippets are often content to spend the day quietly at home, but they still need at least an hour's walk, plus about 20 minutes of free running and play as well. Ideally they should be on leads at certain times, when near livestock, for instance, and definitely near traffic as they have no road sense. Stimulation through off-lead sessions and play is recommended.

Friendly with other pets?
These are gentle, friendly puppies, which get on well with other household pets with little problem. However, they are bred for chasing rabbits, so may be a risk to smaller pets or neighbours' cats.

Is puppy training easy?
Whippets are easy puppies to train for patient and conscientious owners. They are intelligent, alert to their owner and willing to please if training is presented positively with plenty of rewards and encouragement. Harsh training

Character Traits	Poor	Average	Good	Excellent
Attitude to other dogs				
Quietness				
Behaviour at home				
Guarding ability				
Good with children				
Ease of training				
Obedience to owner				

Time to maturity: Up to 4 years
Male height: 47–51cm (18.5–20in)
Female height: 44.5–46cm (17.5–18in)
Weight: 12.5–13.5kg (27–30lb)
Average lifespan: around 14 years

will not be effective because of the sensitive nature of this puppy. Whippets have a strong instinct to chase, so a good recall will be an essential part of early training.

Special puppy care?

Puppies can be naughty, often behaving like small whirlwinds, so patience and attention is needed early to train them in good habits. Whippets suffer quite badly from the cold, so owners need to provide warm coats for wearing outdoors in cold weather.

Possible health problems?

Whippets are healthy and long-lived, but can suffer from heart problems, undescended testicles, and often have difficulty with anaesthetics. Their thin skin is prone to cold and damage by thorny undergrowth when out exercising.

What can we do together?

Whippets are ideal for activities to do together, and enjoy showing, lure coursing, racing, obedience, agility and flyball.

Don't forget!

Whippets have no road sense so must be on leads near traffic. Their thin skin means that they feel the cold in winter.

Medium dogs

● At 9 weeks this puppy (left) looks similar to his 6-month-old friend (right) but has lots of growth and development to catch up on.

Bull Terrier *Other names: English Bull Terrier*

This 'gladiator' of the dog world was bred from terriers and Bulldogs for bull and bear baiting and fighting in the 19th century. Endowed with great courage and stamina, they were totally fearless with a driving determination to match their muscular, solid, powerful bodies. Later breeding produced the modern, more elegant show strain, with distinctive triangular eyes and egg-shaped heads, but with the same characteristics of physical power and strong will. Bullies are loveable clowns, fun-loving and people-orientated. They enjoy playing the fool, but are boisterous and may become destructive when bored. Experienced owners will enjoy their robust, eager-to-please, stable temperament, but they are hard to live with if not properly trained. Their strong personality make them unsuitable for novices, and owners should consider public opinion concerning bull breeds and current breed-specific legislation about owning one.

Colour choices?

All white, or white with coloured patches on the head, also black, brindle, red or tri-colour. In coloured dogs, the colour must predominate over white, which can take the form of markings on the chest, under-body, tail tip, socks and face blaze.

How much grooming?

Weekly brushing with a hound glove or a bristle brush to remove dead hair should suffice.

Do they make good pets?

Bullies make excellent pets in the right hands, and are very people-orientated. They can be boisterous, exuberant, independent, stubborn and wilful, and so are not really suitable for inexperienced or older owners. Bullies are playful and affectionate and make outstanding pets if properly trained, but are unsuitable for families with young children who may tease them.

What home suits them?

Adaptable to either town or country living, sturdy fencing around

● *The powerful physique of adult Bullies means they need watching around other dogs.*

the garden is essential. Access to space for walking is important as Bullies need time to run off-lead to burn off their excess energy.

What sort of owner?

These puppies need an owner with an assertive demeanour, who will be firm in training and not stand any nonsense. Owners will appreciate their comical, mischievous ways, but need to be experienced to handle their intelligence and stubborn streak.

How much exercise and stimulation?

Bullies are active and need plenty of exercise. They may, however, enjoy lazing around their home, and often need encouraging to go walking or they may suffer from obesity. Their intelligent minds need plenty of exercising too.

Friendly with other pets?

This breed needs to be very well socialised as puppies to mix with other family pets. Some may be perfectly happy in their company, others may need to be kept alone. Bullies have strong prey drive, and may be unsafe around cats. Male and female Bullies usually live together quite happily, but take care introducing second dogs at a later date; dogs of the same gender especially may cause disruption to family dynamics.

Is puppy training easy?

Strict, firm but gentle handling is needed, as they can be difficult to train. Reward-based training with lots of positive reinforcement using food and toys is best. Not likely to be outstandingly obedient, but with patience Bull Terriers can achieve satisfactory levels of obedience.

Character Traits	Poor	Average	Good	Excellent
Attitude to other dogs				
Quietness				
Behaviour at home				
Guarding ability				
Good with children				
Ease of training				
Obedience to owner				

Time to maturity: 3 years
Male height: 46–61cm (18–24in)
Female height: 46–61cm (18–24in)
Weight: 24–28kg (52–62lb)
Average lifespan: 11–13 years

Special puppy care?

These puppies have powerful jaws and will happily chew literally anything, so strong toys need to be carefully selected to keep their interest away from valuable belongings. Pure white puppies may suffer from deafness; it is not immediately apparent when very young, so this needs to be checked before buying.

Possible health problems?

Bull Terriers can suffer from kidney and heart problems, patella luxation (dislocating kneecaps), skin problems (allergies to certain foods, fleas and mites) and deafness can occur in white dogs.

What can we do together?

Useful as a guard dog, Bullies and owners will enjoy time spent walking together or just being good companions.

Don't forget!

These dogs can exhibit behavioural problems if training is inadequate. As a powerful breed Bull Terriers can arouse negative public opinion when taken out, so owners have a responsibility to be conscientious with training.

● *Until these 6-week-old puppies are older, their true nature and temperament may be difficult to determine.*

Brittany
Other names: Brittany Spaniel

Descending from the historic Chien d'Oysel from northern France, Brittanys were depicted in hunting scenes in many tapestries of the 17th century. Later versions of these Breton farm dogs, sometimes known as Fougeres meaning 'high spirited' and possibly bred with English Setters, were valued for their unique qualities of hunting, pointing and retrieving game. Their excellent ability for scenting and tracking, along with their medium size, made them popular in the USA in the 1930s for hunting woodcock. Hard-working, tireless and willing to work most terrains, Brittanys are good all-rounders. Brittanys did not reach Britain until the 1970s but they are now prized there as good-natured companions. Their keen, energetic enthusiasm for life does demand a suitable outlet for their high energy, but with an intelligent, even temper they make gentle, affectionate companions as family pets.

Colour choices?
Usual colours (with spots, ticking or flecks) are orange and white, liver and white, black and white, tri-colour (black, tan and white or liver, white and orange). Black is considered a fault in America.

How much grooming?
The medium-length, single, flowing coat sheds very little, and is usually low maintenance. Ten minutes of brushing and combing twice weekly and regular attention to cleaning and checking ears is fine. Feathering on the ears and legs needs attention, particularly after working in undergrowth as debris will need removing. Bath only when needed.

Do they make good pets?
Brittanys make excellent pets if they have plenty of exercise, appropriate activity and a 'job in life', otherwise they can be hyperactive and too energetic to live with. Puppies can be too exuberant and boisterous for small children, although they respond well to older children who can maintain better control.

● With good training and socialisation, Brittanys will become well-adjusted adults.

What home suits them?
They suit country life, because they need space for off-lead running, long walks and organised activity. A reasonably sized, well-fenced garden is the ideal solution. Although suitable in terms of size, Brittanys are too active for apartment living and are not indoor dogs.

What sort of owner?
Ideal for active owners, this puppy needs lots of energy-busting country walking in all weathers, together with training and stimulating activity to appeal to their intelligent minds. Only owners prepared to accept the commitment of a high-energy dog should consider this breed.

How much exercise and stimulation?
Plenty of exercise is needed on a daily basis. Long walks of one to two hours' duration including free running is ideal, as well as activities designed to stimulate the mind and use up their boundless energy.

Friendly with other pets?
Friendly with other dogs if well socialised as puppies, Brittanys are also good with cats. However, small pets such as rabbits and guinea pigs may be at risk because of their hunting background.

Is puppy training easy?
Brittanys are gentle-natured, sensitive puppies responding well to calm, consistent, reward-based learning. Eager to please, quick to learn and highly trainable, they should not be handled roughly, and they will respond best if given plenty of encouragement.

Character Traits	Poor	Average	Good	Excellent
Attitude to other dogs				
Quietness				
Behaviour at home				
Guarding ability				
Good with children				
Ease of training				
Obedience to owner				

Time to maturity: 2 years
Male height: 48–51cm (19–20in)
Female height: 46–48cm (18–19in)
Weight: 13.5–18kg (30–40lb)
Average lifespan: 13–15 years

Special puppy care?

Puppies need plenty of socialising with gradually increasing levels of activity to prevent them from becoming hyperactive. Insensitive training can be detrimental to well-being, so be gentle and kind using plenty of encouragement and rewards to achieve success.

Possible health problems?

Generally healthy and hardy as a breed, Brittanys can be susceptible to epilepsy, eye problems, hip dysplasia (malformation), haemophilia and some skin disorders.

What can we do together?

Brittanys' bright, intelligent minds will respond to owners who encourage them in activities such as flyball, obedience, fieldwork and agility.

Don't forget!

Plenty of exercise for adults and sensitive training are essential. Brittanys sometimes have a

- *Cute as you could ask for at only 6 weeks of age.*

reputation for being unmanageable, but this is usually the result of lack of exercising and poor training.

English Springer Spaniel

A larger spaniel used for hunting, the Springer was developed for scenting and retrieving game, or flushing out birds to trained falcons, which brought them to the hunter. Springers are good all-round bird dogs, their slightly webbed toes making them powerful swimmers for retrieving water birds. Officially recognised in Britain in 1902, they became the most popular hunting dog.

Springers are available in two strains: working dogs, which have a strong working drive, and are sturdier, smaller and less suitable as family pets, and show strains, more suited to family life. An active, energetic dog with vitality and stamina that loves to work and play, Springers are excitable, strong-willed and boisterous and they need firm training. Excellent companion and family dogs, they must have plenty of physical exercise or 'jobs' to do. They are excellent police sniffer dogs used for detecting anything from drugs to illegal immigrants.

Colour choices?
Coat choices are black or liver (dark brown) with white markings, or white with black or liver markings, or tri-colour with additional tan markings. White areas can be flecked or ticked.

How much grooming?
Working-strain Springers have shorter, coarse coats that shed in autumn; show-bred dogs have softer, silkier coats shedding twice yearly. Daily brushing with a bristle brush and comb removes mud and debris picked up on walks. Ears need checking daily and cleaning weekly, with hair carefully trimmed under their pendulous ears allowing air circulation, and any food picked up from trailing in their bowls removed.

Do they make good pets?
Temperamentally Springers are easy-going family dogs; they love children and are patient, tolerant and always willing to play. Not ideal for busy families, puppies are energetic whirlwinds needing lots of time and attention for training and care.

● *Adult Springers are happiest when given a job or activity to do. For instance, they can be taught tricks.*

What home suits them?
Best in the country with a house and secure garden to play in, and owners who are tolerant of their passion for digging. Apartment life would be impossible for this energetic and active dog.

What sort of owner?
Ideal companions for people who enjoy long walks, jogging or cycling, Springers are unsuitable for older, less active types. Owners must be firm, patient and gentle with this emotionally sensitive dog. Above all, they must have a sense of humour to cope with a Springer's rumbustious behaviour.

How much exercise and stimulation?
Springers are tough, hardy, vigorous, active and swift, and need moderate amounts of exercise daily, come rain or shine.

Friendly with other pets?
This sociable breed with its gentle expression and wagging tail is excellent with other dogs and most household pets if well socialised early, although he may not pass up the opportunity to chase the cat.

Is puppy training easy?
Springers are delightful to train because they are intelligent, quick to learn and eager to please. They are sensitive so training must be firm, gentle, encouraging and with plenty of praise to maintain motivation and interest. Training must start early to harness their exuberant energy, but must never be harsh. Generally, Springers are willing, non-aggressive dogs that are biddable and devoted to owners when suitably trained.

Character Traits	Poor	Average	Good	Excellent
Attitude to other dogs				
Quietness				
Behaviour at home				
Guarding ability				
Good with children				
Ease of training				
Obedience to owner				

Time to maturity: 2.5 years
Male height: 48–51cm (19–20in)
Female height: 48–51cm (19–20in)
Weight: 22–24kg (49–53lb)
Average lifespan: 13–15 years

Special puppy care?

Early training is essential to prevent problems with over-exuberance, which can make puppies a nuisance. Take care not to over-walk puppies in a bid to tire them out, as young bones and joints can suffer. Springers' inclination to flush game may encourage puppies to ramble in thickets, which can cause injury.

Possible health problems?

Springers are quite a healthy breed but may suffer eye problems, fucosidosis (a metabolic disorder), phospho-fructokinase deficiency (causing muscle cramps), hip and elbow malformation. All these illnesses tend to be rare, and can be tested for prior to purchase.

Medium dogs

What can we do together?

Companion pet for long walks or jogging and cycling. Hunting trials for working specimens, obedience, therapy and service training.

Don't forget!

Start training puppies early to prevent problems with bad behaviour getting out of hand.

● *These two don't look like potential canine whirlwinds at 8 weeks, but they may become that if not trained properly.*

Norwegian Elkhound
Other names: Norwegian Moose Dog

The Elkhound is one of several ancient Spitz breeds, but this one is acknowledged as Norway's national dog. It dates back to the time of early Scandinavian hunters who kept Spitz-type dogs with thick coats to withstand subzero temperatures for hunting large game in snow-bound forests and rugged mountains. Even earlier, remains suggest Elkhounds were Viking farm dogs, although they now have a more modern conformation in breeding. A sporting breed, they are courageous, hardy, energetic, friendly and loving to their owner, with a reputation for being child-friendly. They are excellent guard dogs who know when to take action, but are also independent and strong-willed, and need firm handling in training. Elkhounds are particularly people-orientated dogs, very protective of small children, and great playmates for families. Their friendly disposition and unswerving loyalty and affection for their owner makes them ideal family pets.

Colour choices?
Silver or grey, with black tips on longer hair, and lighter grey on the chest. Or brilliant black with lighter markings on the chest, front legs and feet. Both colours have areas of darker marking between the shoulder and elbow.

How much grooming?
This harsh, thick, abundant coat is virtually indestructible and without smell, but it sheds continuously, and moults copiously twice yearly when grooming daily with sturdy brushes and combing is necessary. Twice weekly suffices otherwise. Pay particular attention to thicker hair on the neck and underbody to prevent matting and dirt build-up. Elkhounds will tolerate 'vacuum cleaning' to remove loose hair.

Do they make good pets?
Compact and powerfully built, Elkhounds are friendly and intelligent, and their medium size is ideal for families. They make good pets because they are good-natured, very people-orientated,

● *The Elkhound needs firm handling to manage its independent nature.*

patient, tolerant and protective towards children.

What home suits them?
Elkhounds need homes in the country or suburbs, with well-fenced, large gardens. These active, powerful dogs need space for exercising or they are likely to become bored, destructive and noisy. Their sharp, loud bark may upset close neighbours.

What sort of owner?
Elkhounds form inseparable bonds with their owners, who should not leave them at home alone. The best owners are outdoor types, who love walking, understand their exercise requirements and are prepared to groom regularly while tolerant of their copious moulting.

How much exercise and stimulation?
This breed needs lots of exercise (one or two hours daily) which should include off-lead running and active play. Take care if they pick up interesting scents as they will go off hunting. Elkhounds can be trained to run beside a bicycle for exercise, but not as puppies to avoid any risk of bone and joint problems.

Friendly with other pets?
Most Elkhounds are good with other pets, providing introductions and socialising are done early, but rabbits, guinea pigs and other small domestic pets may be at risk.

Is puppy training easy?
Their independent streak and high intelligence could be challenging for novices. Respect must be earned and training with a firm but kind approach is best, as they are

Character Traits	Poor	Average	Good	Excellent
Attitude to other dogs				
Quietness				
Behaviour at home				
Guarding ability				
Good with children				
Ease of training				
Obedience to owner				

Time to maturity: 3 years
Male height: 48–53cm (19–21in)
Female height: 48–53cm (19–21in)
Weight: 19.5–23kg (43–50lb)
Average lifespan: 12–15 years

sensitive if treated harshly, although they do need to understand their family rank position. Sessions should be short to avoid boredom, and made fun with plenty of rewards to maintain interest and enthusiasm. If trained appropriately, Elkhounds do learn obedience, but trying to make them 'Come' when they catch a scent may be difficult.

Special puppy care?

Puppies need training not to pull on the leash before they grow into powerful adults, and grooming early encourages bonding and preparation for dealing with moulting.

Possible health problems?

Generally a healthy breed, Elkhounds suffer from hip dysplasia, kidney disease, eye problems, and some have problems with sebaceous cysts (blocked pores or hair follicles).

What can we do together?

These good-natured companion dogs are excellent trackers, and could be trained for agility, however obedience trials are not their forte!

● *Already powerful at 7 months, this puppy needs to be carefully trained and encouraged in obedience.*

Don't forget!

Essential early training encourages suitable levels of obedience. Grooming daily during the moult will reduce hair shed at home.

Medium dogs

Chow Chow

Popular in its native land of China, the Chow has been around for over 2000 years and is thought to be the oldest breed originating from grey wolves. Used for war, hunting, guarding and as draught dogs by the Huns, Mongols and Tartars, they also came in useful for the pot when times were hard. Its first introduction to England in 1760, was as a zoo animal, although later Queen Victoria's gift of a specimen Chow assured them of popularity as household pets. In the USA Chows became popular with the rich and famous during the 'Roaring Twenties', to the extent that modern breeding practices have unfortunately led to several health problems. This aristocratic teddy bear of a dog is highly civilised, aloof, strong-willed, stubborn, dominant and very reserved. They are, however, absolutely devoted to their family, very protective, well mannered at home and a loyal companion.

Colour choices?

Chows are black, blue, cinnamon (light tan to brown), red (light gold to deep red-brown), cream or white, with lighter colouring on the underside of rumps and tails. Sometimes nuanced, never spotted or parti-coloured. A Chow's most distinctive feature is its blue-black or purple tongue and gums.

● *Fully grown, Chows resemble dignified teddy bears.*

How much grooming?

A Chow's dense, double coat can be smooth or rough, needing daily grooming to keep it clean. Brushing and combing is best for denser coats, reaching into the fur down to skin, with more attention paid to thicker areas. A curry brush is easiest during the twice-yearly moult. Extra care is needed with puppy coats during shedding. Grooming smooth coats, which are upstanding plush hair, takes less time.

Do they make good pets?

Some make great family dogs, others not; a lot depends on the puppy, and the methods of early training and socialising. Chows are one-person dogs, and are not particularly affectionate or demonstrative. They need owners who really understand them, and are not a good choice for novices.

What home suits them?

Quiet, orderly homes with an established routine are best. Chows enjoy country life, but can adapt to towns or apartments if given long, daily walks to burn off energy.

What sort of owner?

Owners must appreciate a Chow's individuality – this is a typically independent Oriental breed. Time spent on grooming, training and socialisation teaches puppies to reach their true potential as loyal companions. Owners must earn their Chow's respect and be experienced, assertive and confident enough to demand it. Strong bonds can be formed, but even so Chows are distant and not naturally demonstrative.

How much exercise and stimulation?

Chows do not enjoy being active, and exercise needs are moderate, but they do enjoy daily walks, maybe half an hour twice daily. Care in hot weather is necessary as Chows have a tendency to overheat under their heavy coats.

Friendly with other pets?

Not ideal for forming friendships with smaller household pets as they have a strong prey drive; early socialisation as puppies should allow tolerant relationships to develop satisfactorily between other household dogs. They occasionally show aggression to dogs of the same gender.

Character Traits	Poor	Average	Good	Excellent
Attitude to other dogs				
Quietness				
Behaviour at home				
Guarding ability				
Good with children				
Ease of training				
Obedience to owner				

Time to maturity: 2.5 years
Male height: 48–56cm (19–22in)
Female height: 46–51cm (18–20in)
Weight: 20–32kg (45–70lb)
Average lifespan: 14–15 years

Is puppy training easy?

Chows need firm, patient, consistent and gentle training from a young age. As puppies they appear well behaved, and inexperienced owners assume that this is the norm, but neglecting early training causes problems later. Adults can be independent, obstinate and dominant, only co-operating when it suits them. It may be difficult for inexperienced owners to change bad habits.

Special puppy care?

Early training must not be neglected, and early socialisation helps to overcome their extreme suspicion of strangers.

Possible health problems?

Poor breeding practice in some lines has caused eye problems, lymphoma (malignant tumour), hip dysplasia (malformation), diabetes, cancer, autoimmune disease and skin melanoma. The thick coat can lead to flea problems.

Medium dogs

What can we do together?

Hunting, guarding and being a loyal companion are the Chow's forte.

Don't forget!

Home insurance in the USA has increased for Chow owners, due to badly trained Chows biting people. Generally, public perception is poor and Chows are included in breed-specific dog control legislation.

Less than 3 months old, but the thick plush coat already needs regular grooming.

Portuguese Water Dog
Other names: Portuguese Fishing Dog

True water dogs, they originally came from the Algarve in Portugal, where they worked with fishermen by herding fish into their nets and retrieving tackle. Early stories from 1297 describe a Portuguese Water Dog saving a drowning sailor. They accompanied the fishing fleet to colder waters around Iceland, where their long coats were ideal for the extremes of temperature they endured.

Excellent swimmers and divers, they can be used for hunting water game. By 1930 the breed was on the decline, but it has become popular again recently and one was chosen as President Obama's family dog. This breed is energetic, impetuous and tough, needing lots of exercise, but they make great pets because they are loving, intelligent and easily trained with firm handling. They enjoy their owner's companionship both indoors and out, and make good watch dogs, although they are friendly towards strangers.

Colour choices?

Solid white, black or brown, or black or brown with white markings. Parti coloured Portuguese Water Dogs are rare but they are found in the United States. In Portugal white markings rarely cover more than 30 per cent of the body.

How much grooming?

These dogs are high maintenance. They have single, hypoallergenic coats, either wavy or curly, and some have both types on different parts. They never shed, and the coat grows indefinitely if not trimmed, which sometimes causes problems around the eyes. Daily grooming is needed, with complete trimming bi-monthly to prevent tangles or skin allergies. Usually a 'lion' cut is favoured with hindquarters, muzzle and base of the tail shaved, or a 'retriever' cut which is trimmed short all over.

Do they make good pets?

These are biddable dogs and quiet in the home, and make excellent family pets. They have a loud, distinctive bark, and invite play and interaction with their owner with an appealing 'expressive panting' sound like 'ha-ha-ha'. Very intelligent, they make ideal companions, and are sometimes used as assistance dogs for the hard of hearing.

● Energetic, impetuous and tough, adults will need plenty of walking and sport to satisfy their need for activity.

What home suits them?

Ideal for country living, Portuguese Water Dogs enjoy gardens for activity and play, with long walks close by. They are excellent jumpers, making high fencing

necessary, and intelligent – if they cannot go over fences, they go under them! True to their name, they are brilliant water dogs, so expect lakes, rivers and seaside to be viewed as potential swimming pools. Owners may need suitable outdoor drying space.

What sort of owner?

People who want their dog constantly at their side, and appreciate an intelligent, independent dog who needs an intense, loving bond. Owners should be prepared to commit to lots of coat care, and enjoy engaging in plenty of activity. Owners must also appreciate that they enjoy 'counter surfing' if food is around! Puppies are bouncy and active, so unsuitable for older or less active owners.

How much exercise and stimulation?

Plenty of exercise through walking playing or swimming is needed and their high intelligence requires adequate mental stimulation.

Character Traits	Poor	Average	Good	Excellent
Attitude to other dogs				
Quietness				
Behaviour at home				
Guarding ability				
Good with children				
Ease of training				
Obedience to owner				

Time to maturity: 2 years
Male height: 50–57cm (19.5–22.5in)
Female height: 43–52cm (17–20.5in)
Weight: 16–25kg (35–55lb)
Average lifespan: 12–15 years

Friendly with other pets?

These dogs are always friendly with other family pets if introduced properly, but do remember their hunting origins. Portuguese Water Dogs are gregarious and loneliness can cause boredom and destructive behaviour.

Is puppy training easy?

Training skills are quickly learned, and they can master numerous tasks including supporting people with hearing problems and epilepsy. However, firm handling is essential because they are wilful, and usually know their owners' shortcomings.

Special puppy care?

Take care with toys, as puppies are destructive; chewy rawhide toys are often safer for playing. Puppies failing to thrive should be checked for genetic conditions that may affect them when young.

Possible health problems?

Generally healthy and breeders do health check, but they can suffer from juvenile dilated cardiomyopathy (puppies aged from two weeks to seven months) which causes heart failure, and hip and eye problems.

What can we do together?

Obedience taught early is best, they also do well in agility and hunting.

Don't forget!

Remember to make sure puppies know who is boss, and only buy from a reputable breeder.

● At 8 weeks old this beautifully marked puppy will make a lovely specimen for showing.

Samoyed

Other names: Nordic Sled Dog, Bjelkier

Samoyeds are a working breed that originated among Samoyedic people of Siberia who were nomadic reindeer herders. They used them for sledding, herding, guarding and keeping their owners warm. Samoyeds date from at least 3000 years ago, and are one of the most ancient dog breeds, although they were unknown in the West until 1889. They are energetic, active dogs and enjoy taking part in a wide variety of activities, such as sledding, mushing, agility and tracking. If denied suitable activity, they may become bored and destructive. Samoyeds have hypoallergenic coats, and when groomed the Angora-like hair can be used for fly-fishing lures or knitting warm sweaters. However, this coat does require lots of grooming, which may not be ideal fo busy families. They are versatile and adaptable, and their sparkling white coat, charming characteristic 'smile' and friendly temperament contributes to a happy, sweet-natured and perfect companion dog.

Colour choices?

Typically white, but cream or biscuit-shaded are acceptable. A range of other colours (black, brown and spotted) were once included, but white predominates.

How much grooming?

Samoyeds have double-layer coats that moult copiously twice yearly. They need daily brushing and combing through to the soft warm undercoat and skin to keep them clean and free from mats and tangles. Curry combs are best when the coat is shedding. Neglected coats get into such a state they need professional help to rectify. Owners need to tolerate moulting because hair sheds everywhere.

Do they make good pets?

These are friendly, gentle, sensitive and affectionate dogs, that make excellent pets for the right owner. Good with children, they love family life and enjoy being the centre of attention. Their sensitive, fun-filled, gregarious temperament does not like being ignored or left alone.

● *If kept well groomed, these beautiful dogs grow into ideal show companions.*

What home suits them?

Samoyeds need sufficient space in a country or town home with a garden. A well-fenced garden is ideal, as their energetic working life reflects the need to run around in open space, and they are inclined to escape from the garden if bored.

What sort of owner?

This dog needs an owner who is prepared to accept daily coat maintenance and still have hair to clear away during moult seasons. They thrive on affectionate humans who keep up with their energy levels. A demanding breed, they are unsuitable for those leading sedentary lives who just seek canine companionship.

How much exercise and stimulation?

Samoyeds are not satisfied unless they get plenty of exercise and appropriate mental stimulation. They are intelligent dogs and benefit from being involved in energetic and stimulating activity with their owner.

Friendly with other pets?

Samoyeds usually get on well with other household pets, but any introductions should be made while puppies are still young. Some males can be a little dominant, and some are inclined to chase rabbits or local cats.

Is puppy training easy?

Not always easy to train, Samoyed can be wilful, but if training starts early and owners find an activity that suits them both, all will be well. They have no natural inclination to obedience and need

Character Traits	Poor	Average	Good	Excellent
Attitude to other dogs		■		
Quietness	■			
Behaviour at home			■	
Guarding ability	■			
Good with children				■
Ease of training		■		
Obedience to owner		■		

Time to maturity: 2 years
Male height: 51–56cm (20–22in)
Female height: 46–51cm (18–20in)
Weight: 23–30kg (50–66lb)
Average lifespan: 14–15 years

firm, consistent handling with lots of patience and attention.

Special puppy care?

Puppies will need grooming and training from the start if their owner is to accustom them to continuous coat maintenance and good behaviour. Take care with puppies that their energy levels do not lead to over-exercising growing bones.

Possible health problems?

Samoyeds do have some health issues such as kidney problems (Samoyed hereditary glomerulopathy), hip dysplasia (malformation of the hip sockets), diabetes, eye, heart and skin problems. Generally, however, they are healthy and robust.

What can we do together?

There are lots of activities that energetic owners will enjoy, such as sledding, agility, carting, obedience, showing, flyball, tracking and mushing. Also non-competitive herding tests and herding trial competitions.

So easy to love at 7 weeks old!

Don't forget!

Samoyeds have heavy shedding coats and require a lot of daily grooming. Always buy from reputable breeders who health-check their stock.

Medium dogs

Sporting
characteristic
Sammy' smiles, these puppies
love being the centre of attention.

Australian Shepherd

Surprisingly Aussies are an American breed, not Australian as their name suggests. After the Californian gold rush caused mass migration, several arrived on the west coast of the United States, together with the herds of Australian sheep they worked. These 'little blue dogs' earned themselves a reputation for being active, hardy and fast. They were exceptional working dogs. Closely resembling a Border Collie, they are bred in very attractive colours of marbled (merle) and pastel shades. An intelligent, tenacious breed with strong herding and guarding instincts, they enjoy open spaces and have unlimited energy, and are capable of covering up to 60km (40 miles) a day. They need plenty of exercise to satisfy their needs. Although friendly, loyal and affectionate, they can be strong-willed and need proper socialising and firm training. They make ideal family dogs if properly trained, but this is not a good choice for novice owners.

Colour choices?

A brilliant range of blue merle (marbled grey and black), red merle (marbled cream and liver red) either solid, or sometimes with tan points, and/or white markings on the face, collar, legs, chest and underbody; red or red bi-colour with white; black or black and tan; or tri-colour (black, tan and white). Eye colours offer varieties of brown, blue or different colours (one blue, one brown).

How much grooming?

Aussies have medium-length coats, straight or wavy hair with manes, leg and tail feathering. Use a stiff bristle brush and groom several times a week to remove any dead hair.

Do they make good pets?

Aussies make excellent pets, because they are affectionate, gentle, good-tempered and very loyal, but need plenty of exercise to maintain this good nature. Unsuitable for busy families, small children may not cope with Aussies' rough play. They expect to spend most of the time with their owner.

● *Between 8 weeks (right) and maturity, there is a lot of growing to be done.*

What home suits them?

Not made for an indoor life, apartments and town dwelling are unsuitable for Aussies. Open spaces and country living are best with somewhere to run off-lead and where long walks are available.

What sort of owner?

This breed needs experienced owners, prepared to walk long distances or jog several miles daily. Ideally, an owner happy to do agility, or with sheep to herd, and who is not out at work all day, would be best. Nicknamed 'velcro' dogs, Aussies need company.

How much exercise and stimulation?

Typically high energy, an Aussie wants a lot of exercising. Two to three hour walks a day may be needed and other activities include to stimulate their minds. They enjoy working and learning, and are ideal for owners who jog daily, but remember to also include obedience and tricks, which is great for mental stimulation.

Friendly with other pets?

Early socialising is best to introduce puppies to other pets, but usually they get on well. Some are dominant, and need to be watched initially. Small pets or cats may be at risk from their chase instinct.

Is puppy training easy?

With firmness, lots of patience and a slow and steady approach, Aussies achieve very high standards and are eager to please. Training regimes need to help them understand a purposeful task, not just learn by obedience, and should include plenty of praise and encourageme

Character Traits	Poor	Average	Good	Excellent
Attitude to other dogs				
Quietness				
Behaviour at home				
Guarding ability				
Good with children				
Ease of training				
Obedience to owner				

Time to maturity: 3 years
Male height: 51–58cm (20–23in)
Female height: 46–53cm (18–21in)
Weight: 16–32kg (35–70lb)
Average lifespan: 12–13 years

Special puppy care?

Puppies and adults become destructive if not trained and kept occupied most of the time. Avoid over-exercising puppies, and grade activity so levels increase with maturity. Start training and activities early to prevent the onset of destructive behaviours.

Possible health problems?

Aussies are healthy but can suffer from cancer, eye problems (juvenile cataracts, collie eye anomaly, glaucoma), respiratory and skin problems, epilepsy, hypothyroidism (insufficient levels of thyroid hormone), hip and elbow dysplasia (malformation) and toxicity to certain medication chemicals. Some merle breeds have blindness and hearing loss.

What can we do together?

Ideal dogs to train for agility, flyball, frisbee, trailing and herding (even ducks, geese and rabbits). They also make good service and therapy dogs.

Active, sporty and full of energy.

Don't forget!

Buy only from reputable breeders who undertake any necessary health checks.

● *10 weeks is the ideal time to start training for obedience.*

Siberian Husky *Other names: Arctic Husky*

Siberian Huskies are a working breed, originating from Spitz ancestors, and were used as sled dogs in Siberia. Bred by Chukchi tribes in northeastern Siberia, their thickly furred, double coats cope well with the harshly cold environment in the Arctic. Early in the 1900s Huskies arrived in Canada during the gold rush, and were used for sport in sled dog racing, in which they became distinguished champions. Huskies gradually gained popularity, spreading to the USA by 1930 and Europe and Britain by the 1960s. With a wolf-like appearance and a howl to match, Huskies are independent and keen to roam. They also have great endurance with strong hunting instincts. Huskies have excellent temperaments, great stamina, amiable characters, and are docile and never work-shy. They adapt themselves happily anywhere, and are becoming increasingly popular as affectionate and playful family and companion dogs, although their gentleness makes them ineffective as guard dogs.

Colour choices?

Any colour is acceptable, distinguishing features are beautiful coat markings and striking facial masks with a 'spectacle' pattern. Puppies look attractive, but markings often change with maturity. Husky eyes are ice-blue, dark blue, amber, brown or sometimes they have one blue and one brown eye.

How much grooming?

Their easy-care double coats need a thorough weekly brushing with a pin-wire brush. The short, straight guard hair of the longer topcoat both protects them against cold weather and acts to reflect summer heat. Huskies moult heavily twice a year, and brushing daily will help to deal with this. There is minimal 'doggy' smell if coat care is good.

Do they make good pets?

Huskies are affectionate, good-natured and very playful, although young dogs may be too rough for small children. They need plenty of activity, walking and training time to maintain this good nature and are

● *An adult and a 7-week-old puppy.*

not the best choice for novices. If well trained and exercised, they make great family pets.

What home suits them?

Definitely not city dogs, Huskies need large garden spaces and very secure fencing because they can jump, dig and chew their way out. Homes need countryside close by for energetic walks, preferably away from livestock that may receive unsolicited attention.

What sort of owner?

Ideal for outdoor-loving owners, Huskies benefit from experienced handling. Suitable owners are firm, patient and confident with dog training, and should expect to participate in energetic canine activities, and enjoy long walks.

How much exercise and stimulation?

Physical and mental stimulation is essential as Huskies are potentially destructive unless thoroughly exercised, and great escapologists when bored. They need plenty of brisk walking – around 6 to 7km (4 miles) per day minimum. On-lead walking is best to prevent roaming and hunting. Some Huskies enjoy running beside a bicycle or participating in energetic activities for exercise and stimulation.

Friendly with other pets?

Not considered safe around any livestock, Huskies may be challenging with other household pets because of their strong hunting drive to chase moving prey. Early socialisation for puppies and introductions to well-mannered dogs should prevent problems.

Character Traits	Poor	Average	Good	Excellent
Attitude to other dogs				
Quietness				
Behaviour at home				
Guarding ability				
Good with children				
Ease of training				
Obedience to owner				

Time to maturity: 18 months
Male height: 53–60cm (21–23.5in)
Female height: 51–56cm (20–22in)
Weight: 16–27kg (35–60lb)
Average lifespan: 12–15 years

Is puppy training easy?

Huskies are intelligent and independent, but not easy to train because they are not naturally obedient. They do best with positive reinforcement training. Socialisation and training must start early to be successful and patience is essential.

Special puppy care?

Carefully graded exercise is needed for puppies, gradually building up until they reach adulthood to prevent problems with bone and joint growth. Puppies should be introduced to coat care and formal training quite early for it to be successful.

The facial markings are characteristic.

Possible health problems?

Generally very healthy, but Huskies can suffer from eye problems and hip dysplasia (malformation of the hip sockets), as well as gastric and respiratory problems and injuries associated with high-intensity activity.

Medium dogs

What can we do together?

Competitive sled or cart racing, hunting and back packing, or simply good companions for long walks or cycling expeditions.

Don't forget!

Take care to keep Huskies on leads near livestock, and prevent them escaping from the garden in case they go roaming.

● *Alert and watchful, these 7-week-olds are keen to investigate everything around them.*

Rough and Smooth Collie
Other names: Scotch Collie

Collies are descended from a variety of herding dog originating in Scotland and Wales. The name Collie is thought to derive from 'Colley' an early breed of Scottish black-faced sheep; other sources believe it to be an association with their beautiful thick mane or collar. Available in two coat types, either long-coated or smooth-coated, the long-coated Rough Collies are usually more popular, and many owners will know them from the canine star of the many *Lassie* films. Present-day Collies have been continually bred with the intention of improving their conformation for showing and not herding sheep, so few are now used for this purpose. Smooth Collies, particularly those with merle coats blending into different backgrounds, were used as messenger dogs during the First World War. Good-natured, reliable, energetic, friendly dogs, they are exceptionally devoted to their owners and make wonderful family dogs.

Colour choices?

Available colours are sable and white, blue merle, tri-colour and white. Many have white collars, legs, feet and tail tips. In the United States white is also accepted.

How much grooming?

Smooth coats are very low maintenance; rough coats need more time but are still relatively low maintenance. Brushing several times a week with a good bristle brush is best. Puppies should be groomed daily with a soft brush for socialisation purposes. Never shave or cut Collie coats. Neutering may cause softer coats and so increase the necessary grooming time.

Do they make good pets?

Collies have a reliable, kind nature which makes them ideal pets, quiet at home but quick to bark an alert to strangers. They are sociable and friendly with people, and always ready to join in whatever their owners are doing. Socialising to prevent shyness is essential. Collies are normally excellent with children.

The coat of this adult Rough Collie needs regular grooming to maintain its condition, unlike that of the Smooth Collie (top right).

What home suits them?

Collies prefer open fields and countryside, which is where they are happiest. They fit into most homes, including apartments, but must be well exercised in smaller homes.

What sort of owner?

This gentle, sensitive dog needs owners who respect his good nature and friendly outlook, and sensible children who will not tease him. Collies are people-orientated dogs and do best alongside owners who give them time and enjoy having them close by.

How much exercise and stimulation?

Collies are very adaptable and will take as much exercise as they are given, but generally moderate amounts of exercise are required. Around an hour daily, which should include a free run when the dog is old enough, is ideal.

Friendly with other pets?

Collies enjoy sharing their home with other pets. They are friendly, non-aggressive and happily spend their day accompanied by other canine pals if owners are not around, although they prefer human company whenever possible.

Is puppy training easy?

Easy to train and quick to socialise, Collies learn new tasks or obedience techniques quickly and efficiently, particularly if motivated with titbit rewards. Training should be firm, but gentle, as puppies are sensitive to an owner's mood and respond best to a positive atmosphere. Collies are sound-sensitive and can hear a whistle

Character Traits	Poor	Average	Good	Excellent
Attitude to other dogs				
Quietness				
Behaviour at home				
Guarding ability				
Good with children				
Ease of training				
Obedience to owner				

Time to maturity: 2 years
Male height: 56–61cm (22–24in)
Female height: 51–56cm (20–22in)
Weight: 18–29kg (40–64lb)
Average lifespan: 11–14 years

up to a mile away; training to desensitise puppies to different noises is beneficial.

Special puppy care?

Lead training should start early and socialisation begin as soon as possible, as some dogs can be a little shy and nervous as adults if they have not been socialised well in early puppyhood.

Possible health problems?

Collies have a genetic disposition to react badly to certain medications (anaesthetics), pesticides and other chemicals. They suffer from eye problems (collie eye anomaly which should be tested for at six to eight weeks), hip dysplasia (malformation), and a blood condition, grey collie syndrome, which affects puppies with grey merle colouring. Collies also suffer from

bloat, epilepsy, thyroid problems and some develop allergies.

What can we do together?

Collies are ideal for agility, obedience, showing, flyball, tracking

● *These 7-week-old puppies are ready for socialisation to help them develop.*

and herding competitions, and are also used for search and rescue and as therapy and guide dogs.

Don't forget!

Avoid choosing grey merle-coloured puppies as they die young. Puppies need eye testing prior to homing.

Medium dogs

Airedale Terrier *Other names: Waterside Terrier, Bingley Terrier*

Originating around 1850 in Airedale, Yorkshire, Airedales are the largest of all terriers. They were developed as a large game terrier suitable for country pastimes such as otter, boar and deer hunting. Recognised as a distinct British breed in 1886, Airedales proved their worth in the First World War as messengers, ambulance dogs and sentinels. By 1920 Airedales were one of the most popular breeds in Britain and the USA. With legendary courage, always alert, they are good guard dogs, but are sometimes dominant and may be aggressive to other dogs. Airedales form close bonds with their owners, are loving and gentle with children, and make excellent family companions, providing their need for training and plenty of exercise is recognised. Often used as working, service and therapy dogs, they have proved their value in army and police roles and have also been trained as search and rescue dogs.

Colour choices?

Usual colour is black and tan, with puppies born black and gaining their tan colour from around ten weeks. Adult dogs will have black (or grizzle) on the body saddle, top of the neck and tail.

How much grooming?

Airedales have a 'broken' topcoat with harsh, wiry and stiff hair (never soft) with a soft undercoat. Grooming daily is recommended plus professional hand-stripping two to three times yearly. Puppies need stripping from six months. Use a bristle brush and curry comb to work through thicker parts of the coat.

Do they make good pets?

Puppies are boisterous and quite hard work early on, and so unsuitable for young families. However, they are great companions and valiantly protective of their owners. They suit active families with time for grooming, mental stimulation and physical exercise. Strong-willed and stubborn, they

● *Strong, sturdy, alert and active, the adult Airedale is the largest of the terriers. He needs firm, patient training to achieve complete obedience.*

can also be noisy and destructive if left alone too long. They will always remain a puppy at heart.

What home suits them?

Airedales need space for play, exercise and training in securely fenced gardens to burn off their energy. Preferring a country life with plenty of walking and off-lead exercise, Airedales do adapt to town living but owners must be thoroughly committed to their need for high levels of exercise.

What sort of owner?

This breed needs total commitment, and owners willing to devote plenty of time and attention to their Airedale and competent to provide the right sort of training. A physically strong owner is essential to handle this powerful dog – one who enjoys an active life with plenty of walking is best. A sense of humour helps as these dogs are great characters, but likely to make mischief. They are occasionally rowdy and sometimes disruptive.

How much exercise and stimulation?

Airedales need half an hour's brisk walk twice a day as well as free running sessions, because of their high energy levels. Regular play sessions and long walks are good, and this dog is an ideal companion for jogging, hill walking, hiking or any other active form of exercise.

Friendly with other pets?

Early socialisation is essential for successful introductions to any family pets, but Airedales have a

Character Traits	Poor	Average	Good	Excellent
Attitude to other dogs	▓			
Quietness		▓		
Behaviour at home			▓	
Guarding ability				▓
Good with children		▓		
Ease of training		▓		
Obedience to owner			▓	

Time to maturity: 2 years
Male height: 58–61cm (23–24in)
Female height: 56–59cm (22–23in)
Weight: 20–23kg (44–50lb)
Average lifespan: 12–13 years

strong chase instinct and puppies may be too boisterous to be safe around smaller pets.

Is puppy training easy?

Firmness, time and patience with training is essential, because Airedales are not dogs who are naturally obedient. Any training should be fun and stimulating with plenty of rewards. They dislike repetitive training; owners must never be harsh, but always patient and flexible in their methods.

Special puppy care?

These energetic, powerful dogs should not be overwalked as puppies to allow bones and muscles to mature gradually. Otherwise damage could result.

Possible health problems?

Generally a hardy breed, but can suffer from hip malformation (dysplasia), skin allergies, cancer, eye and cardiac problems.

What can we do together?

Lots of walking, adoring pal, companion for jogging, hiking, tracking and hunting. In a working context, service training and livestock guarding.

Don't forget!

Airedales are a physically strong, powerful breed and need owners who are strong in mind and body to handle them properly.

Medium dogs

Black initially, puppies gain their tan colouring as they grow.

● *Looking innocent at 3 months old, but already contemplating mischief!*

Dalmatian
Other names: Spotted Coach Dog, Carriage Dog

The origins of this breed are difficult to pin down – it possibly came from the Dalmatian coast of the Adriatic, hence the name. In the 18th century English landowners found a role for Dalmatians as fashionable carriage dogs, energetically running miles beside horses or under the rear of carriages, ready to clear the way and guard against attacks by highwaymen. In the 1890s Dalmatians in America accompanied horse-drawn fire engines, although with increasing mechanisation they became chiefly pets and mascots. This breed's outgoing, friendly nature and distinctive spotted appearance have won it popularity as an exceptional household companion. Dalmatians are sensible, dependable, intelligent, loving, courteous and playful. They are appropriately protective family pets, but also energetic and lively. They need the right owner who will spend time in their company, and provide lots of active walking to satisfy their love of exercise.

Colour choices?
Born white, puppies develop spots within three weeks of birth. Show puppies must have evenly distributed coin-sized, round, black or liver (brown) spots on a white background, with spots merging on the ears. Puppies with body patches are sold as pets and unsuitable for showing.

● *This 4-year-old Dalmatian sports the 'right' size spots on his body.*

How much grooming?
The short, fine, dense, glossy coat benefits from regular weekly grooming with a hound glove or curry comb, because Dalmatians tend to shed all year round. With minimal coat oil they do not smell and stay relatively clean, without the need for regular bathing.

Do they make good pets?
Temperamentally they are perfect companion dogs. Their association with humans, horses and other stable animals has instilled an instinct for correct behaviour, and they are amenable to discipline. Dalmatians are usually well-behaved and trouble-free house dogs, naturally friendly, playful and gentle, although young children may find puppies too boisterous for them.

What home suits them?
With plenty of energetic exercise Dalmatians are adaptable to living in small town homes with gardens. They are, however, happier with the freedom of country living and large, securely fenced gardens for energetic play, with plenty of long walks available nearby.

What sort of owner?
Dalmatians are unsuitable for couch potatoes. They need active owners taking regular, energetic, country walks. Better with company, on their own Dalmatians can be destructive, and express their loneliness loudly and vocally. Ideal family dogs, but unsuitable for young children or frail elderly because puppies are often too boisterous.

How much exercise and stimulation?
These are tough, athletic, energetic dogs with loads of stamina, bred for daily cross-country running with horses, and they are at their happiest when exercised several miles daily. Without exercise they may be destructive at home, using strength and energy to wreck furniture. Stimulation is necessary for their active, intelligent minds

Friendly with other pets?
Dalmatians have an affinity with horses, and most other animals if they are well socialised. However, smaller pets and dogs may find them too bouncy and energetic.

Is puppy training easy?
Always willing to please and attentive to handlers, Dalmatians

Character Traits	Poor	Average	Good	Excellent
Attitude to other dogs			▓	
Quietness		▓		
Behaviour at home			▓	
Guarding ability			▓	
Good with children				▓
Ease of training		▓		
Obedience to owner			▓	

Time to maturity: 2 years
Male height: 58–61cm (23–24in)
Female height: 56–58cm (22–23in)
Weight: 23–25kg (50–55lb)
Average lifespan: 11–13 years

can be strong-minded and stubborn; owners need patience and good leadership to bring out their best. Dalmatians are not difficult to train if handled firmly and obedience is started early.

Special puppy care?

Puppies should not be over-exercised to burn off their high energy, or maturing young bones and joints could be damaged. Puppies are bouncy and boisterous, and early socialisation needs care to prevent problems. Diet needs attention because Dalmatians eat anything and everything, causing problems with obesity.

Possible health problems?

Dalmatians can suffer from hyperuricaemia causing kidney and bladder stones, deafness (which should be tested for before purchase), hip dysplasia (malformation) and arthritic conditions.

What can we do together?

Owners may enjoy showing, jogging, agility, flyball and horseriding companionship. Playing games with a football or a handball may also appeal to many active owners.

Peaceful here, but puppies can be boisterous.

Don't forget!

Buy puppies only from reputable sources, and request sight of hearing test certificates of the puppy's parents. Show puppies are chosen for spots, not patches, on the body.

● *White at birth, at 8 weeks these puppies already have the characteristic spots emerging on their coats.*

Medium dogs

Large dogs

This group consists of breeds such as retrievers and setters that are ideal for training to participate in canine activities. With the right temperaments, they can make wonderful pets suitable for family homes. However, when fully grown many need larger homes and gardens than other breeds. With smooth, wire and shaggy coats to select from, there are plenty of choices for the prospective owner.

Golden Retriever

Goldies acquired recognised breed status in Britain in 1913 having descended from golden-coloured puppies in black retriever litters in mid 18th-century Scotland. Goldies were recognised for registration in USA in 1925, and have since become hugely popular family pets. Unfortunately, their gentle disposition and ideal temperaments for families with children have also made them money spinners for puppy farmers, leading to increasing health and temperament problems in recent years. Hardy, diligent and eager, they will retrieve game even in bitterly cold weather to please their owner and are at home on land or in water. Most common of all retrievers as a family pet, Goldies are great all-rounders, as well as handsome, kind and cheerful family dogs. They are often used as guide, therapy and 'sniffer' dogs. They need mental and physical stimulation, have a great sense of humour but can be exuberant.

Colour choices?

Originally Goldies had to be the shade of a gold guinea, but standards were changed and now allow any shade of gold or cream.

How much grooming?

Top coats are water-resistant and wavy, some thicker than others, with a soft undercoat. They need weekly grooming with a hard brush and comb, particularly around the feathering on legs, necks and tails to remove countryside debris. Some shedding occurs most of the year, but also profusely twice a year. Ears need checking and cleaning weekly to prevent infections occurring.

Do they make good pets?

A good temperament is the Goldie's hallmark; they should be kind, friendly and confident. They are ideal family pets, very patient with children, and amiable with all family members, including visitors to their home. Goldies are also prized for being calm, biddable, sociable, intelligent, eager to please and extraordinarily willing to learn.

● Eager to please and quick to learn, Goldies do well in training.

What home suits them?

Too active for apartments, Goldies readily adapt to well-fenced gardens in town or country homes, providing they have mental stimulation and plenty of exercise to burn off their excess energy.

What sort of owner?

Active, affectionate owners only should purchase a Goldie, as they thrive with kind, easygoing owners and well-behaved children, who respect their gentle disposition and do not mind dog hairs on the furniture. As puppies Goldies can be exuberant and energetic, and owners should expect to spend time training them to become calm, confident, well-mannered adults.

How much exercise and stimulation?

Goldies have the high energy levels typical of working breeds, but care is needed with puppies under nine months to limit over-exercise to prevent damage to young bones and joints. Daily exercise, in all weathers, is needed for adults, and should include mental stimulation: participation in events like agility, obedience or flyball is ideal.

Friendly with other pets?

Goldies are extremely friendly with other dogs, cats and household pets. They are so even-tempered that they can be used as surrogate mothers for other species.

Is puppy training easy?

Goldies are exceptional dogs to train being intelligent, eager to please and quick to learn. They often excel at agility and obedience trials. They have a sense of humour and are only occasionally stubborn. Training should start early, and should be firm but gentle, fun and reward-based.

Character Traits	Poor	Average	Good	Excellent
Attitude to other dogs				
Quietness				
Behaviour at home				
Guarding ability				
Good with children				
Ease of training				
Obedience to owner				

Time to maturity: 2 years
Male height: 56–61cm (22–24in)
Female height: 51–56cm (20–22in)
Weight: 27–36kg (60–80lb)
Average lifespan: 12–13 years

What can we do together?

Goldies do well in obedience, agility competitions, flyball and field trials. They also excel as service dogs.

Don't forget!

Only buy from reputable breeders who carry out the necessary health checks on the parents of their stock.

Special puppy care?

Youngsters can be a bit of a handful, but gentle training and fun distractions backed up with positive reinforcement should pay dividends.

● *As young puppies develop, learning starts naturally through the process of playing with their littermates.*

Taking a well earned break after playing!

Possible health problems?

Overbreeding in some lines has caused problems, but buying from reputable breeders helps. Generally, they suffer from cancer, hip and elbow dysplasia (malformation), dislocating kneecaps, ligament ruptures, eye problems, heart disease, epilepsy, haemophilia and skin allergies.

4-week-old puppies buddying up.

Large dogs

Labrador Retriever

Labrador Retrievers are natives of Newfoundland and Labrador in Canada, after which region they are named. They were originally used as fishermen's dogs. Imported to Poole, England in the 19th century, they proved so versatile as working dogs that kennels started breeding and training them for hunting. Labradors are one of the most popular dogs in the world, both as hunting Retrievers and as family pets. However, in some countries, they are two distinct types: one used in field trials, the other as show specimens. Field trial specimens tend to be lighter in weight, smaller, more lively and are harder to integrate into family life, unless well trained. Labradors are active, intelligent, agile and confident, with exceptionally good temperaments. Their delightful, warm personalitie and low aggression level make them one of the best all-rounder dogs, ideal as workin Retrievers or as family pets.

Colour choices?
Black, chocolate or yellow (cream to fox-red) are the only colours available.

How much grooming?
Labradors have short, dense, water-resistant, easy-care coats, which are slightly oily. They benefit from weekly grooming with a slicker or bristle brush to remove dander and dead hair. As they tend to moult continuously, some owners may find training them to stand quietly to accept 'hoovering' of their coat helps to remove some moult.

Do they make good pets?
Easygoing, kind, even-tempered, sociable, tractable dogs, Labradors need plenty of time and attention from families, because left alone they are destructive and chew just about anything. They are very good with children, but perhaps a little clumsy and boisterous with small children as puppies. Not the best guard dog, as they are easygoing and trusting even with strangers. They tend to 'mouth' hands when playing with children, so hand washing will be essential.

● *Fit, alert Labradors like this need feeding correctly to avoid risks of obesity.*

What home suits them?
With sufficient levels of exercise and mental stimulation, Labradors are happiest with their owner. They are not inclined to jump over or dig under fences, but secure fencing around gardens is necessary as they may wander off with friendly strangers. Owners may find it necessary to remove ornaments from low tables to prevent breakages from tail wagging.

What sort of owner?
Owners must commit to long daily walks, in any weather, and acceptance of mischievous puppy ways as they grow into exuberant adults. Patienc with training and grooming is essential, as is the realisation that homes may be messy with muddy paw prints and moulting hair.

How much exercise and stimulation?
Plenty of walking is needed, up to two hours daily, and mental stimulation. Labradors can be lazy, and often overeat and become obese. But with the right levels of exercise and stimulation, these charming dogs continue to delight well into old age.

Friendly with other pets?
Early socialisation and proper introductions are necessary, but Labradors are ideal companions fo other pets. They are retrievers, anc may carry small pets in their mout but are unlikely to harm them.

Is puppy training easy?
Early lead training prevents pulling when fully grown, and Labradors a easily trained, keen to please and learn quickly, providing sessions are

Character Traits	Poor	Average	Good	Excellent
Attitude to other dogs				
Quietness				
Behaviour at home				
Guarding ability				
Good with children				
Ease of training				
Obedience to owner				

Time to maturity: 3 years
Male height: 56–62cm (22–24.5in)
Female height: 54–60cm (21–23.5in)
Weight: 25–34kg (55–75lb)
Average lifespan: 11–13 years

fun and reward-based to maintain interest. Frequent daily sessions are best, as they get restless without activity. Breaking up training time avoids the onset of boredom.

Special puppy care?

Labradors will eat anything and are persistent when demanding treats; avoid giving in to this because of the risk of obesity. Good healthy diets taking account of different growth stages is best.

Possible health problems?

Labradors suffer from hip and elbow dysplasia (malformation), patella luxation (dislocating kneecaps), eye problems, hereditary myopathy (muscle fibre deficiency), autoimmune disease, deafness and obesity.

What can we do together?

Labradors are ideal companions for playing ball (obsessively!), agility, frisbee and flyball. Also good search and rescue and therapy dogs.

Don't forget!

All breeding stock should be hip- and eye-tested.

● *Cheeky puppies, like these two at 8 weeks, have life ahead of them.*

Boxer
Other names: German Boxer

The original ancestors of Boxers came from dogs used for fighting and defending their owners herds from wild animals. Later versions developed from crossing that original version, the German Bullenbeisser (now extinct), with English Bulldogs. The resulting Boxers developed from these strains in the 1880s. Their high intelligence meant they were ideal for training as service dogs, and they were used by German forces during the First World War as messengers, pack carriers, attack and guard dogs. Proving also to be ideal family dogs, Boxers have become one of the most popular breeds in the United States in the last few years. These are fun dogs, loveable clowns who are very affectionate. They are energetic and likely to be playful well into old age. Owners must commit to give them enough exercise, have patience to cope with their exuberance and offer plenty of training. This is not a breed for someone seeking a peaceful life.

Colour choices?
Colours are fawn or brindle (black stripes on fawn background) with or without white markings, which should not exceed one third of base colours. Black muzzles, and white markings ('flash' marks) usually white underbody and feet. White Boxers occur, but suffer from deafness.

How much grooming?
A Boxer's short, dense coat is low maintenance, needing only occasional brushing with a hound glove to remove dead hair.

Do they make good pets?
Energetic, impetuous, and dominant, Boxers make good pets if trained early, and should not live in rowdy households, as they can be unmanageable. If well trained, Boxers are loyal, loving, humorous and playful with older, sensible children. They are too boisterous for small children and the elderly.

What home suits them?
Adapting to both town or country dwelling, Boxers need space and

● *Adult Boxers still have plenty of 'bounce' and need firm training.*

plenty of exercise, and so are unsuitable for apartments. Secure high fencing around large gardens is best, as puppies are excellent escapologists. Boxers suffer from extremes of temperature, so provide shade to prevent overheating in summer and keep homes warm in winter.

What sort of owner?
Unsuitable for novices, Boxers prefer experienced, active owners who appreciate dogs that are extremely affectionate and loyal. Owners need a sense of fun and the commitment to spend time in energetic walking and training. Kindness is essential as Boxers are sensitive dogs, and firmness is needed to control the occasional whirlwind of activity.

How much exercise and stimulation?
Boxers are high-energy dogs – they need plenty of walking, up to two hours daily. Activity should be good fun for both dogs and owners, and it will provide essential mental stimulation.

Friendly with other pets?
Early socialisation is best as Boxers can be dominant with other dogs of the same gender. Smaller pets find them too boisterous for comfort. Generally they are good-natured and friendly.

Is puppy training easy?
Training should start very early and needs to be firm, kind, consistent and patient as Boxers can be challenging because they are strong-minded and stubborn. Kindness is essential, and mutual respect between dog and owner should develop for successful results. Training must be fun-based, as this loveable clown tends to make a game of obedience and avoids serious learning.

Character Traits	Poor	Average	Good	Excellent
Attitude to other dogs				
Quietness				
Behaviour at home				
Guarding ability				
Good with children				
Ease of training				
Obedience to owner				

Time to maturity: 2–3 years
Male height: 57–63.5cm (22.5–25in)
Female height: 53–59cm (21–23in)
Weight: 25–32kg (55–70lb)
Average lifespan: 9–12 years

Special puppy care?

Puppies often mirror their owners' moods and their attention span is short. They endear themselves to owners, who may not be as firm as they should be. Do not overwalk puppies to prevent injury to young bones and joints.

● *This row of obedient 8-week-old puppies are making a good start with training to 'Sit'.*

Possible health problems?

They are sensitive to certain medications so always check with your vet. Other health issues are eye and heart problems, cancer, hip dysplasia (malformation), epilepsy, gastric and intestinal problems, and allergies (related to dietary intolerance). White puppies may suffer from deafness.

What can we do together?

Great companions for jogging or running, Boxers also enjoy agility, obedience and flyball. They train well as service and therapy dogs.

Don't forget!

Buy from reputable breeders who perform health checks to ensure healthy stock.

Large dogs

Hungarian Vizsla
Other names: Hungarian Pointer

Vizslas are Hungary's national dog, with a long history as an ancient Magyar hunting breed and favoured sporting dog of Hungarian nobility. There are two modern varieties: a short-haired version and a wire-haired strain (now a separate breed) which dates from around 1930. The Short-haired Vizsla became better known, and with rising popularity in France, was registered in Europe from 1938. These are lively, adaptable dogs with an excellent scenting nose. They tend to stay close to their owner, and are famed for their ability as upland bird dogs, very skilled over rough terrain in pointing and retrieving game. Over the years these beautiful dogs have gained popularity as a companion breed. Their even temper, outgoing personality, friendliness and sociable attitude make them ideal family pets, providing their needs are met – plenty of exercise, stimulation, human contact and lots of company. They don't like being left alone.

Colour choices?
Solid golden/russet colouring in different shades. Small white patches on chest and neck are allowed, but not desired in show puppies.

How much grooming?
Weekly brushing of the short smooth coat will suffice. Ears need checking regularly, and skin checked for cuts and thorns after hunting or rambling in scrub and brambles. Vizslas rarely have any doggy smell.

Do they make good pets?
These high-energy puppies can be demanding, but are gentle, caring and loving. They bond well with owners, are good with children, and are often called 'velcro' dogs because they are so loyal, affectionate and owner-orientated. Vizslas often cry if neglected or lonely, and are not happy if left home alone.

What home suits them?
Vizslas put their owners first, so home is most important; while life in the country is preferred, they can adapt to town living. Country homes

Vizslas' gentle nature and kindly disposition make them easy to live with.

with space for regular exercise and well-fenced, secure gardens are best. They do jump fences if bored.

What sort of owner?
These are not part-time dogs, and meeting their demands for exercise and stimulation is a lifetime commitment. Good owners and families are involved with their Vizsla daily, and spend weekends doing canine activities. They should expect full-time companionship and interaction with their puppy.

How much exercise and stimulation?
Vizslas need plenty of exercise and stimulation daily, with time to gallop and run in open space. Staying healthy and happy requires high levels of exercise and stimulation and Vizslas thrive on attention, exercise and interaction. Puppies need limited short walks and play when very young.

Friendly with other pets?
Vizslas are hunting dogs, so expect family pets to be at some risk, unless they have been well socialised with good introductions as puppies. There may be an inclination to chase cats, although these are usually friendly dogs.

Is puppy training easy?
A sensible approach to training puppies is necessary; their natural instinct is pointing and retrieving, which can be utilised for

Character Traits	Poor	Average	Good	Excellent
Attitude to other dogs				
Quietness				
Behaviour at home				
Guarding ability				
Good with children				
Ease of training				
Obedience to owner				

Time to maturity: 2 years
Male height: 57–63.5cm (22.5–25in)
Female height: 53–60cm (21–23.5in)
Weight: 20–30kg (44–66lb)
Average lifespan: 12–14 years

involvement in activities that contribute to good training. They can be wilful and distractible, but are eager to please, responding well to firm, patient handling.

Special puppy care?

These are sad puppies if left home alone, and will cry and become very destructive if they are lonely. Some puppies may mouth

● *12 weeks old, but take care not to let them over-exercise.*

owners' arms or legs, and can be clingy; training puppies early on to accept being left on their own for short periods is essential.

Possible health problems?

Vizslas can suffer from hip malformation (rarely), epilepsy, cancer, sebaceous adenitis (a skin disease), hypothy-roidism (lack of thyroid hormone), heart and eye problems, skin and certain food allergies.

Large dogs

What can we do together?

Owners can choose from many activities, but they have a special talent for competitive obedience, tracking and agility.

Don't forget!

Buy from responsible breeders and avoid over-exercising energetic youngsters to prevent damage to young bones and joints.

Flat-Coated Retriever

Originating in Great Britain in the 19th century as land and water retrievers, Flat-coats are strong swimmers and natural water dogs, marking, retrieving and delivering game with admirable style. They are often considered more elegant and stylish than other retrievers. They were not recognised as a separate breed until around 1860. They later achieved popularity in the United States, although numbers dwindled between the wars, but the effort of enthusiasts rescued them and by 1960 they were again popular as brilliant companion and family dogs. These lively, intelligent gundogs love attention and companionship, but they are not couch potatoes, preferring to be active and gainfully employed in plenty of activity and walking. Flat-coats continue to be youthful, playful and mischievous well into old age, which accounts for their popularity as family pets. Owners must be prepared to meet their needs for plenty of exercise.

Colour choices?

Solid black or liver (brown).

● The black gleaming shine of the adult Flat-coat's mantle is a joy to groom because it oozes health and condition.

How much grooming?

Flat-coats have easy-care, medium-length, weatherproof coats that need brushing and combing two or three times weekly right down to the skin. Feathering on the head, under the body and tail needs combing to remove tangles. More frequent combing is needed during seasonal moulting.

Do they make good pets?

These puppies enjoy being the centre of attention and being around their families most of the time. They love children, although they may be too boisterous for toddlers or hurt them with their wagging tails. Flat-coats are exuberant, outgoing and confident, with a strong wish to please, and make excellent companion dogs for active families.

What home suits them?

Flat-coats are unsuitable for city life and definitely unsuitable for apartment living; they prefer space and activity in the countryside. Well-fenced large gardens and long country walks suit them best.

What sort of owner?

Owners should be firm and sensitive to this active dog's need for exercise, and should be able to appreciate their sense of humour. Flat-coats are unsuitable for working families planning to leave them home alone, as they can be destructive and noisy if bored.

How much exercise and stimulation?

Adult Flat-coats need either one good long walk daily or several moderate walks to satisfy their need for plenty of exercise. They also need off-lead running and will enjoy a regular swim. They prefer to stay near their owner when out walking, and so are unlikely to disappear on their own private pursuits.

Friendly with other pets?

Very friendly disposition to other dogs and household pets, but they need to be socialised early and introduced correctly for the relationship to develop as it should. Take care with boisterous puppies though, as they may be too rough for other small pets, and unknown cats may be considered fair game for chasing.

Is puppy training easy?

Eager and quick learning, the Flat-coat should be treated with firmness and consistency or they are inclined to play the fool and clown around. Short sessions with

Character Traits	Poor	Average	Good	Excellent
Attitude to other dogs				
Quietness				
Behaviour at home				
Guarding ability				
Good with children				
Ease of training				
Obedience to owner				

Time to maturity: 3 years
Male height: 58–61cm (23–24in)
Female height: 56–58cm (22–23in)
Weight: 25–36kg (55–80lb)
Average lifespan: 12–14 years

plenty of variety and little repetition are best. This puppy has a sensitive nature, and so any overbearing treatment during training will simply be counter-productive.

Special puppy care?

Over-exercising exuberant immature youngsters must be avoided, as there is a risk of injury to young bones and joints. Gradually increase exercise duration to allow for growth without risk of damage.

Possible health problems?

This breed has a higher risk of cancer than average. Other conditions Flat-coats may suffer from are hip dysplasia (malformation), dislocating kneecaps, eye problems and epilepsy. Eye testing and hip scoring are recommended for this breed.

What can we do together?

Flat-coats are great family dogs and good companions, but can also be used for hunting. Some are used as therapy companions and in the services as 'sniffer' dogs.

Don't forget!

Always buy from reputable breeders who complete necessary health checks on their breeding stock.

Large dogs

Even at 6 weeks, these puppies benefit from patient handling and socialisation to help them develop into friendly family dogs.

German Short-haired Pointer

Developed in Germany between the 17th and 19th centuries, Pointers are noted for their powerful fast gallop, great endurance, hunting ability over any terrain and tolerance of cold. They are excellent working dogs for hunting, pointing and retrieving game and boast a stylish appearance. Believed to descend from similar species as other pointers, they were popular at one time with German, French and Spanish nobility. The current breed has existed since 1880, and today GSPs are recognised worldwide for their versatility and virtues as excellent family dogs. Energetic, sociable and even-tempered, they are attached to owners, love children, are good guard dogs and excel as companion pets. GSPs can be stubborn and strong-willed, and need their physical and mental needs satisfied or they can be destructive. Plenty of exercise and time spent grooming and training will be needed.

Colour choices?
Coat colours are solid black or liver, black and white, liver and white. Bi-colours are ticked, spotted or both.

How much grooming?
The short, flat, dense coat, protected by guard hairs, is water-resistant and low maintenance, despite shedding constantly. Occasional brushing removes dead hair. Bath only when needed. The floppy ears need regular checking and cleaning.

Do they make good pets?
Intelligent, bold, and affectionate, even slightly eccentric, they are cooperative and easily trained dogs. Puppies are boisterous and demanding, so they may not suit young family members, but active families who keep them busy with suitably energetic activities should have no problem with them.

What home suits them?
Unsuitable for small homes and apartments, GSPs are happier in country homes with high-fenced, large gardens. They enjoy digging!

● *These 3-year-old GSPs will be good company for one another if their owner decides to go out for a while.*

They are athletic, and benefit from open space nearby for plenty of daily exercise. GSPs can live outside if necessary but prefer to be indoors with their family.

What sort of owner?
Inactive, inexperienced or working owners are unsuitable, as GSPs form strong bonds with their owners, and dislike being left alone for too long. They can be destructive and make mischief if bored or lonely. An active owner, who enjoys walking whatever the weather, will suit them best. The high energy levels will not suit elderly, frail owners or families with young children.

How much exercise and stimulation?
GSPs need plenty of vigorous exercise, around two hours daily with off-lead running, plus other suitably stimulating canine activities such as agility. Unused energy can be channelled into undesirable destructive behaviours.

Friendly with other pets?
GSPs get on well with other dogs, although there may be some gender disagreements between dominant males, or females in season. With their hunting background, smaller pet animals may be at risk, and early socialisation is essential to prevent problems. During exercise, owners should take care if their GSP shows interest in countryside prey or a neighbour's small animals.

Is puppy training easy?
GSPs are easy to train as biddable and well-behaved family members

Character Traits	Poor	Average	Good	Excellent
Attitude to other dogs				
Quietness				
Behaviour at home				
Guarding ability				
Good with children				
Ease of training				
Obedience to owner				

Time to maturity: 2 years
Male height: 58–63.5cm (23–25in)
Female height: 53–58cm (21–23in)
Weight: 27–32kg (60–70lb)
Average lifespan: 14–16 years

● *Life at 10 weeks old is about exploring and learning how to behave.*

They need firm training, and agility or obedience competitions are ideal for making the most of their superb ability to learn and eagerness to please, as well as for stimulating their intelligent minds.

pecial puppy care?

Take care with puppies under nine months – don't exercise them too hard to prevent damage to young joints. Fresh water must always be available as these active puppies often drink copious amounts.

ossible health problems?

GSPs can suffer from hip dysplasia (malformation), eye problems, epilepsy, cancer, gastric torsion (bloat) and skin problems.

Damage (cuts and abrasions) to skin while out hunting is also a risk.

What can we do together?

Owners may enjoy GSPs as running companions and for hunting, carting, bikejoring, showing, agility and obedience competitions.

Don't forget!

GSPs can suffer from separation anxiety and are high maintenance in terms of exercise and training needs.

● *Even at 10 weeks this puppy's large pendulous ears will need attention to keep them clean and free from infection.*

Large dogs

A peaceful moment sitting quietly.

Standard Poodle

The early 15th century version of the Standard Poodle was bred for hunting, but they are now known for their companionship and classy looks. Fashionable French ladies in Louis XIV's court loved their elegant and refined charm. Today there are four popular coat clips, Lion, Dutch, Lamb and Puppy clip, but the original style was created to protect large joints from the cold when retrieving game from water. Highly intelligent dogs, and with a great sense of humour, Poodles make a popular choice for owne wanting to participate in obedience, agility and sledding, as well as providing support for the disable In recent generations, smaller sizes have been bred (Miniature and Toy) which some pet owners may fin better accommodated to apartment living. Virtually identical except in size, all make excellent family dog Apart from the extensive coat care required, Poodle are great companions and ideal pets for novices because they are easy to train.

Colour choices?

Usually solid colours of black, blue, white, brown, café-au-lait, grey, silver and apricot; less common are parti-colours (solid colours and white), phantom (black and tan markings) and tuxedo (solid colour tuxedo markings and white).

How much grooming?

Poodles have single coats of fine, soft, thick hair which require extensive grooming and clipping; a slicker brush and wide-toothed comb are best on this coat. Most pet owners find Lamb or Puppy clips, done every six weeks, the easiest to maintain. The coat is moisture-resistant and produces little moult, so needs grooming daily to remove dead hair. Bathing is needed regularly.

Do they make good pets?

Poodles are very popular because of their merry, outgoing and good-natured approach to life, and they make excellent pets. They are loyal and intelligent, but can be possessive. They make obedient

● *Adult Poodles can be trimmed in different coat trims to suit their owners.*

pets if trained well. Puppies need supervision by adults, because they can be vulnerable to young or boisterous families.

What home suits them?

Although Poodles are very adaptable, Standards may be a little on the large size for apartment living and will suit a larger house and garden better. Very companionable by nature, Poodles prefer homes with plenty to do and interesting company.

What sort of owner?

A Poodle owner must be committed to grooming and providing company. Puppies should be treated as proper dogs, not as a fashion accessory or toy. They need affection, training and quite a lot of attention, without being pampered or over-indulged.

How much exercise and stimulation?

Energetic and intelligent, they have a great sense of fun, but as a large active breed they need to be walked regularly and provided with adequate levels of mental stimulation. Short outings as puppies building up to longer walks as adults is the best policy.

Friendly with other pets?

Very accepting of other househol pets, but mischievous puppies mus be discouraged from becoming an irritant to older pets. Small pets are at less risk at home if early socialisation is practised.

Is puppy training easy?

Highly intelligent, Poodles are an ideal breed for training by anyone in the family. Puppies will be quick to learn and can be trained to do tricks, as well as obedience.

Character Traits	Poor	Average	Good	Excellent
Attitude to other dogs				
Quietness				
Behaviour at home				
Guarding ability				
Good with children				
Ease of training				
Obedience to owner				

Time to maturity: 2 years
Male height: 58–66cm (23–26in)
Female height: 53–61cm (21–24in)
Weight: 20–32kg (45–70lb)
Average lifespan: 12–14 years

Special puppy care?

It is most important that puppies are groomed daily to prevent hair becoming matted and painful to remove, even if they are clipped. Early training and mental stimulation is particularly recommended as they will become mischievous if bored. Noisy households with young children may cause stress to puppies.

Possible health problems?

There are various inherited health problems, although Standard Poodles are usually recommended as the most healthy of all the sizes, so only buy from reputable breeders who do regular health checks on their breeding stock. The most common

problems are eye, heart, thyroid and joint conditions, Addison's disease (failure of the adrenal glands), Cushing's disease (a hormonal disorder) and epilepsy.

What can we do together?

This breed does particularly well in agility, obedience, tracking, herding. Some owners may also enjoy showing their Poodle, although the latter involves a lot of grooming time.

Large dogs

Don't forget!

Buy only from reputable breeders.

● *Puppies can be trained from 2 months to perform simple tricks.*

● *This shaggy 2-month-old apricot-coloured Poodle already has a thick coat that will soon need to be tidied.*

Chesapeake Bay Retriever

Although rare in Europe, the Chesapeake Bay Retriever is an old American breed that derived from two Newfoundland puppies that were rescued from an English ship wrecked off the coast of Maryland in 1807. Used for hunting wildfowl in swampland, they are hardy with webbed feet and powerful chests which can break ice when swimming to retrieve fowl in water. First recognised as a breed in the United States in 1878, Chesapeakes were declared the official state dog of Maryland in 1964. These are good all-round dogs, tireless when working, superb when hunting, reliable guard dogs, ideal as 'sniffer' or therapy dogs, and great companions. Chesapeakes are devoted to their owner and his family, but they do need their working drive satisfied to be happy. Exercise, socialisation and training will be an important part of their development in early life, or they may become excessively shy or sometimes aggressive with strangers.

Colour choices?

Three basic colours: brown, from light to dark, deadgrass colour (straw to bracken) or sedge (red gold to strawberry blond). Small amounts of white – under body, on the chest, toes and back of the feet – are allowed.

How much grooming?

Chessies have double, wavy outer coats and soft woolly undercoats, feeling slightly oily which makes the coat waterproof, and often with a slight musky odour. This low-maintenance coat needs brushing weekly with a rubber or short-toothed brush. Grooming too often damages its waterproof properties. Bath every three to four months with a mild shampoo.

Do they make good pets?

Chessies are intelligent, alert, intensely loyal, with quiet good sense, affectionate protective natures and bright, happy dispositions. Some can be vocal or may 'smile' by grinning with their teeth bared to express their pleasure.

● *This 9-week-old puppy will need to spend time socialising with adults (right) and learning manners in preparation for later training and habituation*

What home suits them?

A country home suits this energetic working dog best, with a well-fenced-in large garden or extensive grounds. Town life is possible providing plenty of long walks are provided, but they are definitely not suited to apartment living.

What sort of owner?

Owners need to be strong-natured as this breed has a powerful working instinct, and is not ideal for novices. Owners need to be active and enjoy plenty of exercise in any weather and have experience of working and training dogs of strong character. Not a part-time breed, this puppy needs company and work to keep him happy.

How much exercise and stimulation?

Chessies need plenty of exercise and stimulation involving activities which appeal to their working instincts. Exercise should be athletic, energetic and interesting for mental stimulation, preferably with some swimming included.

Friendly with other pets?

As a working, hunting breed, they may see small animals, and sometimes cats, as ideal for chasing. Chessies can be dominant and males particularly may be territorially aggressive, so plenty of early socialisation is essential.

Is puppy training easy?

An intelligent and attentive breed that learns skills quickly. Consistent daily, obedience training with a firm approach, without allowing the puppy's independent nature to take over, is best. Playtime before,

Character Traits	Poor	Average	Good	Excellent
Attitude to other dogs				
Quietness				
Behaviour at home				
Guarding ability				
Good with children				
Ease of training				
Obedience to owner				

Time to maturity: 2 years
Male height: 58–66cm (23–26in)
Female height: 53–61cm (21–24in)
Weight: 25–36kg (55–80lb)
Average lifespan: 10–13 years

during and after may be necessary to maintain interest. Rules for obedience should be established for puppies, but they will not respond to harsh discipline.

Special puppy care?

Some puppies can be boisterous and have a tendency to mouth hands, so encourage children to wash their hands after playing with them. Care is needed not to over-exercise puppies to prevent damage to growing bones and joints.

Possible health problems?

Chessies are a hardy breed but may suffer eye problems, hip dysplasia (malformation), von Willebrand's disease (a blood disorder) and alopecia (hair loss).

What can we do together?

As an active and very versatile dog, Chessies will do well in field trial competitions, hunt tests, tracking, showing, obedience and agility.

Don't forget!

Chessies will be unhappy unless kept well occupied, and need to be effectively socialised and trained, or they may become dominant.

● *Learning a 'Down' will be one of the first training tasks.*

Alert and ready for action!

Italian Spinone
Other names: Italian Wire-haired Pointer, Italian Griffon

One of the most popular show dogs in its native Italy, the Spinone is the oldest griffon-type pointer. Its exact origins are unknown but it is thought to have developed in the Piedmont area of Italy around 500 years ago. The name Spinone is derived from the Italian for 'thorn' which denotes the thick, thorny undergrowth that game hides in. The Spinone, protected by its thick skin and coarse hair, is an excellent hunting companion in these harsh terrains, and also in water, and is a versatile hunter, pointer and retriever. Spinones almost became extinct during the Second World War, but were nursed back to popularity by small groups of enthusiasts, and are now well-loved and very individual members of many families. Spinones are inclined to drool, and have a particular 'doggy' smell, and so are not ideal for house-proud owners. They also need substantial amounts of exercise. Their calm, friendly, playful nature delights many families.

Colour choices?
Colour variations are solid white, white with orange or brown markings, and roan (white with flecked colour – either orange or brown with or without markings). Skin colouring on nose, lips and paw pads varies with different coat colours. Shades or combinations of black markings are undesirable.

● *Well protected from thorny undergrowth, this adult Spinone's coat will need regular brushing after walks.*

How much grooming?
Coats are tough, wiry, oily, weatherproof and close-fitting, without an undercoat. Grooming twice a week is sufficient to remove dander and shed, with some stripping of dead hair needed during periods of moult. Spinones should not be over-groomed, as the coat is likely to become, long, soft and silky, which is undesirable.

Do they make good pets?
Spinones are docile, affectionate dogs with an easygoing nature. They are gentle, patient, playful and dependable with children, but puppies can be boisterous and may overwhelm small children. A very loyal family dog, as adults they display little aggression to strangers or other pets, but they do need early socialisation and lots of exercise or they may be destructive. They are inclined to scavenge food. They can also be highly vocal and 'talkative'.

What home suits them?
Unsuitable for apartment living, Spinones prefer to be country dwellers with space to run around. Small, well-fenced gardens are acceptable, provided regular long walks are available. They prefer living indoors but need space to accommodate the 'doggy' smell.

What sort of owner?
Spinones need patient, gentle owners willing to be fully involved with their care, and committed to constant companionship with plenty of active walking. They are definitely not dogs for house-proud owners.

How much exercise and stimulation?
They need plenty of physical activity and mental stimulation. Adults need one to two hours minimum walking and galloping daily. Length of walks for puppies should be built up gradually until at least nine months old to prevent damage to developing joints and bones.

Friendly with other pets?
These are sociable dogs, and with early socialisation and proper introductions they get on well with other dogs and household pets. They are hunters with strong chase instincts, however,

Character Traits	Poor	Average	Good	Excellent
Attitude to other dogs				
Quietness				
Behaviour at home				
Guarding ability				
Good with children				
Ease of training				
Obedience to owner				

Time to maturity: 2.5 years
Male height: 60–70cm (23.5–27.5in)
Female height: 58–65cm (23–25.5in)
Weight: 29–39kg (64–86lb)
Average lifespan: 12–14 years

and need educating not to give chase to neighbours' cats.

Is puppy training easy?

These loyal, intelligent, sensitive puppies have had working roles for centuries, and are easily trained and very biddable, but can be stubborn. They need firm training and are slow maturing, so need training sessions little and often. Treat them sensitively as their feelings can easily be hurt. Motivational training with positive reinforcement is best.

● This puppy is just the right age at 12 weeks to start training to an acceptable standard using food rewards or clicker training. If properly trained, he will make a super family pet.

Special puppy care?

Puppies under nine months should not be over-exercised to prevent risk of damage to young bones and joints. These are demanding puppies and very destructive if bored.

Possible health problems?

Spinones are relatively healthy, but suffer from hip dysplasia (malformation), arthritis, eye problems (ectropion and entropion) and cerebellar ataxia which affects control of the limbs. Parents should be tested for this before breeding, as puppies die under a year old. Stomach problems if stealing food.

Large dogs

What can we do together?

These are perfect companions for running or jogging, and good hunting dogs.

Don't forget!

Spinones can be demanding and will be destructive if bored; they are also scavengers and food-stealers.

German Shepherd Dog *Other names: Alsatian*

Developed more than 100 years ago from ancestral working and herding dogs, these fine shepherd dogs originated in the Bavarian hills of Germany. They successfully proved their worth during the First World War as guard dogs, and as search and rescue specialists. This versatility continues to this day: German Shepherds perform valuable roles in police and military work, alongside security guards, in search and rescue, and as therapy dogs. German Shepherds are now one of the world's most popular dogs, although they were previously vilified in some quarters for their German origins. Introduced into the UK and USA after the First World War, German Shepherds became popular family dogs, valued for their even-tempered nature, unfailing loyalty and devotion to their family. They are proud, courageous, intelligent companions enjoying the company of their human friends. They must have plenty of exercise, stimulation and training.

Colour choices?

Colours are solid black, sable, bi-coloured (tan with black saddles) or tri-coloured (black with combinations of reddish brown, tan or light grey). White (which often suffer deafness), blue or liver colours are unacceptable for the breed standard, and so not registered by Kennel Clubs.

● *A 7-week-old puppy with an adult GSD.*

How much grooming?

Outer coats are weatherproof, straight and harsh, lying over a softer, thick undercoat and need brushing twice weekly to maintain condition, with extra attention paid to thicker areas. Long-coated Shepherds need daily grooming, but this type of coat is unacceptable for showing.

Do they make good pets?

Shepherds need the right owner to turn them into ideal family dogs. Properly trained, they are loyal, obedient and protective of their family. Early socialisation prevents any tendency to nervousness or dominance, but having active owners helps. They are unsuitable for frail, elderly owners.

What home suits them?

Unsuitable for apartments or small homes, German Shepherds appreciate country homes but adapt to town homes with space for walking. They dislike being confined within four walls, and need stimulation and activity and human company to thrive.

What sort of owner?

This highly intelligent dog needs owners who are willing to commit time to training, walking, grooming and companionship. They are unsuitable for owners who go out to work. Shepherds need physical and mental activity daily; solitude leading to boredom is unkind to such intelligent, active dogs.

How much exercise and stimulation?

Adult dogs need up to two hours daily, which should include time off-lead for running. Youngsters should not be over-exercised to prevent damage to young bones and joints and benefit from several short walks daily, gradually building up to longer, less frequent walks.

Friendly with other pets?

Generally, with appropriate socialisation and supervised introductions, German Shepherds do well with other household pets but they are boisterous. Family dynamics need handling carefully to prevent upsets.

Is puppy training easy?

Shepherds are supremely willing to learn, eager for purpose, and with an excellent working ability. They are very intelligent dogs,

Character Traits	Poor	Average	Good	Excellent
Attitude to other dogs				
Quietness				
Behaviour at home				
Guarding ability				
Good with children				
Ease of training				
Obedience to owner				

Time to maturity: 2 years
Male height: 61–66cm (24–26in)
Female height: 56–61cm (22–24in)
Weight: 34–43kg (75–95lb)
Average lifespan: 12–13 years

responsive to training and enjoy spending time learning obedience skills to perfection. Many are able to participate in advanced training classes, and have potential for competition success.

Special puppy care?
Take care that puppies do not upset other pets as this could cause friction later as they mature. Start training early as dominant German Shepherds can turn quite pushy if untrained, or can become nervous through poor socialisation.

Possible health problems?
Earlier inbreeding did these lovely dogs no favours; they suffer from hip and elbow dysplasia (malformation), arthritis, ear infections, gastric torsion (bloat), von Willebrand's disease (a blood disorder), anal furunculosis (ulcerated anal tissue) and skin problems. The inbred sloping toplines of some show specimens may

result in impairment of hind leg action and poor gait.

What can we do together?
Agility, competitive obedience, companion dogs for walking and

● *Cute intelligent puppies at 8 weeks, destined to be loyal to the right owner.*

hiking, guide and guard dogs, tracking, service dogs and loyal, affectionate pets.

Don't forget!
These are bright dogs that need great training and plenty of exercise.

Large dogs

Old English Sheepdog *Other names: Bobtail*

This is a large breed, and one of England's most ancient pastoral herding dogs. They originated as tough shepherd's and cattle drover's dogs in southwest England. Appearing in British show rings from 1873, the breed was recognised in USA in the 1880s. They subsequently gained popularity worldwide when the rich and famous began to take an interest in them. Some OES are naturally bobbed (tailless), others will be found with full-length tails as docking is now banned in many countries. Friendly, faithful, even-tempered dogs, with intelligence and a boisterous nature, these ultimate shaggy dogs love children and are an ideal choice for many families. They are high maintenance, and need physical and mental stimulation and lots of grooming, but in the right family they make super pets and great companions. Like many working breeds, they need lots of company to prevent them becoming bored and destructive.

Colour choices?

Shades of grey, grizzle, black, blue or blue merle on the body and hindquarters. Head, neck, forequarters, underbody and paws are white. Puppies have black and white coats, true colour developing as the puppy coat sheds as the dog grows.

How much grooming?

Bobtails require plenty of grooming (three or four hours a week for pets); owners may prefer trimming professionally to a short, neat outline. Coats are hard-textured, shaggy, curl-free, profuse, with water resistant undercoats. Tangles need gently teasing out by hand, and grooming with stiff brush and combs. Dead hair needs brushing out to prevent mats. Show puppies need training for grooming sessions (around 15 hours weekly) to maintain show condition.

Do they make good pets?

Playful, quiet, dignified, but never boisterous, Bobtails make good children's companions and

● *A full adult coat like these (3 years) is impractical for the average family, and owners may prefer their pet to be trimmed to a neat short outline.*

playmates. They are intelligent, sociable and adapt to most situations, but some have clownish energy and are clumsy with small children. They may try herding people together, but their intentions are always friendly.

What home suits them?

Bobtails have amiable, home-loving natures; they adapt and fit best in farm and countryside locations with open spaces. With proper exercise and training they can be accommodated to a town lifestyle, if owners meet their needs appropriately.

What sort of owner?

Bobtails are unsuitable for owners who are out all day, as they are gregarious and could be bored and destructive if left alone. They need active owners who are not house-proud, enjoy long walks, and who will spend time on exercise and training. Commitment to regular grooming is essential.

How much exercise and stimulation?

These dogs need daily exercise (two hours a day), plus active play to reduce their energy levels adequately. Never overwalk puppies to avoid damaging young bones and joints; energy is better channelled into play activities.

Friendly with other pets?

Good with other pets, Bobtails will need early socialisation and supervised introductions for the

Character Traits	Poor	Average	Good	Excellent
Attitude to other dogs				
Quietness				
Behaviour at home				
Guarding ability				
Good with children				
Ease of training				
Obedience to owner				

Time to maturity: 2 years
Male height: 61–66cm (24–26in)
Female height: 56–61cm (22–24in)
Weight: 29.5–30.5kg (65–67lb)
Average lifespan: 10–12 years

correct dynamics. Unlikely to chase family cats, but the neighbours' cats may be fair game. Smaller animals may feel threatened by their size and the risk of being squashed.

Is puppy training easy?
Moderately easy to train, this puppy is keen to please, and a quick learner with a great thirst for new and varied activities. Training should be firm with positive reinforcement, or Bobtails can be stubborn, self-willed and uncooperative.

Special puppy care?
Early training will be essential, but never overwalk young dogs. Take care to prevent over-heating.

Possible health problems?
Cancer can be a problem. Bobtails can also suffer hip dysplasia (malformation), eye problems, thyroid and heart disorders, haemophilia, deafness, diabetes, allergies and skin problems. Their thick heavy coat may cause overheating in hot weather.

What can we do together?
Successful sled, tracking and herding dogs, and ideal for agility, obedience, rallying, flyball and competition showing.

Large dogs

Don't forget!
Buy only from reputable breeders who complete health checks.

At 4 months the coat is growing and needs brushing gently daily.

● *Puppies need socialising from early on to develop a confident nature.*

Weimaraner *Other names: Weimar Pointer*

One of the most striking of all the gundog breeds, Weimaraners spring from various hunting dogs of the 17th century. In the 19th century the German court of Weimar specifically bred and refined Weimaraners from carefully chosen native working dogs for hunting purposes. Good all-rounders, Weimaraners were employed to hunt large forest animals (deer, bear, wild boar) and also used for pointing and retrieving game birds. After their introduction into the USA in around 1929, they became popular hunting dogs there, and subsequently found their way to Britain in 1952. Keen-scented, intelligent, powerful, rangy dogs, they need extensive socialisation, but in the right hands are relatively easy to train. They need experienced handlers and are unsuitable for novices but for experienced, strong-minded handlers, and with suitable outlets for their abundant energy, they make marvellous dogs for the right family.

Colour choices?

Nicknamed the 'grey ghost', the only colour is metallic grey, with shades from charcoal blue to mouse grey, silver grey and blue grey. Some have a darker grey stripe ('eel stripe') along their spine. Puppies are born striped, but this soon disappears. Eyes are amber or blue grey.

● *Intelligent and powerful, this 2-year-old bitch should be well trained, obedient and loyal to her owner and a marvellous pet in any family.*

How much grooming?

Brushing with a hound glove twice weekly removes dead hair and buffs the natural coat glossiness to a shine. Long-haired Weimaraners (a variety which appeared in 1973) need brushing and combing of thicker feathering daily.

Do they make good pets?

Weimaraners make good housedogs, and dislike being kennelled outside. They are responsive to handling, happy to guard their family, and are usually gregarious and devoted to their owners. They prefer being with their family most of the time and are gentle and reliable with children. Properly exercised, they are good companions, but sometimes they can prove too boisterous for small children or frail elderly.

What home suits them?

Weimaraners are unsuitable for small homes or apartments, and do better in large country homes with high, well-fenced gardens, with access to open areas for running, galloping or supervised hunting.

What sort of owner?

They are powerful dogs, and only suitable for physically strong and mentally tough-minded owners. Firm, kind leadership is needed, and owners should expect working companions, not placid lapdogs. Owners must be prepared to spend time in the open, whatever the weather, and to keep them gainfully employed, perhaps also participating in canine activities. Bored or dominant Weimaraners are destructive, possessive, over-protective and noisy.

How much exercise and stimulation?

From adolescence, Weimaraners need extensive exercise to satisfy their physical endurance and stamina. Long walks, play and games are appreciated in abundance. Ideal jogging companions, owners may struggle to provide enough exercise for this energetic dog.

Friendly with other pets?

These puppies have a strong instinctive drive to hunt. They may tolerate family cats if introduced and socialised early, but most cats are seen as fair game, and they will not hesitate to chase deer or livestock if an opportunity occurs.

Character Traits	Poor	Average	Good	Excellent
Attitude to other dogs				
Quietness				
Behaviour at home				
Guarding ability				
Good with children				
Ease of training				
Obedience to owner				

Time to maturity: 18–24 months
Male height: 61–69cm (24–27in)
Female height: 56–63.5cm (22–25in)
Weight: 32–39kg (70–86lb)
Average lifespan: 10–12 years

Is puppy training easy?

A consistent, firm, patient approach is best, keeping sessions short and interesting, particularly during the first year. Teaching 'Sit' using positive reinforcement is important to prevent jumping up later on. Weimaraners are stubborn and can be boisterous, but when trained properly are obedient and stay close to their owners.

● *Slight colour variations are evident in 6-week puppies until coats mature.*

A cosy bed keeps young puppies warm.

Special puppy care?

Weimaraners lack undercoat, and puppies feel the chill in cold weather. Puppies may suffer from separation anxiety; training to reduce this problem is necessary. Destructive puppies are best contained in pens or crates when left alone, as they chew and eat anything.

Possible health problems?

Weimaraners are reasonably healthy, but can suffer hip and elbow dysplasia (malformation), eye problems, hypothyroidism (lack of thyroid hormone), heart defects, von Willebrand's disease (a blood disorder), dwarfism and hernia. Rapid growth in puppies also poses problems.

Large dogs

What can we do together?

Hunting, working, jogging, walking and hiking companion.

Don't forget!

These are strong, powerful dogs and unsuitable for novice owners.

Gordon Setter

Other names: Scottish Setter, Black and Tan Setter

These intelligent, noble and dignified dogs were originally bred in 17th-century Scotland for hunting game birds that preferred concealment in undergrowth, instead of taking flight. Partridge, grouse, ptarmigan and woodcock were popular hunting targets, usually on open moors. Then changing British farming methods limited opportunities for this type of hunting, and it is now mainly confined to Scottish moorland. Gordons first appeared in USA in 1842, and were officially recognised in 1892. Considered a good choice for active families, these are calm, docile, affectionate pets. They need sensitive, firm handling as they enjoy roaming after a scent. They can be boisterous and slow maturing, but particularly enjoy being members of a family household. Owners must be prepared to spend time on exercise, grooming, and patient and gentle training of the youngster to develop this dog to its true potential.

Colour choices?

Rich, glossy coal-black with distinctive glossy tan markings (two spots over the eyes, on the muzzle, chest and inside the legs) is the only colour available. A small patch of white on the chest is allowed for showing.

How much grooming?

The hair is silky, and fine on the back, head and front of legs, with longer feathering elsewhere. Time must be spent grooming to remove any undergrowth debris after walks. Brushing and combing daily maintains coats in good condition. Ears need to be checked and cleaned regularly.

Do they make good pets?

Gordons thrive in attentive, loving environments as they are intensely loyal. They make excellent family pets because they love to please, and are patient and protective of their family – sometimes to the point of jealousy. Training may need to continue for longer than with other dogs as they are slower to

● *No longer used primarily for hunting birds, this breed have now become loving and devoted family dogs. They make an enthusiastic addition to any family who can cope with their larger size.*

mature, retaining their puppy ways well into old age. They may be too boisterous for families with young children or elderly owners.

What home suits them?

Unsuitable for apartments, some adapt quite happily to town environments, but this puppy will really appreciate country homes with large well-fenced gardens, and open areas nearby for walking.

What sort of owner?

Owners will love the Gordon's empathy with them, and their enjoyment of 'talking' in response. Time and commitment is needed for training, as well as regular coat care. Owners should not be too house-proud as Gordons enjoy snuffling in undergrowth and may bring mud and debris into the home.

How much exercise and stimulation?

A Gordon's working instinct means that they appreciate vigorous daily exercise, preferably two hours plus daily, which can include swimming. Walking needs grading from gentle exercise for puppies with several shorter walks through the day, increasing to fewer longer walks with maturity. These are intelligent dogs, and socialisation and obedience training is important.

Friendly with other pets?

Their calm, docile nature ensures they are friendly with other pets, although some may find them too

Character Traits	Poor	Average	Good	Excellent
Attitude to other dogs				
Quietness				
Behaviour at home				
Guarding ability				
Good with children				
Ease of training				
Obedience to owner				

Time to maturity: 3–4 years
Male height: 61–69cm (24–27in)
Female height: 58–66cm (23–26in)
Weight: 20–36kg (45–80lb)
Average lifespan: 10–12 years

boisterous. Small household pets may be overwhelmed, and some Gordons can be jealous of other pets around their family, although with good early socialisation and supervised introductions, these problems should be overcome.

Is puppy training easy?

Gordons are quick to learn and eager to please, but need firm, patient, gentle handling as they can be sensitive. Agility training, ideal for adult exercise, should not start until at least 18 months of age to prevent damage to young joints.

These large paws indicate the size this puppy will reach when adult.

Special puppy care?

Avoid overwalking puppies to reduce any possible damage to young bones and joints.

Possible health problems?

Gordons are generally fairly hardy but can suffer from hip dysplasia (malformation), hypothyroidism (lack of thyroid hormone), gastric torsion (bloat) and eye problems.

● *Calm and docile at 16 weeks and contemplating a period of play!*

What can we do together?

Hunting as a trained gundog, walking, and lots of fun and games as a loving family pet.

Don't forget!

Make sure puppies are walked away from the danger of traffic as they like to roam ahead of owners following scents. Keep them on a lead when near the road.

Large dogs

Rhodesian Ridgeback

Other names: Lion Dog, African Lion Hound

In the 1860s settlers to Africa brought their own hunting dogs, which were crossed with the indigenous Hottentot dogs of the Khoikhoi people of Rhodesia. These hunting dogs were distinguished by the ridges of hair on their spine, growing in reverse directions to the rest of the coat. They were fierce, courageous hunting dogs able to track and hold lions at bay and to hunt wild pigs or baboons. They were forerunners of Rhodesian Ridgebacks. Ridgebacks achieved recognition in Africa in 1922, and in Britain not long after, although they did not reach America until the 1950s. The handsome dogs of today are protective and strong-willed, and make excellent watch dogs, but they are also loyal and devoted companions. Very much a 'people's dog', Ridgebacks need strong-minded, experienced, confident owners who will spend time and effort on early socialisation, and appropriate training and exercise for this powerful, independent, dog.

Colour choices?
Light to red wheaten colour, with dark muzzles and ears; a small white patch on the chest is allowed. White on paws is undesirable for show puppies.

How much grooming?
The short, sleek, glossy coat can be maintained by a once-weekly brush with a hound glove.

Do they make good pets?
With good socialisation, Ridgebacks make excellent pets. They are calm, affectionate, rarely bark, and are good with respectful, older children. But these dogs really are unsuitable for novices, and are best owned by experienced dog handlers, who provide the right level of training and socialisation. Their guarding instinct should not be over-encouraged as they can be aggressive if it is allowed to run unchecked. They can be mischievous, but are loving and intelligent and with the right owner do really well as companion dogs.

● *Ridgebacks have a distinctive ridge of hair down the spine. They were bred to hunt big game and guard property.*

What home suits them?
Country homes are best for these puppies, unless plenty of walking is available for town dwellers. Ridgebacks are athletic dogs, and need sturdy high fencing as they are quite likely to jump clear over fences, if bored.

What sort of owner?
These strong-willed dogs are very demanding – they need confident, experienced owners. Time spent on training and socialisation will be well rewarded if the owner is able to produce a well-behaved dog and gain an appropriate level of leadership over them.

How much exercise and stimulation?
Ridgebacks need several brisk daily walks, up to 3km (2 miles) each time, interspersed with free running and play. Owners will need to take care they do not chase joggers, livestock or other dogs for their private enjoyment.

Friendly with other pets?
Ridgebacks have a high prey drive, and small family pets will definitely be at risk. They may be fine if raised with family cats, but other cats in the neighbourhood should beware. This is a dominant breed, and is quite likely to be aggressive with other dogs of the same gender, unless well socialised and trained to accept them.

Is puppy training easy?
Ridgebacks need rigorous training. Owners should be fair, firm, consistent, but not harsh or training will be counterproductive. It is particularly important that training starts early and puppies view their owner as their leader,

Character Traits	Poor	Average	Good	Excellent
Attitude to other dogs				
Quietness				
Behaviour at home				
Guarding ability				
Good with children				
Ease of training				
Obedience to owner				

Time to maturity: 2 years
Male height: 63.5–68.5cm (25–27in)
Female height: 61–66cm (24–26in)
Weight: 29–34kg (65–75lb)
Average lifespan: 10–12 years

● *From this age (6 weeks), puppies develop their natural behaviours. Good training is necessary to prevent unwanted habits becoming established.*

otherwise they can be strong-willed and stubborn. Reward-based training will add motivation and works best.

Special puppy care?

Puppies under six months should not be over-exercised because of the risks of damage to young bones and joints.

Possible health problems?

In America, breeders are expected to perform health screening for hips, elbows, thyroid and eyes, with cardiac and hearing tests optional. Ridgebacks are also known to suffer from dermoid sinus (abnormal tissue on the neck), degenerative

myelopathy (a spinal cord disease affecting the legs), hypothyroidism (lack of thyroid hormone) and gastric torsion (bloat).

What can we do together?

Lure coursing and agility are fun, and appreciated by both owners and Ridgebacks. They are excellent walking companions.

Don't forget!

Buy from reputable breeders prepared to perform the necessary health checks.

Large dogs

● *This tiny puppy's eyes and ears will not open for several more days.*

Bullmastiff

Bullmastiffs have to be the original designer dog. Bred from crossing Mastiffs and Bulldogs, they combine qualities of being fast, active, large and heavy. These impressive, powerful dogs were bred in the 19th century, and used for guarding property. Sometimes dubbed the 'Gamekeeper's Night Dog', they were used in Victorian Britain to tackle problems with violent intruders and poaching on large estates. These agile, solid, courageous and fearless dogs certainly have the looks to deter criminals. They were recognised in Britain by the Kennel Club in 1924 and in the USA in 1933. Despite their fierce appearance, they are much loved because they are excellent companions, family dogs and home guardians. Today's Bullmastiff, were it not for its size, would enjoy life as a lapdog! It is dignified, loyal and affectionate and makes a gentle member of the right family. However, they need firm training and are not a choice for novices.

Colour choices?
Fawn, red or brindle solid colours are available. White is undesirable although a small white mark on the chest is acceptable.

How much grooming?
Regular brushing of their short, coarse hair with a firm bristle brush, ten minutes twice a week, removes dead hair and dander. Cleaning and drying face folds prevents skin infection. Check feet for damage weekly as these are heavy dogs. Some slobber, so wiping the mouth regularly is necessary.

Do they make good pets?
This big, powerful dog has strong protective instincts and so is not a good choice for families with younger children. Some may be overly protective, placing visiting children at risk, and may misinterpret rough play from strangers. They can be excellent, companionable family pets if well trained by the right owner and in the right home environment. If left alone they will be unhappy but, being stoical by

● *This breed was designed as a formidable guard dog.*

nature, are more likely to sleep than become destructive.

What home suits them?
Large country homes with strongly fenced gardens are best, as Bullmastiffs can barge their way through flimsy fences and hedges. Shady trees are good because they do not tolerate hot weather. Bullmastiffs are unsuitable for small homes and apartments. They are quiet dogs, seldom barking, so are not likely to upset neighbours.

What sort of owner?
Bullmastiffs need strong, experienced owners to prevent this puppy becoming a real liability. Their fearless, guarding instinct needs ear socialisation, and firm direction from an owner prepared to put in the time and effort to make sure this protective character does not encourage aggressive tendencies.

How much exercise and stimulation?
While their exercise needs are moderate, they need regular daily walking to prevent laziness and health-threatening obesity. Puppies should have gentle walks gradually increasing in distance as they get older.

Friendly with other pets?
Bullmastiffs will be friendly but the size alone places small animals at risk. Early socialisation will be necessary to encourage family relations; closely supervise and take care when introducing puppies to prevent any adult dominance and aggression, which may occur with other same-gender dogs.

Is puppy training easy?
Bullmastiffs are strong and can be

Character Traits	Poor	Average	Good	Excellent
Attitude to other dogs		▓		
Quietness			▓	
Behaviour at home			▓	
Guarding ability				▓
Good with children			▓	
Ease of training		▓		
Obedience to owner		▓		

Time to maturity: 3.5 years
Male height: 63.5–69cm (25–27in)
Female height: 61–66cm (24–26in)
Weight: 45–60kg (100–133lb)
Average lifespan: 9–11 years

stubborn, so it may be moderately difficult. Training must start early and owners must be firm, patient and consistent, providing short, non-repetitive sessions using treats for motivation. Harsh training or bullying simply will not work.

● *Only 12 weeks old, this puppy is already large and active.*

Special puppy care?
Puppies should not be subjected to long walks until at least two years old to prevent damage to young bones and joints. Early socialisation is a must for Bullmastiffs.

Possible health problems?
Their size makes bone and joint conditions a serious problem. Other conditions they suffer from are hip dysplasia (malformation), eye problems, cancer and gastric problems (bloat), hypothyroidism (lack of thyroid hormone). This dog has a relatively short lifespan.

What can we do together?
Obedience, agility, tracking and carting.

Large dogs

Don't forget!
This breed is unsuitable for novice owners. Bullmastiffs need careful, early socialising and training to make good family dogs.

Bullmastiffs are a powerful breed and will demand a lot of time and commitment from the right owner.

Rottweiler

Rotties earned their name as the 'butcher's dog of Rottweil' from tradesmen in this thriving market town in southern Germany. This powerful breed was developed as a droving dog, to herd cattle from farms to market, and guardian, to bring their master and his cash (tied securely around their necks) safely home. Rotties have fearsome looks, and for their size are one of the strongest breeds of dog in the world. They have a powerful sense of duty, a natural guarding ability within their territory, and make excellent dogs for service work in military and police use, as therapy and guide dogs, and for search and rescue. Despite this, they have developed a bad reputation because of irresponsible ownership by unsuitable people. However, with good socialising and training they can be trained to an excellent standard. With proper discipline, love and attention, they are brilliant companions and family dogs.

Colour choices?

Black with tan markings above the eyes, on muzzles, cheeks, chest, under necks, on legs and base of tail.

How much grooming?

The low-maintenance coat needs brushing twice weekly to keep its healthy shine and remove dead hair. Female Rotties shed prior to being in season, males usually have a yearly seasonal moult.

Do they make good pets?

Happy, well-balanced Rotties are fabulous family dogs, but need an experienced owner to train them to be well disciplined. This is not a suitable dog to let children take responsibility for, or for novice owners. Walking them needs a strong, confident owner, who knows how to handle them with assurance. In the wrong hands, Rotties can be aggressive and dangerous, and sometimes a real liability.

What home suits them?

This is a versatile breed, but big dogs need space and Rotties are no

● *These two 7-week-old puppies still need time for weaning, socialising and learning some manners through play before they leave for a new home.*

exception. They are totally unsuitable as apartment dogs. Securely fenced gardens will be essential, whether in town or country, and access to plenty of space for walking will be needed daily, in all weathers.

What sort of owner?

Rotties need firm, consistent leadership from a calm, assertive owner, plus plenty of affection. Time has to be devoted to training and exercise. Owners will need experience of dog handling to take on this big character, and to provide sufficient physical and mental stimulation. Unsuitable for novices and child handlers.

How much exercise and stimulation?

Modern owners are unlikely to be able to offer the many miles of exercise that Rotties' ancestors would have enjoyed (anything up to around 65km/40 miles); however, several miles daily to maintain good health is ideal.

Friendly with other pets?

The dominant nature of the Rottie is likely to place other family pets at some risk, particularly same-gender dogs, even with excellent socialising and training. More docile Rotties, if introduced early enough, may do all right with supervision.

Is puppy training easy?

Formal training must be started early because Rotties are strong-willed, but training is extremely rewarding for conscientious owners who are calm and confident. Training will be easiest if it is non-confrontational, and owners earn respect by being firm and sympathetic using reward-based incentives.

Character Traits	Poor	Average	Good	Excellent
Attitude to other dogs				
Quietness				
Behaviour at home				
Guarding ability				
Good with children				
Ease of training				
Obedience to owner				

Time to maturity: 2 years
Male height: 63.5–69cm (25–27in)
Female height: 58–63.5cm (23–25in)
Weight: 41–54kg (90–120lb)
Average lifespan: 9–11 years

What can we do together?

Well-trained Rotties are successful in obedience competitions and herding trials, and they make good walking or jogging companions.

Don't forget!

In some European countries, Rotties have developed bad reputations and are placed on dangerous dog lists, and may be banned or unavailable.

Special puppy care?

Puppies should not be over-exercised to reduce their energy levels to avoid the risks of damage to young bones and joints. It is essential that training starts as early as possible with puppies to prevent dominance issues later. Bad habits learned as puppies will grow with them.

Just 8 weeks old and no bad habits yet!

Large dogs

● *A puppy's paw size is often an indicator of its future size when fully grown.*

Possible health problems?

Rotties can suffer from hip and elbow dysplasia (malformation), cruciate ligament and eye problems, and cancer. Obesity caused by a poor diet can lead to heart failure, arthritis, respiratory problems, diabetes and skin disease.

Bloodhound
Other names: Ardennes Hound, Flanders Hound

One of the greatest tracking dogs, Bloodhounds are second to none as scent hounds.

These dogs were developed in the 9th century from St Hubert Hounds in the Ardennes region of Belgium. The presence of Bloodhounds in Britain in 1066 is attributed to William the Conqueror. The Bloodhound's name alludes to its noble breeding as great care was taken with maintaining pure bloodlines. Later specimens formed hunting packs for French kings indulging their love of sporting pursuits. Present-day Bloodhounds look very similar to their ancestors, and are generally good-natured dogs and very affectionate. Though they are kind, gentle and pleasant companions, Bloodhounds are powerful dogs, ruled by their noses, and are difficult to walk off-lead as they follow any interesting scent and are often deaf to recall. They eat vast amounts, are destructive when bored, slobber copiously and bay loudly when lonely.

Colour choices?
Colours are black, liver, or red, all with tan. Some have small white markings on the chest, feet or tail tip.

How much grooming?
The short coat is low-maintenance, requiring brushing with a hound glove once weekly to remove dead hair and dander. Regular grooming reduces unpleasant 'doggy' smells. Their pendulous ears hang down into food bowls and collect mouth slobber and need cleaning daily. Expect slobber to reach the corners of the room when a Bloodhound shakes his huge head.

Do they make good pets?
These affectionate, calm, even-tempered, gentle puppies are companionable family dogs, although stubborn and difficult to train. However, size and a clumsy gait may accidentally bowl over or trample small children or frail elderly, so they are not ideal for all families. Bloodhounds can tend to be one-person dogs, and may not bond with everyone. Some are food-possessive.

● *Powerfully built for hunting, Bloodhounds are well known for their tracking abilities and will enjoy being out and about detecting scents to follow.*

What home suits them?
Unsuitable for small flats or houses, Bloodhounds need country dwellings with large gardens and long daily walks. Secure fencing will prevent them escaping to follow every new smell. Neighbours are unlikely to appreciate their magnificent, melodious voice.

What sort of owner?
Bloodhounds are best for owners with specialist breed experience who can harness their natural ability in tracking activities, and devote time to exercise and training. This puppy needs considerate owners who are not rough or insensitive.

How much exercise and stimulation?
Never over-exercise puppies, and start with graded exercise levels to prevent damaging bones and joints. Adult Bloodhounds require extensive walking. They feel compelled to follow interesting scents, so must be kept on long leads to prevent them disappearing, or they must be walked in safe and secure areas.

Friendly with other pets?
Very good-natured dogs, Bloodhounds get on well with most pets, although they can be clumsy and their sheer size may put small animals at risk.

Is puppy training easy?
Expect difficulty in training as they are stubborn and wilful, and complete obedience is unlikely. Owners should be firm, kind and incredibly patient in training – Bloodhounds are gentle and sensitive to every kindness or correction. Puppies and

Character Traits	Poor	Average	Good	Excellent
Attitude to other dogs				
Quietness				
Behaviour at home				
Guarding ability				
Good with children				
Ease of training				
Obedience to owner				

Time to maturity: 2.5years
Male height: 63.5–69cm (25–27in)
Female height: 58–63.5cm (23–25in)
Weight: 36–50kg (80–110lb)
Average lifespan: 9–11 years

adolescents may be more wayward until mature, and need consistent, sensible guidance.

Special puppy care?

Ensure puppies learn a recall to prevent them straying too far following scents, and never over-exercise to burn off their abundant energy. When choosing, avoid puppies with

A Bloodhound's large nose is excellent for scent detection when hunting.

excessive skin folds and runny eyes. Adolescents need firm, kind leadership.

Possible health problems?

Bloodhounds suffer from eye problems, ear infections, hip dysplasia (malformation), skin allergies, and gastro-intestinal problems (bloat). Not walking them within an hour of feeding can help. Bloodhounds also suffer from overheating.

Large dogs

What can we do together?

Quiet and gentle, but contemplating a life of fun and frolic.

Man-trailing is a favoured sport done in national working trials (Britain and Europe). Single Bloodhounds are used for hunting.

Don't forget!

Never use harsh treatment in training, as this ruins their gentle temperament.

● *This 6-week-old puppy already has head folds and large ears that will need attention.*

Bernese Mountain Dog *Other names: Bernese Cattle Dog*

This ancient breed, which dates back to Roman times, developed in the canton of Bern in Switzerland. Bernese are one of a small group of Swiss national dogs, and the best known and most popular outside Switzerland. They were bred to accompany Alpine herders and dairymen called Senn. Mainly farm dogs, Bernese were draught animals used to pull carts and to drive cattle from farms to Alpine pastures, and to haul small carts of goods to market for the weavers of Bern. Rescued from near extinction in the 19th century, Bernese gained recognition in the USA and Britain in the 1930s and have now achieved worldwide popularity. Noted as appealing family dogs, they are people-orientated, gentle, tolerant and loving companions, but these big, powerful, intelligent dogs can be demanding. Bernese need to be kept occupied, can be strong-willed, and are unsuitable for inexperienced owners.

Colour choices?

The distinctive tri-coloured coat is black with a white facial blaze and white on the chest, at the sides of the mouth, on the front feet and tail tip. A white 'Swiss cross' marks the chest with a kiss of white on the neck. Tan marks appear above the eyes, on the sides of the mouth, paws and chest.

● *Adult and a 14-months-old juvenile.*

How much grooming?

Bernese need brushing twice weekly. They shed all year with seasonal changes causing the heaviest moult. During heavy shedding, daily brushing to reduce hair fall helps. Bathing is usually done bi-monthly, sometimes more frequently.

Do they make good pets?

Bernese make excellent pets as they are very tolerant of children climbing over them during play, although puppies may be too boisterous for young children. Generally, Bernese make ideal family pets because they are placid, docile, good-natured, self-confident, affectionate and stranger-friendly.

What home suits them?

Unsuitable for small homes or apartments, Bernese need space outdoors, but do not like to live outdoors as they are very people-orientated, needing company most of the time. Very warm houses and gardens without shady trees are not good as the heavy coat makes overheating a problem.

What sort of owner?

These strong-minded, powerful dogs need experienced owners prepared to spend time on training them and keeping them occupied. They are unsuitable for novices or those without the time to devote to the relationship.

How much exercise and stimulation?

Outdoor dogs at heart, Bernese need activity and exercise. When motivated, they move quickly but have little endurance and tend to stay near their owner. Bernese are used to working and need stimulation in the form of activities such as hiking or herding. An hour's walk or a long hike will be appreciated by adults.

Friendly with other pets?

Bernese are boisterous puppies and need socialising sensibly, but otherwise they are mostly compatible with other pets and get along just fine. Some males can be dominant and may need corrective training to curb this tendency.

Is puppy training easy?

Training varies according to individual dogs, but usually moderate difficulty may be experienced. Owners must be firm, patient, gentle and consistent. Plan to train employing regular interesting, but short, sessions.

Character Traits	Poor	Average	Good	Excellent
Attitude to other dogs				
Quietness				
Behaviour at home				
Guarding ability				
Good with children				
Ease of training				
Obedience to owner				

Time to maturity: 18–24 months
Male height: 63.5–70cm (25–27.5in)
Female height: 58–66cm (23–26in)
Weight: 40–41kg (87–90lb)
Average lifespan: 6–8 years

Already large, even at 12 weeks old.

Bernese do have minds of their own, but they also have a willingness to please, and a sense of humour.

Special puppy care?

As puppies grow they need to be well socialised and owners must appreciate that they will grow into large, powerful dogs. Young puppies should not

● *Left alone, puppies may become destructive if bored. It is best to train them early to stay home alone or temporarily contained in a crate.*

be overwalked and exercise should be graded to avoid problems with developing bones and joints, particularly as young dogs in this breed can be prone to musculoskeletal problems.

Possible health problems?

Bernese have a high incidence of cancer. They also have eye problems, hip dysplasia (malformation),

Large dogs

hypoadrenocorticism (lack of a particular hormone), arthritis and musculoskeletal problems (cruciate ligament rupture is fairly common).

What can we do together?

Owners may enjoy non-competitive herding trials, cart pulling, agility and hiking. Some are used as therapy dogs and for police work.

Don't forget!

Buy only from reputable breeders producing stock that is health-checked.

Alaskan Malamute

One of the oldest dog breeds, Malamutes are the official state dog of Alaska. Bred as utilitarian dogs, they were used for hunting bears, guarding caribou herds, finding seal blow holes, hauling heavily loaded sledges and for companionship. Life was varied and their human keepers – an Inuit tribe called Mahlemuts for whom they were named – reputedly kept them for centuries. Arctic exploration increased interest in Malamutes because of their incredible ability to withstand impossible weather in frozen snow and icy blizzards. Today Malamutes are primarily used for sledge racing or hunting. Although not originally intended as family pets, they are affectionate, playful, gentle with children and attached to people. This is a powerful dog, who may be stubborn at times, and needs firm training. Their dignified nature and friendly demeanour make them excellent companions for sensible families.

Colour choices?

Either solid white, or grey shades through to black, or shadings of sable to red, with white markings on underbody, face, legs and feet. Face markings form a cap or mask, and coat shading is either mantled or splash coated.

How much grooming?

Brushing this dense coat twice weekly using a curry comb will usually suffice. Daily grooming during the annual seasonal shedding is necessary as hair comes out in clumps. These dogs seldom have a doggy smell.

Do they make good pets?

Not good guard dogs, Malamutes rarely bark, are not aggressive and are generally very sociable dogs. Size puts small children at a disadvantage as they may get injured accidentally, although Malamutes are patient and gentle. They need to be active and are likely to be destructive unless gainfully employed in active tasks such as sledding.

● *Malamutes are unsuitable for novices or owners who do not like an active life.*

What home suits them?

Malamutes dislike being shut in small spaces, and apartments or town life is unsuitable for them. Larger country homes with space to run and walk are best. Close neighbours may not appreciate their enjoyment of a good howl, so isolated or detached properties are a better proposition.

What sort of owner?

Malamutes are ideal for owners who enjoy being active, out in all weathers and involved in back-packing, sled-racing and hunting; this is not a dog for stay-at-home people. Owners need to be strong-willed and ready to enjoy a Malamute's company full-time.

How much exercise and stimulation?

Adult Malamutes will need in excess of 8km (5 miles) of walking daily, and still be happy for more. Walks near livestock should definitely be avoided – remember these dogs enjoy hunting and have strong prey drives.

Friendly with other pets?

Not ideal for keeping with other pets or even other dogs, because Malamutes have natural hunting instincts and are likely to chase smaller animals. Even those happy around other pets should be supervised carefully.

Is puppy training easy?

Malamutes are highly intelligent dogs but can be difficult to train. Owners who understand their independence, resourcefulness and natural behaviours and who can keep them motivated will be

Character Traits	Poor	Average	Good	Excellent
Attitude to other dogs				
Quietness				
Behaviour at home				
Guarding ability				
Good with children				
Ease of training				
Obedience to owner				

Time to maturity: 18–24 months
Male height: 63.5–71cm (25–28in)
Female height: 58–66cm (23–26in)
Weight: Up to 57kg (125lb)
Average lifespan: 12–15 years

successful, but natural obedience will be hard to achieve. Trainers should start early, show plenty of patience and no harshness. Definitely not a dog for owners with no experience of training strong-willed dogs.

● *Puppies will be ready for training from 8 weeks, which is this pup's age.*

Special puppy care?

Take care with puppies to build up walking activities gradually until puppies are fully developed at 18 to 24 months old, or young bones and joints could be permanently damaged. Early careful socialisation should help to control natural hunting behaviours. Signs of illness in puppies should be checked out immediately as some conditions in this breed affect young dogs.

Possible health problems?

Malamutes suffer from hip dysplasia (malformation), eye problems, epilepsy, kidney and congenital heart problems and skin disorders.

What can we do together?

Owners will enjoy recreational sledding (known as mushing), skijoring, bikejoring, carting and canicross with their dogs. Malamutes also enjoy weight pulling and agility.

Don't forget!

This is not a novice's dog and it needs plenty of time devoted to training and vigorous activity.

● *Not easy pets to train, but this puppy has strength, brains and beauty and is very appealing.*

English Setter *Other names: Laverack Setter (show specimens), Llewellin Setter (working).*

The oldest of English-bred setters, this breed was used in the 16th century for hunting game birds in wetlands and swamps. At a time when falconry hunting was popular, they approached game (usually woodcock) quietly, and crouched down to mark the position of the prey in a similar way to how they 'point' when working as gundogs today. The best known and most common of modern setters, they typify idyllic English country scenes with their quiet, elegant and hand-some appearance. More popular now as companion dogs, they have friendly temperaments, sociable natures, and are calm, gentle and fun-loving. English Setters radiate grace and intelligence from within a beautiful white and flecked coat. Given their hunting background, they can be energetic as youngsters. They are highly intelligent, need plenty of exercise and companionship, and are unsuitable for house-proud owners unable to cope with mud and mess, or wanting a quiet life.

Colour choices?
White coats with ticked or flecked colouring (known as 'belton'), without heavy patches. Colouring is black and white (blue belton), orange and white (orange belton), lemon and white (lemon belton), brown and white (liver belton), or tri-colour (black, tan or brown and white). Puppies are born white, colour develops later.

How much grooming?
Regular grooming removes dead hair, tangles and debris from their long, silky hair. Neutered pets need more grooming because coats become thicker and woollier. Ears need checking and cleaning regularly.

Do they make good pets?
Great pets and willing participants in family activities, but small children may be overwhelmed by their exuberance and bounce. However, with careful training and exercise they will suit most families. Some are one-person dogs, and have a habit of wheedling food and privileges from owners, which should be

● An orange belton adult, showing the smooth silky coat of a mature dog, that will need regular grooming to keep it looking good.

resisted. Smaller working specimens are usually more active than those specifically bred for show purposes.

What home suits them?
English Setters dislike being confined, preferring the outdoors where they can express their exuberance and vivacious nature, so country homes are better. Unsuitable for apartments, they do adapt to town living providing enough time is allowed for walking and periods of running free.

What sort of owner?
These are dogs for active owners, who enjoy walking reasonable distances in any weather. Owners must be firm, patient and provide plenty of company for these sociable dogs. Confidence and consistency is needed as they sense an owner's weakness.

How much exercise and stimulation?
Easily covering lots of ground – many miles when out running free – and dependable in any terrain, exercise is important for this dog. Space to run is essential, but a good recall is necessary to prevent them tearing off on an interesting solo expedition. Highly intelligent, they need mental stimulation to maintain happiness .

Friendly with other pets?
English Setters are very sociable and friendly with other pets, but early socialisation will teach them manners, such as not chasing the family cat or being too bouncy with small household pets.

Is puppy training easy?
Meek owners may find them rather wilful and stubborn in

Character Traits	Poor	Average	Good	Excellent
Attitude to other dogs				
Quietness				
Behaviour at home				
Guarding ability				
Good with children				
Ease of training				
Obedience to owner				

Time to maturity: 2.5–3 years
Male height: 65–69cm (25.5–27in)
Female height: 61–65cm (24–25.5in)
Weight: 25–30kg (55–66lb)
Average lifespan: 11–13 years

training; a firm, patient, gentle approach with handling is the best method. Reward-based, patient and repetitive training will normally pay dividends.

Special puppy care?

Puppies can be very demanding and are slow maturing, so training may continue for longer than for an average breed.

Lack of exercise, attention or stimulation are likely to trigger their potential for being tearaways and very destructive.

This puppy's watchful eyes are always on his owner.

Possible health problems?

English Setters can suffer from hip dysplasia (malformation), eye problems, hypothyroidism (lack of thyroid hormone) and skin allergies. Some puppies are born deaf.

Large dogs

What can we do together?

These very sociable dogs are ideal as walking, jogging and hiking companions, as well as being great all-round family dogs for playing.

Don't forget!

This is a boisterous, exuberant breed that needs plenty of walking and firm, authoritative training.

Blue belton puppy showing at 16 weeks early signs of flecks and ticking as his coat matures.

Giant and Standard Schnauzer

Standard Schnauzers originated around 500 years ago in the German provinces of Württemburg and Bavaria. Crossed with other breeds at different times during the early years of their development, both larger and smaller sizes were produced, although both conform to similar standards. They were used for vermin hunting or guarding farms, factories or homes. Schnauzers were not popular outside Germany until the 1950s, with little interest shown in Britain until 1960, although American owners took to them much earlier. Giant Schnauzers are more popular in Europe than the Standard. The versatility of Schnauzers is a bonus because owners can choose between sizes according to their circumstances. Schnauzers, particularly Giants, are strong-minded and benefit from experienced owners. Both sizes make excellent family pets when well trained but need experienced, strong-minded owners, not novices.

Colour choices?

Black, pepper and salt, or black and silver, with a dark mask. There are no white markings; pure white and parti-colour Schnauzers are bred, but not recognised as standard.

How much grooming?

Coats are high maintenance and need hand-stripping, not trimming, to retain the wiry top coat over a softer undercoat, although puppy owners may prefer trimming. A stiff brush through the coat daily starting when a puppy, combing the whiskers and legs and washing the beard after meals is best.

Do they make good pets?

Schnauzers are powerful, high-spirited, strong-willed, energetic and quite dominant; inexperienced owners or those with young children may find the larger Schnauzers rather a handful. Schnauzers are loyal and obedient, making excellent family dogs, but the Giant's size and dominant nature make them unsuitable for novice families or as first dogs.

● *Bred for working, not boring routine, Giant Schnauzers, and the smaller Standards, are energetic and high-spirited dogs.*

What home suits them?

Giant Schnauzers need a large garden and plenty of walking as they grow up to satisfy their exercise needs. Standard Schnauzers suit smaller homes and gardens better, but still need plenty of exercise. Giants, particularly, are unsuitable for apartment living.

What sort of owner?

Schnauzers' strong will and dominant nature demand owners who give firm discipline from the start, allowing plenty of time for socialisation and training to command loyalty and obedience.

How much exercise and stimulation?

Puppies need gently increasing amounts of exercise; Giant Schnauzers, particularly, should not be over-exercised as their bigger size and greater weight can give rise to bone growth problems. In adult life one to two hours a day may be needed, with a little less for the Standard. Schnauzers do not appreciate being confined indoors, and need regular vigorous exercise to stay fit, as well as extensive socialisation and stimulation for their mental well-being.

Friendly with other pets?

Schnauzers can be dominant, so introductions to other family pets need care, and socialisation must be accomplished early on. Male dogs can be overly dominant with other male dogs, so problems can occur.

Is puppy training easy?

Giant Schnauzers are powerful and strong-minded but learn quickly with the right training. Firm handling is essential to prevent them challeng

Character Traits	Poor	Average	Good	Excellent
Attitude to other dogs				
Quietness				
Behaviour at home				
Guarding ability				
Good with children				
Ease of training				
Obedience to owner				

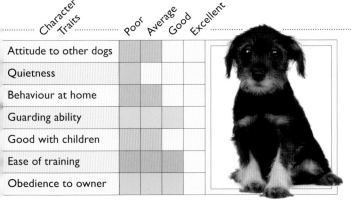

Time to maturity: 2.5 years
Height: Giant 60–70cm (23.5–27.5in) Standard 45–50cm (18–20in)
Weight: Giant 30–40kg (66–88lb) Standard around 15kg (33lb)
Average lifespan: Giant 10–12 years Standard 13–14 years

their owners for leadership. Training should be fun with some rewards, and without excessive repetition to prevent boredom. Calm, confident owners will be well rewarded. Plenty of puppy training through games and play is essential.

Special puppy care?

Puppies up to 12 months need less walking and more play to learn obedience. Plan exercise regimes with care to prevent damage to growing bones. Schnauzers are excellent guard dogs, but can bark a lot, so conditioning acceptable behaviour early on can help to prevent problems later.

Possible health problems?

Usually healthy, the Giant's size can cause hip dysplasia; other conditions include hypothyroidism, cataracts, epilepsy, skin problems and digestive disorders.

● *At 10 weeks old, these puppies are in need of regular stimulation, and will benefit from early socialisation and training.*

What can we do together?

Schnauzers are devoted, loyal companions, and ideal guard dogs. Well-trained dogs have been known to achieve success in obedience trials.

Don't forget!

This breed (particularly Giants) are dominant, territorial and very protective dogs, so you must start socialisation early.

Large dogs

Coat colour will mature as these puppies grow.

Dobermann *Other names: Dobermann Pinscher*

This very elegant, fast, fearless dog was developed by the German Louis Dobermann in the later 19th century as a vigilant guard dog to accompany him on his rounds when he collected taxes. As working dogs, Dobes have been used for farm activities such as herding, tracking, retrieving and as police dogs. During the Second World War the US Marines made the 'devil dog' its official war dog, although this fierce reputation belies their loyalty to their owner, traine obedience and trustworthiness with children. At heart, Dobes dislike conflict and can be emotionally sensitive. In the wrong hands, if badly trained or abused, they can be a dangerous liability. They are capable of being strong-minded, dominant and compulsive and are not for inexperienced or novice owners. Well trained, Dobes are stable, composed and sociable, performing to high standards of obedience with experienced handling.

Colour choices?

Choices are black and tan, blue and tan, brown and tan, isabella (fawn) and tan. Other colours may be available, but are not recognised for registration.

How much grooming?

The short coat is low maintenance and needs only a once-weekly wipe with a hound glove or stiff bristle brush to keep it glossy, in good condition and free of loose hair. Bathing is only needed occasionally.

● *In the right hands, Dobermanns are devoted and reliable family pets, although not for novices or young families.*

Do they make good pets?

When well trained, Dobes make excellent family pets, but be aware – training needs lots of time, patience and dedication. They enjoy being part of a family group, but need to be well supervised through their adolescent phase when they can be very rowdy with children, so Dobermanns are not recommended for homes with young children.

What home suits them?

Due to their size and active nature, Dobermanns need a fair amount of space and would not be suitable for small homes or apartments. They will need a well-fenced garden with plenty of space for playing and running free, with good walks nearby to release high energy levels.

What sort of owner?

Dobes need experienced owners who are fair, patient, strong-willed and confident leaders, and very committed to spending time on training. This is not a dog to leave alone for long periods of time, and some may become territorial if left to their own devices for too long. Novices and inexperienced dog owners would be well advised not to consider this dog as a choice for a companion.

How much exercise and stimulation?

Dobes are very active, energetic dogs, and will need at least two hours of exercise daily, plus time for running free. They need daily training sessions, and a variety of challenges to stimulate their highly intelligent minds.

Friendly with other pets?

Dogs reared from puppies should tolerate other household pets well but they need to be well socialised and introductions must be made when they are still puppies. Males may be dominant, and can be aggressive with each other.

Is puppy training easy?

A Dobermann is very intelligent and strong-willed, but also highly trainable in the right hands; owners must maintain calm, confident

Character Traits	Poor	Average	Good	Excellent
Attitude to other dogs				
Quietness				
Behaviour at home				
Guarding ability				
Good with children				
Ease of training				
Obedience to owner				

Time to maturity: 2 years
Male height: 66–71cm (26–28in)
Female height: 61–66cm (24–26in)
Weight: 30–40kg (66–88lb)
Average lifespan: 10–12 years

leadership, providing just the right challenge through reward-based training to prevent boredom. Owners must earn respect and be firm, calm, authoritative and patient.

Special puppy care?

Owners should buy from responsible breeders who view good temperament as a priority, and follow this up with early socialisation and good training.

Possible health problems?

Dobes have a higher than average incidence of health problems and are prone to heart defects, hypothyroidism (low levels of thyroid hormone), eye problems, von Willebrand's disease (a blood disorder), wobbler syndrome (spinal malformation), hip malformation and gastric torsion (bloat).

What can we do together?

Loving pet, walking companion, service dog and guard dog.

● *Playing with other dogs will boost confidence.*

Don't forget!

These are devoted, reliable dogs, but they can be dominant, so need good handlers and excellent training to achieve their potential as good companion dogs.

A 10-week-old puppy makes a typical play bow.

Irish Setter *Other names: Red Setter*

This breed was developed in 18th-century Ireland by crossing spaniels, setters and retrievers for use as working dogs. Originally red and white, the beautiful coat developed into its present chestnut red during the 19th century. Irish Setter popularity grew with their introduction to the USA and as their capabilities as hunting dogs, with tireless staying power, became evident. Early use in falconry for marking game birds later evolved into modern hunting practices, and they were trained as gundogs. Irish Setters are fun-loving and good tempered. Their racy lines and glamorous silky coats have ensured their popularity as eye-catching, affectionate dogs which fit well into family life. Puppies can be excitable, and in the wrong hands this big and boisterous personality may cause problems. Well trained, and with their boundless energy firmly focused through obedience, they have eye-catching beauty, are great companion dogs and ideal family pets.

Colour choices?
The colour is chestnut to mahogany red, with white on chest, throat, chin or toes allowed.

How much grooming?
The long, silky coat needs moderate care. The undercoat is thicker in winter with a fine top coat, and feathers on ears, chest, legs and tail. Brushing daily is best, while thicker parts of feathering need combing. Tying the ears back, or providing raised food bowls, helps to prevent them getting soiled with food.

● *A Setter's beautiful feathered tail wags constantly. It is even liable to knock ornaments off furniture at home.*

Do they make good pets?
Slower maturing than other breeds, puppies can be too boisterous for small children. They make super pets for families prepared to spend time and effort developing their potential, but can be exuberant. Well trained with plentiful exercise, they are great family dogs for active families.

What home suits them?
Best in country homes, Irish Setters need space, away from traffic, for off-leash running. Well-fenced, large gardens are essential. They adapt to town environments, but only if they are well exercised regularly.

What sort of owner?
Owners need to be patient with these slow-maturing, exuberant dogs, as they are not particularly obedient. Firmness, lots of exercise and consistent training are necessary to cope with their clown-like personalities. Irish Setters need constant company or they can become neurotic and destructive.

They should not be left at home alone, and thrive on company.

How much exercise and stimulation?
An active, exuberant breed, puppies are a real handful, needing plenty of exercise with long daily walks, and off-lead running. Working-stock Irish Setters can be more active than show-bred stock. Lack of activity and mental stimulation causes boredom, which may lead to high levels of destructive behaviour.

Friendly with other pets?
Wonderful family dogs, when socialised and trained, they get on well with children, other dogs and pets, and are happy greeting visitors to their home. The only problem may be their energy and enthusiasm for play, which is too boisterous for children and may overwhelm small household pets.

Is puppy training easy?
Irish Setters have a reputation for being difficult in training. They

Character Traits	Poor	Average	Good	Excellent
Attitude to other dogs				
Quietness				
Behaviour at home				
Guarding ability				
Good with children				
Ease of training				
Obedience to owner				

Time to maturity: 2.5–3 years
Male height: 66–71cm (26–28in)
Female height: 61–66cm (24–26in)
Weight: 25–34kg (55–75lb)
Average lifespan: 11–15 years

naturally work ahead of owners as working retrievers, and often play 'deaf'; positive reinforcement with good recalls works best. Eager to please and highly intelligent, they thrive on stimulation derived from walking and companionship. Giving them 'jobs' to do works well, and makes training fun.

training. Successful training may take longer than with other breeds. Walking reduces energy levels but build up exercise gradually to avoid damaging young bones and joints.

Special puppy care?

Puppies demand a lot of commitment as they need company and patient

Possible health problems?

Generally healthy, but Irish Setters can suffer from hip dysplasia (malformation), eye problems, epilepsy, cancer, hypothyroidism (lack of thyroid hormone), gastric torsion (bloat), von Willebrand's disease (a blood-clotting disorder) and intestinal problems.

Large dogs

What can we do together?

Hunting, and companionable walking and hiking.

● Already eye catching, this 11-week-old puppy will grow quite large. He will be constantly on the go as he gets bigger.

Don't forget!

Not for owners wanting instantly obedient puppies as training takes time and patience. Expect to find mud and leaves brought indoors on their paws and coats.

Akita/Japanese Akita-Inu

Other names: Japanese Akita, Akita Inu

Akitas are the largest of three Japanese Spitz breeds developed in the Akita prefecture on the island of Honshu. Their ancestors were medium-sized hunting dogs; later they were used for dog fighting and this dominant strain remains in their character. Facing near extinction during the First World War, interest in Akitas increased in recognition of their significance as part of Japan's national heritage, and was spurred by the introduction to America of new gene pools. American and Japanese Akita bloodlines have now diverged so much that they are recognised as two different breeds in Europe (Akita and Japanese Akita Inu). Akitas are impressively powerful, magnificent and dignified animals with strong characters and a natural guarding ability. They make excellent pets for people who enjoy close relationships with powerful dogs, but owners must be very experienced and confident in handling them.

Colour choices?

American Akitas are usually white, red, black, silver, grey, pinto (white and another colour) or brindle, with or without black masks. Japanese Akitas must be red, fawn, sesame, brindle or white, without black masks on the face.

● Powerful and independent, Akitas are great dogs when trained well, but they are not the right choice for a first-time owner.

How much grooming?

The thick coarse coat needs thorough brushing twice weekly. The twice-yearly heavy seasonal moult needs daily grooming to remove dead hair from the coat.

Do they make good pets?

Akitas are strong, independent, dominant and powerful, usually aloof with strangers, but affectionate in a family context. Akitas are not ideal around children, because their low tolerance of teasing or rough handling makes the risks too great.

What home suits them?

These puppies are better in country homes because they require space and a secure garden. Close supervision is needed near livestock.

What sort of owner?

Owners need to be very experienced with handling such large, dominant, powerful dogs. They need dedication to own dogs as challenging as this, and must spend plenty of time socialising, training and exercising their Akita. Owners must be committed to companionship with them, and prevent them from becoming bored or they will be destructive.

How much exercise and stimulation?

Akitas need a minimum of two to three hours daily exercise, preferably much more. Off-lead walking is definitely risky near livestock, and challenges from other dogs met by chance may cause Akitas to respond aggressively.

Friendly with other pets?

Akitas are highly dominant unless they are with the opposite sex of their own breed; same gender rivalry can be dangerous. They were originally bred to live and work alone or in pairs. Other small pets will definitely be at risk from the Akita's strong prey drive.

Is puppy training easy?

This breed has natural dominance and is very strong-minded, so training will be very difficult. It must start early, and socialisation even earlier . Bullying will not work – owners must be very patient and firm, using reward-based guidance to motivate these puppies to respond well. Badly trained Akitas are a liability and may cause legal problems as some countries list them as a dangerous breed.

Special puppy care?

Start training early, and make sure this puppy responds well and doe

Character Traits	Poor	Average	Good	Excellent
Attitude to other dogs				
Quietness				
Behaviour at home				
Guarding ability				
Good with children				
Ease of training				
Obedience to owner				

Time to maturity: 2.5 years
Male height: 66–71cm (26–28in)
Female height: 61–66cm (24–26in)
Weight: 36–59kg (80–130lb)
Average lifespan: 10–14 years

not get bored. Good discipline may only be possible through constant supervision, consistency and unwavering attention.

Possible health problems?

Akitas suffer from a wide range of health problems, but two significant ones are pseudohyperkalaemia (a rise in potassium levels) and immune sensitivity to chemicals in vaccinations, drugs, anaesthetics and insecticides. Owners contemplating this breed should question breeders closely and research the literature on other conditions affecting Akitas.

● *Docile-looking teddy bears at just 7 weeks. These dogs are described in Japan as 'tender in heart and mighty in strength'.*

What can we do together?

Today Akitas participate in obedience trials, good citizen programmes, tracking trials, agility competitions, weight pulling, hunting and showing. Some have also been used as therapy dogs.

Don't forget!

Unsuitable for novices, Akitas should only be considered by experienced owners.

Large dogs

Greater Swiss Mountain Dog

Greater Swiss Mountain Dogs are the oldest and largest of all mountain dogs. They are thought to have developed from breeding indigenous dogs with imported mastiffs. Large and heavy boned, their physical strength made them ideal dogs for Alpine farmers, and they were used for cattle herding, hunting and as heavy-duty draught dogs by farmers who needed a substitute for horses to pulling carts and wagons.

They were believed to have died out in the 19th century when mechanisation increasingly made them redundant, but sufficient stock was found in 1900 to resurrect the breed and rescue it from extinction. GSMDs are versatile, outgoing, keen to please, easily trained, and good guard dogs – although not territorial. Loyal, gentle and exceptionally good with children, they are relatively healthy compared to other large breeds. They make great family dogs, but size and exercise needs render them unsuitable for many family homes.

Colour choices?

There is only one colour combination: tri-colour coats of black, with symmetrical markings of tan/rust and white.

How much grooming?

The short, double, waterproof coat, which comes in varying degrees of thickness, is less oily than other breeds, and smells less doggy. GSMDs moult all year, with copious seasonal shedding twice a year. They require regular brushing using a rubber curry comb and a heavy-duty brush, with more grooming during heavier shedding.

Do they make good pets?

These are happy dogs with an enthusiastic nature. They are sociable, active, calm and dignified. They love people and are particularly good with children. They enjoy being part of a family provided that the family is active and enjoys exercise as much as the dog does.

What home suits them?

This breed will not suit many

These gentle giants enjoy being at the heart of a loving family.

● *Exercise is essential for this dog.*

modern homes, because they are simply too big. They need country homes or farms with space for plenty of exercise, or working pastimes, to keep them happy. Generally not house dogs, they prefer to be kennelled outside.

What sort of owner?

GSMDs are attentive, alert and active, and need owners who respect these qualities, and keep them gainfully employed in stimulating activities. Easy to train, they serve many useful purposes around farms and estates.

How much exercise and stimulation?

Plenty of exercise and stimulation is needed, usually 5–10km (3–6 miles) daily spread over two or three walks. These are natural working dogs, enjoying the stimulation of performing farm or carting tasks.

Friendly with other pets?

With very low aggression and a reluctance to bite, GSMDs are usually very accepting of other dogs and household pets. However, as with any breed, early socialising and sensible introductions to other animals will be necessary.

Is puppy training easy?

Training should use patient, reliable training techniques to teach manners and physical self-control. Owners must build trust through positive reinforcement, and avoid harsh methods. GSMDs can be stubborn and determined, and may be boisterous as youngsters; they should be socialised early, and provided with suitable activities as part of training.

Character Traits	Poor	Average	Good	Excellent
Attitude to other dogs				
Quietness				
Behaviour at home				
Guarding ability				
Good with children				
Ease of training				
Obedience to owner				

Time to maturity: 2–3 years
Male height: 65–72cm (25.5–28.5in)
Female height: 60–69cm (23.5–27in)
Weight: 48–64kg (105–140lb)
Average lifespan: 10–12 years

Special puppy care?

Some female puppies (but occasionally males too) are difficult to house-train, and lack bladder control until six months, or older. They tend to eat or lick anything, even if inedible, and need supervising to prevent them eating something harmful.

Possible health problems?

Longer living than some larger breeds, GSMDs can suffer from hip and elbow dysplasia (malformation), gastric torsion (bloat), spleen disorders, epilepsy, eye problems and osteochondrosis (degenerative joint disease).

What can we do together?

This puppy prefers a job to do, and most owners will enjoy participating with them in agility, carting, tracking, herding trials, obedience, weight-pulling, walking, hiking and backpacking. They are also used as drovers, draught and rescue dogs.

Don't forget!

With a limited gene pool due to low breeding numbers, potential owners should buy from reputable breeders who check for health problems.

● *Looking forward to a future as a loyal family companion, this 6-month-old puppy is already learning some basic skills in a 'Down'.*

Large dogs

Proper development of such a large dog as this depends on good nutrition and care.

Newfoundland

Newfies were originally bred by working fisherman in Newfoundland, Canada. Their exact origin is unknown, but they are thought to descend from Scandinavian 'bear dogs' imported into Canada by immigrants. Exceptional and powerful water dogs, braving rough ocean waves and storm tides, their importance for carrying ship's lines and fishing nets ashore was exceptional, as was their legendary ability to save human lives at sea. They were valuable working dogs on ships, and so their popularity spread. In England, their fame was bolstered by Sir Edwin Landseer who featured them in his paintings. Sweet-tempered, gentle, friendly and very loyal family pets, these huge dogs are expensive to feed, tend to drool, need a lot of space and shed copiously everywhere. They are unsuitable for many families as their size alone poses a problem. These puppies need space, constant company and loving, easygoing owners.

Colour choices?
Black or brown, with white splashes on chest, toes and tail tip. The only bi-colour choice (recognised as a separate breed in Europe) is 'Landseer' – white with black markings, the black head has a narrow white blaze, saddle, rump and upper tail.

How much grooming?
Newfies have flat, coarse, oily, water-resistant coats, with dense undercoats. Regular (twice weekly) brushing and grooming right down to skin is needed, removing accumulations of mats in undercoats. Extra grooming is needed during times of extreme moulting twice a year.

Do they make good pets?
The Newfie's temperament is near perfect, and his mellow disposition makes him one of the kindest dogs. Very affectionate, deeply attached to families, adoring children, they are watchful and capable of keeping children safe, but not territorial. Children must

● *These two fine specimens at 9 years (left) and 19 months are examples of the only bi-colour choice available. The Landseer was named after Sir Edwin Landseer, a fashionable London painter.*

not take advantage of their gentle nature or be allowed to ride on this puppy as it causes back problems

What home suits them?
These are huge dogs and only suitable for larger homes with well-fenced gardens. Puppies need space to accommodate their giant size when fully grown and, because of the heavy, hot coat, cool areas to rest, even in winter.

What sort of owner?
Newfies want to be part of the family, and owners must commit to spending time and attention on exercise and grooming. Ideal for including in family activities and trustworthy with children, they do need supervising with toddlers to prevent accidental injury. Unsuitable for house-proud owners because of potential mess indoors. Conscientious owners who groom regularly and provide suitable accommodation are best.

How much exercise and stimulation?
Moderate exercise is needed. Newfies are not active and an hour's walk a day is ideal, with opportunities for swimming. Puppies under 12 months should not over-exercised to prevent damage to young bones and joints.

Friendly with other pets?
Pleasant and docile, with early socialisation and proper introductions Newfies live successfully with other household

Character Traits	Poor	Average	Good	Excellent
Attitude to other dogs				
Quietness				
Behaviour at home				
Guarding ability				
Good with children				
Ease of training				
Obedience to owner				

Time to maturity: 2.5 years
Male height: 69–73.5cm (27–29in)
Female height: 63.5–69cm (25–27in)
Weight: 50–68kg (110–150lb)
Average lifespan: 8–10 years

pets. Take care with small pets to avoid the risk of this gentle giant treading on them.

Is puppy training easy?
Newfies reach emotional maturity around the age of two, and are sensitive and gentle. Training must start early because of their size, but is very easy. Firmness, patience and positive reinforcement and encouragement work best.

Special puppy care?
Puppies should be trained early to learn good behaviours and obedience in readiness for maturity.

Owners, who need physical strength, should lead-train them early to avoid being dragged along by an unruly adult.

Possible health problems?
Due to their size, the risk of hip, elbow and other joint problems is higher. Newfies also suffer from heart disease, lip fold infections and eye problems.

What can we do together?
Loyal, devoted and playful companions, they also enjoy carting (pulling a wheeled carriage) and swimming.

Don't forget!
Owners must give careful thought to how this puppy will be housed when fully grown.

● *Already quite large at 12 weeks, these three will need kind, patient owners who will provide the space they need to grow and develop.*

Large dogs

Greyhound *Other names: English Greyhound*

Considered the oldest breed in the world, Greyhounds are sighthounds and they were used for royal sports as early as ancient Egyptian times. Brought to Britain by the Phoenicians, their name is probably derived from 'Greek hound'. Greyhounds were popular with the aristocracy, and frequently appear on the crests of many noble families. Used for competitive sports such as hare coursing and speed running, they achieve a top speed of 72km/h (45mph). Greyhound racing, popular from around 1920, continues today, although mechanical hares are used now. Despite their aptitude for running and their sporting pedigree, Greyhounds enjoy a relatively sedentary life, preferring to be curled up on the sofa rather than actively running around. Their gentle, affectionate nature and adaptability make them ideal family dogs. It is often possible to rehome 3- to 5-year-olds who have been retired from track life.

Colour choices?
Around 30 recognised colours, all variations of white, black, fawn, red, brindle and blue, either as solid colours or combinations.

How much grooming?
The single, fine coat needs regular brushing with a hound glove to remove dead hair. After grooming, the coat should look clean, smell fresh and lie flat against the body.

Do they make good pets?
Greyhounds are loving, quiet and loyal, enjoying their owners' or other dogs' company. Gentle and loving with children, they appreciate respect and prefer quiet lives; children must learn to treat them kindly, although Greyhounds can be boisterous as youngsters. Greyhounds suffer from separation anxiety, and may be happier with another dog to share their days.

What home suits them?
Town or country homes suit Greyhounds equally well, with space to run off-lead daily. They

● *Well-muscled and powerful, this young dog is approaching maturity.*

are happiest lying in the warm, sleeping up to 18 hours, and don't need much space, often adapting to apartment living, providing they have daily exercise. High, secure garden fencing is necessary to prevent them escaping.

What sort of owner?
Gentle, sensitive owners who appreciate quiet, friendly and extremely loyal dogs will find these puppies calm, good-natured companions. Giving retired racing Greyhounds a second chance brings a sense of reward and pleasure. Owners who are patient, sensitive and firm with training are best suited to Greyhounds.

How much exercise and stimulation?
Greyhounds do not need miles of walking; they need short, sharp sprints rather than endurance running. They need to expend their energy, and youngsters need mental stimulation because they can be hyperactive and destructive. Lead-walking and free running in enclosed spaces, as they have no road sense, is ideal.

Friendly with other pets?
Some Greyhounds have high prey drives, and wear muzzles when out as they may chase small animals and cats, but this depends on individuals. Others live happily with other family pets, but all need socialising and introducing properly to prevent problems. Greyhound charities will advise owners on this.

Character Traits	Poor	Average	Good	Excellent
Attitude to other dogs				
Quietness				
Behaviour at home				
Guarding ability				
Good with children				
Ease of training				
Obedience to owner				

Time to maturity: 2 years
Male height: 71–76cm (28–30in)
Female height: 69–71cm (27–28in)
Weight: 27–32kg (60–70lb)
Average lifespan: 11–12 years

Finding his feet at 6 weeks.

Is puppy training easy?

Greyhounds are moderately easy to train, but need firm, gentle and sensitive training, as they are not naturally obedient. Teaching a good recall is essential for off-lead running, but with patience and time they are ready learners and willing to please.

Special puppy care?

Puppies feel the cold because their coat/skin is thin, with lean body fat, and they should wear coats in cold weather. Take care around small animals, as they sometimes chase and kill them. Puppy hyperactivity needs careful management to prevent injuries to skin or bones from jumping and running.

Possible health problems?

Hereditary illness is a low risk, and they may suffer from gastric

• *A family favourite and a gentle, dependable companion.*

torsion (bloat), eye problems, skin sores from lying on hard bedding or floors, and inability to metabolise anaesthetics or chemical products against parasites. Fractures and injuries from running can also be a potential risk.

What can we do together?

Gentle, loyal companions, racing and hunting. And just sitting with you.

Large dogs

• *Play will be important for young puppies like this.*

Don't forget!

Do consider giving a home to a retired Greyhound as they can make delightful pets. Teaching a good recall will be important.

Mastiff *Other names: English Mastiff*

Historically 'Mastiff' was a name given to any large heavy dog, but this breed is thought to be of old English origin from pre-Medieval times. Julius Caesar describes them as fighting against his Roman legions when he invaded Britain in 55 BC. Later they served as guards on the estates of the nobility. The breed almost disappeared in the early 20th century, but American enthusiasts managed to restore them as popular family dogs. Today's Mastiff is one of the heaviest breeds, but is most definitely a gentle giant. Although still retaining their territorial instinct for protecting home and family, Mastiffs are calm, dignified and very loving. Tending to be big 'softies' most of the time, they love to please and spending time in the company of their owner. With good training and socialisation, Mastiffs are peaceable, gentle and affectionate. Their size, however, may tell against them, as they need plenty of living space to be comfortable.

Colour choices?
Colour choices are apricot/fawn, silver/fawn, dark fawn/brindle, with black mask on ears, nose and around eyes.

How much grooming?
This short and close-lying coat needs brushing once or twice weekly to remove dead hair, but is otherwise low maintenance.

● Adults will happily sit around enjoying company, but need to be kept fit and given regular exercise.

Do they make good pets?
Good natured, calm and loving, while also courageous and protective, Mastiffs are docile and affectionate with their families and are prized for their patience. However, their physical size alone makes them unsuitable for young children, who may be unintentionally knocked over or injured by a wag of the powerful tail.

What home suits them?
This huge dog needs space and is best suited to country life; this is not a dog for small homes or apartments. Well-fenced gardens and spacious homes are suitable, but don't keep this dog permanently outside as they prefer being near their family for company.

What sort of owner?
Mastiffs need tolerant owners who accept that their size means more mess in the home. They are sensitive puppies, and owners must accept that companionship is a full-time commitment. This breed should be handled by physically fit and strong owners with experience of handling such breeds, as dogs can easily pull their handlers over.

How much exercise and stimulation?
Too much exercise and running are not recommended while puppies are young as this causes damage to bones and joints. Mastiffs would like to lead a couch potato life, but moderate exercise is necessary to maintain them in good health and to prevent laziness or obesity. Socialisation is of great importance with a dog of this size.

Friendly with other pets?
These very good-natured puppies get on well with most other pets providing early socialisation and good introductions take place. Size is a concern, as other pets could be injured in play, unintentionally trod on or knocked over. Some males can be aggressive with other males, so firm training is necessary to prevent this occurring.

Is puppy training easy?
Mastiffs are stubborn, but sensitive, and effective training of such a large dog is essential. Owners must be rigorous and firm, using short fun-filled sessions. Negative association are likely to upset them, so plenty of praise and rewards for good behaviour work best.

Character Traits	Poor	Average	Good	Excellent
Attitude to other dogs				
Quietness				
Behaviour at home				
Guarding ability				
Good with children				
Ease of training				
Obedience to owner				

Time to maturity: 2.5 years
Male height: 75–82cm (29.5–32in)
Female height: 70–76cm (27.5–30in)
Weight: 79–90kg (175–198lb)
Average lifespan: 8–10 years

Special puppy care?

Mastiffs are prone to calluses, arthritis and hygroma (inflammatory swellings on joints), so soft surfaces for sleeping on should be provided. Special diets are needed for puppies to ensure they maintain the correct growth rate, and do not become obese.

Possible health problems?

Not the hardiest or longest living breed, Mastiffs can suffer from hip dysplasia (malformation), gastric problems (bloat), heart disease, ligament ruptures, arthritis, hypothyroidism (low thyroid hormone levels), eye problems, obesity and allergies.

● *Encouraging activity using suitable toys and providing a healthy diet will prevent puppies from becoming overweight.*

What can we do together?

Ideal as a loving companion and vigilant guard dog.

Don't forget!

Given the size of this puppy, veterinary and food bills will all be large to maintain good health. Mastiffs are unsuitable dogs for owners who cannot cope with drooling, snoring and flatulence, which all comes on a large scale because of their size.

Even at 12 weeks these are big puppies.

St Bernard *Other names: Alpine Mastiff*

In the Great St Bernard Pass that links Switzerland and Italy, St Bernards became famous for saving the lives of people trapped in snow high in the mountains. Resident at St Bernard's Hospice in the Swiss Alps from the 17th century, they trained as pack dogs and guides, rescuing lost travellers and finding avalanche victims. Originally Saints were smooth-coated, but rough coats developed with the introduction of Newfoundland crossing to reduce inbreeding problems. The rough-coated variety is the most common today. Saints are devoted companions, but owners must realise that they are taking on one of the heaviest and strongest dogs in the world. This peace-loving, calm, gentle and friendly dog is sociable, devoted to his family and adores children, but his size and the quantity of good-quality food he needs is enough to put off the average family owner. However, they make fantastic pets in the right home.

Colour choices?

Red and white. Red ranges through shades of orange, mahogany brindle and red brindle, with white markings on muzzle, head, collar, chest, legs and tail tip. Black shading appears on face and ears, with ticking and spots.

How much grooming?

Rough-haired varieties have dense, flat-lying coats needing energetic daily brushing through to the skin. Poor brushing leaves dead hair underneath the top coat that is liable to form mats. Smooths need brushing weekly. Saints shed copiously and extra grooming is needed during moulting.

Do they make good pets?

Fantastic dogs, despite their huge size, Saints are extremely gentle and friendly, and are exceptionally tolerant of and careful with children. They make ideal family pets, providing they are cared for with correct feeding and exercise. They are devoted to their owners, and become distressed and destructive if left alone for long periods.

● *Growing completed, this gentle giant is a beautiful specimen of a mature dog.*

What home suits them?

Not recommended for apartment living, they need open space. They must be allowed sufficient room to move and lie down. When they settle down indoors, they rarely move far from their master's feet. Kennelling outdoors is not an option as they want to be near their family. Saints are happiest in larger homes, with well-fenced gardens to keep them secure.

What sort of owner?

Owners need to give time and attention and include Saints in family activities, and must be tolerant of drooling and copious hair shed during moulting. Saints are happiest in family company and are trustworthy with children.

How much exercise and stimulation?

Due to their huge size and fast growth rate, it is important that they receive the right amount of exercise and proper food or they could suffer bone deterioration. Adults are satisfied with a 3km (2 mile) walk daily, but puppy exercise should be limited to frequent short walks until the age of two.

Friendly with other pets?

Saints need socialising with other pets and visitors to their home to prevent any aggressive tendencies. Generally, they get on well with other pets providing proper introductions are made, but care is needed to prevent them treading on smaller pets.

Character Traits	Poor	Average	Good	Excellent
Attitude to other dogs				
Quietness				
Behaviour at home				
Guarding ability				
Good with children				
Ease of training				
Obedience to owner				

Time to maturity: 2–3 years
Male height: 71–91cm (28–36in)
Female height: 66–91cm (26–36in)
Weight: 50–91kg (110–200lb)
Average lifespan: 8–10 years

Is puppy training easy?

Their enormous adult size, and the need to keep adults under control, demands proper training, which must start early. Control must be asserted from the start. Owners should be firm, patient and consistent, as puppies are willing to learn but rather slow to respond.

Special puppy care?

Limit the length of walks for a puppy to prevent damage to young bones and joints.

Possible health problems?

Due to fast growth and heavy weight, Saints need correct feeding or health can suffer. Major health concerns are hip and elbow dysplasia (malformation), cancer, eye problems, epilepsy, dilated cardiomyopathy (heart muscle weakness) and eczema.

What can we do together?

Excellent companion dogs, devoted and loving their family, but not a great deal else!

Don't forget!

Expensive to keep, should never be left alone, not for the house-proud, but still amazing companion dogs.

Large dogs

At 9 weeks, this puppy will be happiest being at the heart of family life.

● *The circumference of puppies' necks will need regular monthly checking as they will need a bigger collar as they grow and put on weight..*

Deerhound

Deerhounds, even in early Celtic times, were highly prized by Scottish chieftains who exploited their power, speed and stamina for coursing or tracking red deer. Deerhounds have been used in Australia for hunting kangaroo and wild boar, and in North America for hunting wolves. Their ancestors were sporting dogs, used by both landowners and poachers, who appreciated their fast, silent hunting skills. As Scottish clans broke up and hunting practices changed, there was less need for the Deerhound's skills, but enthusiasts of the breed helped ensure their survival by developing an interest in showing them. The Deerhound's powerful body can cover rough terrain at tremendous speed, and they need plenty of space to exercise for their health and well-being. Although too big for the average home, these dogs are gentle, calm, dignified, well-mannered (maybe not as puppies) and devoted to their owners.

Colour choices?

Historically, Deerhounds were available in blue, brindle, fawn, grey, red and yellow. Modern dogs are now usually found in varying shades of grey, with a little white on the chest, toes and tail tip.

How much grooming?

The harsh, wiry coat is relatively easy care, but still needs to be brushed regularly, using a slicker brush and metal comb to remove tangles and dead hair. Underbody and facial hair is best tended gently with a comb. Bathing is needed only infrequently.

Do they make good pets?

This is a most attractive dog temperamentally: obedient, biddable, rarely boisterous, quiet and trustworthy. Deerhounds tend to attach themselves to one person and are extremely faithful to them. They are very trusting, never aggressive and love children – although puppies may be too boisterous for toddlers. Time commitments in maintaining

● *Most owners today would agree with Sir Walter Scott, who said about his own Deerhound Maida that they are 'the most perfect creature of heaven'.*

regular exercise for this active dog may need to be a consideration for parents with young children.

What home suits them?

Deerhounds should have access to well-fenced (fencing at least 2m/6ft high), large gardens for free play and running, with plenty of exercise space available close by for longer off-lead runs. Puppies may be destructive if energy levels are high and their exercise needs are not met.

Some may prefer to live outdoors, as they do not tolerate heat well.

What sort of owner?

This breed suits owners who want a devoted companion, are prepared to walk long distances, and happy to sacrifice their sofa for rests in between times. These are gentle dogs, happiest with patient, gentle, easy-going owners, who can expect unswerving loyalty and the close scrutiny of a warm, honest gaze in return.

How much exercise and stimulation?

Long walks of at least an hour, preferably over several miles, which should include off-lead running. Regional clubs organise lure coursing, which provides opportunities for exercising Deerhounds to satisfy their need to run free and fast.

Friendly with other pets?

Deerhounds are very friendly, especially with other sighthounds and most household pets, if well

Character Traits	Poor	Average	Good	Excellent
Attitude to other dogs		▨		
Quietness			▨	
Behaviour at home				▨
Guarding ability	▨			
Good with children			▨	
Ease of training		▨		
Obedience to owner			▨	

Time to maturity: 2.5 years
Male height: 76–81cm (30–32in)
Female height: 71–76cm (28–30in)
Weight: 36–54kg (80–120lb)
Average lifespan: 10–13 years

socialised as a puppy. However, supervision may be needed with unknown pets as they have a strong chase instinct and are very fast. The cat next door may be seen as fair game for a chase.

Is puppy training easy?

Training should be calm, consistent and gentle to achieve the best from Deerhounds; they are the most trainable of sighthounds, although the degree of trainablilty may not satisfy owners with an interest in obedience competitions. Their eagerness to please and quickness to learn are a pleasure for owners wanting a sweet-natured companion.

Special puppy care?

Young puppies should not be over-exercised too early, as their young bones and joints may be susceptible to injury. Starting to teach a recall early is essential, as these dogs love to run and may need to be reminded how far they can venture away from their owner when out and about.

Possible health problems?

The most serious problems this breed experiences are heart disease, osteosarcoma (bone cancer), gastric torsion (bloat), liver shunt (insufficient blood supply), hip dysplasia (malformation) and eye problems.

What can we do together?

Mainly ideal as companion pets, but owners may enjoy lure coursing or long country walks.

Don't forget!

Buy from a reputable breeder who has completed any necessary health checks on their stock, especially in relation to heart disease. Take care exercising puppies, as immature bones are at risk of injury if they are over-exercised.

● *Patient and loyal, these puppies want to be close to their owner, and are unhappy if left alone.*

All puppies look gangly at 5 months, and this one especially so!

Great Dane *Other names: Danish Hound, German Mastiff*

These magnificent, noble dogs are German in origin, and are often called the 'Apollo of dogs' because of their huge size and majestic bearing. One of several large mastiff-type hunting dogs, Danes were bred to run down and fight wild boar. English nobility later appreciated their abilities and elegant style, and they became popular carriage dogs. Subsequently, they were also found useful for guarding South African gold mines, which they did admirably. Today's Great Dane continues to display a superior, but gentle, countenance and is probably the most peace-loving of mastiff breeds, with a kind, affectionate, sensitive nature. They are good with children, but their size – some can weigh as much as a person does – does make the risk of injury to toddlers a possibility. If owners commit time to training and exercising them, however, and have sufficient home and garden space, these sociable family dogs will thrive on human company.

Colour choices?
Acceptable show colours are fawn with black mask, brindle, blue, black, harlequin (irregular patches of black and grey on white) and Boston (black or blue specific body patterns with white shirt front and socks). Merle or other advertised 'rare' colouring is unacceptable, and sometimes occurs in conjunction with deafness.

How much grooming?
Danes have easy-care coats, requiring occasional brushing with a hound glove or firm bristle brush over their smooth, short coat to remove any hair shed.

Do they make good pets?
Not all families appreciate Danes, because youngsters under three years old are boisterous and clumsy and small children or frail elderly may be knocked over or accidentally trodden on. However, with good early socialisation Danes make sensitive, affectionate and peace-loving companions for appreciative families.

● *The colour of this magnificent Great Dane is called harlequin.*

What home suits them?
Large and spacious homes with high-fenced, large gardens will meet Danes' needs. Apartments or small homes are definitely unsuitable, because these dogs need space.

What sort of owner?
Owners need physical strength, and reasonable experience to deal with Danes, who can be stubborn and strong-willed. They are, however, sensitive, gentle and kind and owners must spend time with these puppies, and be patient and confident in handling them.

How much exercise and stimulation?
Moderate exercise is needed, and for owners with sufficient land, Danes may exercise themselves. Some walking should be off-lead for free running, and exercise and stimulation can include agility training. Puppies under 18 months should have limited exercise because their immature bones and joints are at risk of damage.

Friendly with other pets?
Danes are friendly with other household pets, providing early socialisation occurs, and introductions are done properly. Their size and strength is a drawback, because of the risk that they may knock over other pets, or tread on them unintentionally. They are not usually aggressive, unless another pet irritates them.

Is puppy training easy?
These puppies are remarkably tractable, and responsive to command, but early training is best. Danes should be firmly handled,

Character Traits	Poor	Average	Good	Excellent
Attitude to other dogs				
Quietness				
Behaviour at home				
Guarding ability				
Good with children				
Ease of training				
Obedience to owner				

Time to maturity: 2.5 years
Male height: 76–86cm (30–34in)
Female height: 71–81cm (28–32in)
Weight: 45–60kg (100–132lb)
Average lifespan: 7–10 years

and treated with patience, kindness and positive reinforcement. Encouragement and praise works best; harsh, overbearing methods do not. It is important to prevent puppies from jumping up or sitting on people's laps – they may still expect it when fully grown!

Special puppy care?
Puppies grow fast and get large; do not over-exercise them because of risks to their growing joints. They need correct feeding at every stage, taking account of their eventual size and correct development. Soft bedding prevents painful rub sores from occurring on joints.

Possible health problems?
Danes are not long-lived dogs, and may suffer from gastric torsion (bloat), hip/elbow dysplasia (dislocation), tumours, hypothyroidism (lack of thyroid hormone), von Willebrand's disease (a blood disorder), heart disease (breeders can check this prior to homing) and sometimes damage their tail from knocks. Merle-coloured Danes suffer from deafness and blindness.

What can we do together?
Danes and their owners may enjoy agility and flyball and they make good walking companions.

Don't forget!
Buy from reputable breeders with longer-living stock, and choose recognised colours, not merle colours which carry health risks.

● *This litter of 5-week-old puppies shows the range of colours available for owners to choose from.*

Large dogs

Designer dogs

Designer dogs have pure-breed ancestry from two pedigree parents, but they are cross breeds and cannot be registered with the Kennel Club. Many owners find them loveable, but determining adult form in terms of eventual size, health and coat quality can be difficult when choosing puppies. Both parent breeds should appeal to families before a choice of puppy is made.

Yorkiepoo

Other names: Yo-Yopoo, Yorkapoo, Yoodle

Character Traits	Poor	Average	Good	Ex
Attitude to other dogs				
Quietness				
Behaviour at home				
Guarding ability				
Good with children				
Ease of training				
Obedience to owner				

Time to maturity: 18 months
Male height: 18–38cm (7–15in)
Female height: 18–38cm (7–15in)
Weight: 2–6kg (4–14lb)
Average lifespan: 10–15 years

A recent addition to designer selections, Yorkshire Terrier/Poodle crosses appeared in the early 2000s. They have affectionate dispositions and hypoallergenic coats.

Colour choices?

Colours vary from tan to black to white and brown.

How much grooming?

Yorkiepoos have smooth, fine coats of silky, wavy hair which requires brushing daily to keep it free of mats and tangles. Most coats are hypoallergenic, but not all.

Do they make good pets?

They are very confident, love people, and are generally fun-loving and willing to play. Not suitable for young children, Yorkiepoos make excellent companions for older children or the elderly. Barking is a favourite occupation, but can be stopped with training.

What home suits them?

The small size lends itself to apartments and small homes.

How much exercise and stimulation?

Short daily walks and romps suffice, but they can go longer as they have plenty of energy.

Is puppy training easy?

Yorkiepoos are highly intelligent, quick learners so need early training. They excel in agility, obedience, therapy dog training and enjoy performing tricks. Training must be sensitive and use positive reinforcement as strict methods only make them stubborn.

Possible health problems?

Epilepsy, patellar luxation (kneecap dislocation), liver shunt, Legg-Perthes syndrome (hip deformity), hypothyroidism (low thyroid levels), Addison's disease (an endocrine disorder) and atopic dermatitis (skin allergy)

● *This 6-week-ol puppy cou inherit any colour variations from his parent*

Morkie
Other names: Yorktese, Malkie

Time to maturity: 2 years
Male height: 20–30cm (8–12in)
Female height: 20–30cm (8–12in)
Weight: 1.5–4.5kg (3–10lb)
Average lifespan: 12–15 years

This Maltese/Yorkie cross can exhibit a wide variety of looks and personality traits. Early training develops their potential as delightful and obedient companions.

Character Traits	Poor	Average	Good	Excellent
Attitude to other dogs			▓	
Quietness		▓		
Behaviour at home			▓	
Guarding ability		▓		
Good with children			▓	
Ease of training			▓	
Obedience to owner			▓	

Colour choices?
Most are black and tan but apricot, white, brown and Maltese colouring is also seen.

How much grooming?
Coats are long, very soft, and straight. They need brushing two or three times weekly, and hair around the eyes should be cleaned. Ears are dropped or erect, and need cleaning weekly.

Do they make good pets?
Loyal, loving but sometimes bossy, this mix of two breed personalities can be difficult to predict. They should not be spoiled or over-indulged. They often crave attention and may suffer from separation anxiety. Usually ideal for the elderly providing they can be exercised adequately.

What home suits them?
Morkies usually adapt well to apartment living.

● *Take care with young puppies as they are vulnerable to injury if dropped.*

How much exercise and stimulation?
Highly energetic, Morkies love playing, running and some walking, and need exercise to prevent boredom, obesity and poor health. Socialisation brings out their best, encouraging friendliness to strangers and other pets.

Is puppy training easy?
These puppies are intelligent and fearless, and are easy to train. But they can be stubborn, so need patience.

Possible health problems?
Hydrocephalus (water on the brain), patellar luxation (dislocating kneecaps), tracheal collapse (obstruction of the airway), eye problems and heart disease. Avoid obesity by correct feeding.

Looking cute and cuddly, and easy to spoil!

Cavapoo *Other names: Cavadoodle*

Time to maturity: 2 years
Male height: 20–36cm (8–14in)
Female height: 20–36cm (8–14in)
Weight: 4.5–8kg (10–18lb)
Average lifespan: 10–14 years

Originating in the USA in around 1950 by crossing Cavalier King Charles Spaniels and Poodles. Cavapoos have a gentle nature, and luxurious coats.

Character Traits	Poor	Average	Good	Exc
Attitude to other dogs				
Quietness				
Behaviour at home				
Guarding ability				
Good with children				
Ease of training				
Obedience to owner				

Colour choices?

Usually multi-coloured, but mostly light/red-brown, black or white.

How much grooming?

The most distinctive feature is their low-shed, hypoallergenic, luxurious coats, which can be either curly or feathered. Brushing and combing is a daily commitment to remove tangles and mats, and prevent skin problems. Professional trimming several times a year is best as coats can form dreadlocks.

Do they make good pets?

Cavapoos are good-natured, gentle, loving and playful with children and other pets.

They frequently demand attention, are unhappy if left on their own, but make poor guard dogs.

What home suits them?

Ideally sized for small homes with back yards or apartments, but they still need exercise. Their natural curiosity encourages jumping onto furniture.

● *A puppy at 8 weeks with his mother.*

How much exercise and stimulation?

Cavapoos enjoy, but do not crave, exercise, and need stimulation through activity and play.

Is puppy training easy?

Highly intelligent, Cavapoos will excel at obedience if started early.

Possible health problems?

Parent breeds have several health issues. Cavapoo problems include ear, eye and heart disorders, hypothyroidism (low thyroid levels), syringomyelia (fluid in the spinal cord), epilepsy, hip dysplasia (malformation and von Willebrand's disease (a blood disorder).

Shihpoo

Other names: Pooshih

Time to maturity: 2 years
Male height: 20–38cm (8–15in)
Female height: 20–38cm (8–15in)
Weight: 3–4.5kg (7–10lb)
Average lifespan: 14–17 years

This Shih Tzu/Poodle cross was bred for its companionable quality, cute looks, low-shedding coat and small size. It is ideal as a loving domestic pet.

Character Traits	Poor	Average	Good	Excellent
Attitude to other dogs		▓		
Quietness	▓			
Behaviour at home			▓	
Guarding ability		▓		
Good with children		▓		
Ease of training				▓
Obedience to owner				▓

Colour choices?

Any colour or combination of colours are usually available.

How much grooming?

Shihpoos' coats are long, wavy and low-shedding. They need daily brushing and trimming as necessary. Bathing is needed only occasionally as these are clean dogs. Clean ears and eyes regularly.

Do they make good pets?

Intelligent, alert, playful, friendly and affectionate lap dogs, they are always ready to love someone. Not ideal for small children, but they are good family companions, friendly with other pets and courageous guard dogs, although they can be rather yappy.

What home suits them?

These small dogs will suit apartment living or homes in towns or countryside, as long as they have company to keep them happy.

How much exercise and stimulation?

Shihpoos need moderate exercise usually adapting well to their owners' lifestyle. They enjoy a stroll and playtime daily.

Is puppy training easy?

Very easy to train, Shihpoos are quick to learn and enjoy showing off their tricks; some do well in agility and obedience. Training to stop them barking may be needed.

Designer dogs

Possible health problems?

Ear and breathing problems, poor tolerance to extremes of heat and cold.

● *The coats of these 8-week-old puppies will need regular daily attention.*

Cavachon

Time to maturity: 2 years
Male height: 25–32cm (10–12.5in)
Female height: 25–32cm (10–12.5in)
Weight: 5.5–8kg (12–18lb)
Average lifespan: 10–12 years

Originating in the USA, these Cavalier King Charles Spaniels and Bichon Frise crosses are popular for their intelligent, loving nature and cute, teddy bear looks.

Character Traits	Poor	Average	Good	Exce
Attitude to other dogs				
Quietness				
Behaviour at home				
Guarding ability				
Good with children				
Ease of training				
Obedience to owner				

Colour choices?
White and/or shades of brown, with mixed patches, spotting and flecking of these colours.

How much grooming?
Cavachons shed their puppy coats as the adult coat grows in. It is best to groom early, removing tangles with a comb. Adults may be non-shedding, although some have seasonal changes. This luxurious, long, curly coat needs daily attention, with regular baths once/twice month. Professional trimming occasionally required, although some puppy owners learn to do this themselves.

Do they make good pets?
Cavachons are great family dogs, good with children and other pets. Loving, affectionate and sociable, but they maybe not the best guard dog.

What home suits them?
Their size makes them ideal for most homes and apartments, and they can be trained to stay within garden boundaries.

How much exercise and stimulation?
Active and alert, Cavachons enjoy daily walks with playtime, and owners who enjoy teaching them tricks.

Is puppy training easy?
Training is easy, as they are intelligent and biddable, and often good at obedience activities.

Possible health problems?
Both parent breeds have health issues, so ear, eye and heart problems are possible, as are syringomyelia (fluid filled cavities within the spinal cord) and hypothyroidism (lack of thyroid hormone).

● *This charming little teddy-bear-like dog (12 weeks) may not always have a non-shedding coat, and will need grooming daily with some trimming as necessary.*

Make training fun for this puppy as he will respond best to stimulating methods of learning.

Cockerpoo

Other names: Cockapoo, Spoodle

Time to maturity: 2.5 years
Male height: 25–38cm (10–15in)
Female height: 25–38cm (10–15in)
Weight: 5.5–11kg (12–24lb)
Average lifespan: 14–15 years

Cockerpoos result from hybrid crosses between American or English Cockers and Poodles. Bred in the USA since 1950, they even have their own species clubs.

Character Traits	Poor	Average	Good	Excellent
Attitude to other dogs				
Quietness				
Behaviour at home				
Guarding ability				
Good with children				
Ease of training				
Obedience to owner				

Colour choices?

Solid colours of black, tan/buff, red, brown, brindle, sable, silver, cream, white and occasionally merle. Some are white with patches of colour, other spots or ticking (freckles).

How much grooming?

Most have coats somewhere between Poodle and Cocker type, although they may be similar to either parent. All coats need daily grooming using brushes and wide-toothed combs, and monthly bathing.

Do they make good pets?

Popular as family pets, they combine the Cocker's outgoing personality with a Poodles' reduced coat shedding. They can inherit their personality from either parent breed, and generally are intelligent, friendly, playful and loving pets.

What home suits them?

Active and versatile, Cockerpoos prefer homes with gardens, but will adapt quite readily to apartment living.

How much exercise and stimulation?

Cockerpoos do best with regular daily exercise, and intelligent puppies need stimulation through play, walks, training, flyball or agility.

Is puppy training easy?

These puppies love to please, and with early training should do well.

Possible health problems?

Robust and healthy, but they can have luxating patellas(dislocating kneecaps), eye problems and are susceptible to ear infections.

● *These two 7-week-old puppies are just growing their longer coats, but it will be some time before it becomes clear if they have inherited hypoallergenic coats.*

Puggle

Time to maturity: 2 years
Male height: 33–38cm (13–15in)
Female height: 33–38cm (13–15in)
Weight: 8–14kg (18–30lb)
Average lifespan: 10–15 years

One of the three most popular designer dogs, Puggles are Beagles crossed with Pugs. They were developed in 2000 for owners wanting a distinctive type of dog.

	Poor	Average	Good	Excel
Attitude to other dogs				
Quietness				
Behaviour at home				
Guarding ability				
Good with children				
Ease of training				
Obedience to owner				

Colour choices?

Fawn, red, tan, lemon, black or various parti-colours.

How much grooming?

The short, dense undercoat and longer topcoat shed, and so need weekly grooming. Cleaning and drying eyes and skin folds daily prevents the onset of infections; bath as and when needed.

Do they make good pets?

Good-natured, sociable, intelligent puppies, Puggles are playful, cuddly, love people and are friendly with other pets. Their hunting instincts may put smaller pets at risk.

What home suits them?

They adapt to most homes, or apartments if well-exercised, but Puggles bark or howl a lot, and are unsuitable for working owners.

● *Puggles have a tendency to beg for food leading to overeating. Its Beagle parent is prone to this problem, so this puppy should not be overindulged or obesity may result.*

How much exercise and stimulation?

Puggles need good daily walks with play time; exercise and agility prevents them becoming unruly. Walk them on a lead, because Beagle instincts may ignore recalls in preference to interesting smells. Good stimulation and socialisation produces well-rounded dogs.

Is puppy training easy?

Neither parent breed is easy to train. Intelligent but stubborn, Puggles respond to positive reinforcement training using rewards, play and lots of praise. Patience will be essential in training a Puggle to achieve good and consistent results.

Possible health problems?

Breathing problems (if mostly Pug-like), eye problems (cherry eye), hypothyroidism (low thyroid levels), patellar luxation (dislocating kneecaps), hip dysplasia (malformation), epilepsy, allergies.

Schnoodle

Time to maturity: 2 years
Standard height: 38–66cm (15–26in)
Standard weight: 9–34kg (20–75lb)
Miniature height: 25–30cm (10–12in)
Miniature weight: 3–4.5kg (6–10lb)
Average lifespan: 10–15 years
Based on largest and smallest parent sizes

Currently rising to canine stardom, this Schnauzer/Poodle cross is a popular family dog in three sizes, with a low shed coat, and endearing personality.

Character Traits	Poor	Average	Good	Excellent
Attitude to other dogs			■	
Quietness		■		
Behaviour at home			■	
Guarding ability			■	
Good with children			■	
Ease of training				■
Obedience to owner			■	

Colour choices?

Black, grey, silver, brown, apricot, sable, black with white or tan and parti-colours.

How much grooming?

The non-shedding coats are either soft and silky, needing daily brushing, or wiry, needing less brushing; both need trimming bi-monthly. Clean the ears weekly.

Do they make good pets?

Schnoodles are good guard dogs, love car rides, and are clever, friendly, fun-loving, good with children and great family pets.

At 8 weeks old this little Schnoodle is developing a thicker coat that will need brushing daily.

Devoted and affectionate to owners, and friendly towards other pets, they can suffer separation anxiety if left on their own.

What home suits them?

Schnoodles adapt to most locations, but eventual size matters as small dogs suit apartment living, while larger dogs prefer homes with gardens or countryside locations and the opportunity for plenty of activity.

How much exercise and stimulation?

Schnoodles need daily exercise, activity and stimulation.

Is puppy training easy?

Schnoodles are naturally protective, strong-willed, excitable and active, not unlike their parent breeds. Easily trained, they excel at obedience, agility and flyball, and make ideal therapy dogs.

Designer dogs

Excitable and active, training is essential.

Possible health problems?

Addison's disease (an endocrine disorder), gastric torsion, diabetes, epilepsy, Legg-Perthes syndrome (hip deformity), kneecap dislocation, eye disease, ear and anal gland infections.

● *Smaller puppies at this age are likely to be miniatures, but buyers should check the parents' heights.*

Labradoodle

Time to maturity: 2 years
Standard height: 53–63.5cm (21–25in)
Standard weight: 23–30kg (50–66lb)
Miniature height: 36–42cm (14–16.5in)
Miniature weight: 7–13kg (15.5–28lb)
Average lifespan: 12–14 years
Based on largest and smallest parent sizes

A Labrador Retriever and Standard or Miniature Poodle cross that was first bred in 1955. Originally bred as guide/therapy dogs, they are popular family pets.

Character Traits	Poor	Average	Good	Excel
Attitude to other dogs			■	
Quietness		■		
Behaviour at home			■	
Guarding ability	■			
Good with children				■
Ease of training				■
Obedience to owner			■	

Colour choices?

Black, chocolate, cafe, gold, apricot, red, silver, chalk, cream and various parti-colours.

How much grooming?

Labradoodle coats vary between wiry to soft, and can be straight, wavy or curly. Grooming daily is best, using brush and combs suitable for the coat texture. They may have hypoallergenic, non-shedding coats, but not always. They simply shed less, and have less odour. Professional grooming may be necessary.

Do they make good pets?

These are friendly, energetic, enthusiastic, good-natured puppies, and ideal family dogs. Often too rough for small children, their good natured boisterousness is usually fine with other pets.

What home suits them?

Labradoodles are unsuitable for apartment living; homes with gardens are preferable.

How much exercise and stimulation?

Dependent on size, but around one hour daily, and stimulation levels need to be high. Puppies are destructive if bored.

Is puppy training easy?

Sensible, patient and consistent reward-based training is the best approach with this eager-to-please, easy-to-train, intelligent puppy.

Possible health problems?

Addison's disease (an endocrine disorder), hip dysplasia (malformation) and eye problems (research indicates higher incidences in Labradoodles than in their parents). Ear infections may be frequent.

● *At 9 weeks these puppies are ready to go home with new owners.*

Goldendoodle

Time to maturity: 2 years
Male height: 61–66cm (24–26in)
Female height: 56–58.5cm (22–23in)
Weight: 20–32kg (45–70lb)
Average lifespan: 12–14 years

Goldendoodles were developed in Australia and North America as guide dogs for owners prone to allergies by crossing Poodles and Golden Retrievers.

Character Traits	Poor	Average	Good	Excellent
Attitude to other dogs				
Quietness				
Behaviour at home				
Guarding ability				
Good with children				
Ease of training				
Obedience to owner				

Colour choices?

Black, sandy, gold, red, apricot, cream or white.

How much grooming?

Similar coats to either parent, and some in-between. Low- or non-shedding coats require daily grooming with slicker brushes and wide-toothed combs. Use slicker or bristle brushes on shedding coats. Ears need regular cleaning.

Do they make good pets?

Very person-orientated and affectionate with owners and other pets, Goldendoodles are calm and good natured, great with children and good family pets. They are used as therapy/assistance dogs, and suitable for allergy sufferers, although this quality depends on coat type.

What home suits them?

Goldendoodles are usually crossed with standard-height parents (occasionally with Miniature Poodles), but all usually suit larger homes with gardens and walking close by.

How much exercise and stimulation?

These active dogs require daily walks, with stimulation through play and activities such as agility, obedience and bird hunting.

Is puppy training easy?

Highly intelligent, these dogs are very trainable.

● *Puppies like this 7-week-old have coats more like their Poodle parent.*

Possible health problems?

Hip dysplasia (malformation), inherited eye problems, von Willebrand's disease (a blood disorder) and ear infections.

Index

Picture Credits

Perry Harmon: 70tl, 103b.
hjschneider: 141t.
Pavel Hlystov: 18bl, 56c.
horvathta: 181t.
Darren Hubley: 93t.
Tereza Huclova: 156tl.
Anna Hudorozkova: 44cl.
Eric Isselée: 1, 3 (GSP), 5t,
  5b, 6, 7, 11 (puppy eating),
  16t, 18bc, 20b, 23t
  (puppy), 26tl, 26c, 27t,
  28tl, 28c, 29t, 29b, 33b,
  36tl, 37bl, 37br, 38c, 39b,
  41t, 47t, 48tl, 50c, 51t,
  60tl, 60c, 62tl, 63t, 63b,
  64cl, 66tl, 67t, 67b, 68tl,
  69t, 71b, 72tl, 72c, 73t,
  75t, 75b, 80tl, 80c, 81t,
  83b, 84c, 86tl, 86c, 87br,
  88tl, 88c (wire), 89t, 89cl,
  89br, 92c, 94c, 95b, 96tl,
  97t, 97b, 105t, 106tl,
  121br, 122tl, 122c, 124tl,
  126tl, 127t, 131t, 131bl,
  131br, 136c, 137c, 137bl,
  138tl, 144c, 147, 148tl,
  149t, 149cl, 149b, 150c,
  158c, 159cl, 159b, 161t,
  161bl, 161br, 166c, 168c,
  170tl, 170c, 179t, 179b,
  183t, 182c, 188c, 189t,
  194tl, 198c, 200c, 201bl,
  204c, 205t, 208c.
Jagodka: 31b, 79b, 84tl, 96c,
  107t, 107b, 110c, 111b,
  112c, 113cr, 113b, 115t,
  118tl, 118c, 120tl, 121t,
  148c, 189b.
Marina Jay: 31t, 106c, 167t.
Petr Jilek: 182tl, 183b.
Jody: 110tl.
Gail Johnson: 52tl.
JStaley401: 90tl, 212t, 213t,
  213b, 216b.
Dmitry Kalinovsky: 142c.
Sergey Khachatryan: 168tl.
Vasiliy Khimenko: 88c
  (smooth).
Crystal Kirk: 18r, 202tl, 203t.
Dan Kosmayer: 218b.
Paul Krugloff: 11 (wet food).

Pelevina Ksinia: 174c.
Lilia Kulianionak: 35b, 135b.
Oksana Kuzmina: 21t.
Kuznetsov Alexey: 184tl,
  185t.
Erik Lam: 52c, 54tl, 54c, 58c,
  59t, 74tl, 74c, 82c, 87cl,
  91t, 101, 104tl, 108t,
  109cl, 109br, 114tl, 114c,
  116c, 134tl, 136tl, 140c,
  151t, 172c, 180c, 186c,
  196tl, 196c, 197b, 208tl,
  209b, 220t.
LauraVI: 34tl.
Sergey Lavrentev: 40tl, 65t.
Lebedinski Vladislav: 120c.
Lee319: 164t.
Maja H.: 22l.
Makarova Viktoria: 188tl.
Reha Mark: 102tl.
mariait: 79t.
Dorottya Mathe: 47b.
Medvedev Andrey: 49b.
mj007: 117t.
Andrii Muzyka: 78tl.
Ekaterina Nikitina: 53t.
Igor Normann: 82tl.
Okssi: 30tl.
Olga_i: 78c.
Andrey Perminov: 38tl.
Perrush: 70c.
Photobac: 185cl, 185br.
Pongphan R.: 42c.
poutnik: 94tl.
PozitivStudija: 61t.
Quayside: 165t, 214t.
Raffalo: 187t.
Reddogs: 44tl, 193b.
Julia Remezova: 42, 62c,
  144tl, 198tl, 199b.
Robynrg: 58br, 59b.
Rtimages: 217t.
Boris Ryaposov: 23t
  (woman).
Rybin: 71t.
Carlos E. Santa Maria: 46c.
Luis Santos: 215t.
Rena Schild: 192, 219t.
Susan Schmitz: 130c, 132c,
  160c, 202c.
Scorpp: 37t, 42tl.

W. Scott: 117b.
Viorel Sima: 33t, 83t, 150tl,
  151b, 154tl.
sima: 195b.
Snaprender: 76tl.
Nikola Spasenoski: 49t.
steamroller_blues: 64tl,
  195t.
Fernc Szelepcsenyi: 15tr.
takayuki: 3 (woman), 10br
  (woman).
tandemich: 143t.
Katsai Tetiana: 174tl.
Jeff Thrower: 152c.
Tihis: 155t.
Vitaly Titov and Maria
  Sidelnikova: 15br.
Toloubaev Stanislav: 184c,
  194c.
Lars Tuchel: 190tl.
April Turner: 11 (puppy
  head), 11 (dried food).
Nikolai Tsvetkov: 30c, 34c,
  167b.
Utekhina Anna: 35t, 56tl,
  77t, 77b, 137t, 137br,
  201t, 201br.
Rob van Esch: 159t.
Anke van Wyk: 175bl,
  175br.
violetblue: 8 (terrier).
Elliot Westacott: 9tl.
Ivonne Wierink: 171tl.
Marlonneke Willemsen:
  190c.
WilleeCole: 14t, 85t, 100tl,
  100c, 103t.
Wolf Avni: 116tl.
Yan Wen: 36c.
Roman Zhuravlev: 178tl.
Zuzule: 109t, 157t.

Warren Photographic:
3 (Corgis), 3 (Border
Collies), 3 (Cockerpoos),
8br, 9tr, 14 (scanner), 15cl,
16b, 25, 27b, 32c, 40c, 41b,
43b, 48c, 53cl, 53b, 55b, 57t,
57c, 61bl, 61br, 64cr, 65c,
66c, 67tr, 68c, 69b, 71cr,
73b, 81b, 83cl, 85cr, 85b,

90c, 91b, 95t, 95cl, 99, 101t,
103cr, 104c, 105c, 115b,
119t, 119b, 121b, 123b,
125b, 126c, 127b, 138c,
139b, 141c, 143br, 145b,
153b, 154c, 155b, 157b,
162c, 163b, 165b, 178c,
187cr, 187b, 203b, 209t,
211, 212b, 214b, 215b,
217b, 220b, 221b.

**Wikimedia
Commons/Nattieliz:** 39t.

Jacket photographs:
Scott Bolster/Shutterstock:
Schnoodle; LinnCurrie/
Shutterstock: Rottweilers;
HelleM/Shutterstock:
Golden Retriever; Eric
Isselée/Shutterstock: Beagle,
Bedlington Terriers, Border
Collie, Chihuahuas, French
Bulldog, German Short-
haired Pointer, Greyhound,
Lhasa Apso, Poodle,
Yorkshire Terrier; Erik
Lam/Shutterstock: Tibetan
Spaniel (standing);
mariait/Shutterstock:
Miniature Schnauzer;
Dorottya Mathe/
Shutterstock: Havanese;
Sbolotova/Shutterstock:
Siberian Husky (single
puppy); swissmacky/
Shutterstock: woman;
Brandy Taylor/
iStockphoto.com:
Weimaraner; Tihis/
Shutterstock: Hungarian
Vizsla; Utekhina Anna/
Shutterstock: Siberian
Huskies (two puppies);
Warren Photographic: Bull
Terriers, Chihuahua
(mother and puppy), Italian
Spinone, Pembroke Corgis,
Siberian Huskies (mother
and puppy), Tibetan Spaniel
(lying).